# The Monstrous and the Unspeakable

Playing the Texts, 1

*Series Editor*
George Aichele

# The Monstrous
# and the Unspeakable

## The Bible as Fantastic Literature

edited by
**George Aichele & Tina Pippin**

Sheffield
Academic Press

Copyright © 1997 Sheffield Academic Press

Published by Sheffield Academic Press Ltd
Mansion House
19 Kingfield Road
Sheffield S11 9AS
England

Printed on acid-free paper in Great Britain
by Bookcraft Ltd
Midsomer Norton, Bath

British Library Cataloguing in Publication Data

A catalogue record for this book is available
from the British Library

ISBN 1-85075-692-9
ISBN 1-85075-821-2 pbk

# Contents

List of Contributors                                                    7

Introduction: Imagining God
    *Tina Pippin and George Aichele*                11

Bordercrossing: Fall and Fantasy in *Blade Runner and
Thelma and Louise*
    *Mara E. Donaldson*                             19

God the Monster: Fantasy in the Garden of Eden
    *David Penchansky*                              43

A *Teshuva* on Sacred Clowning, from Reb Kugel
    *Judith B. Kerman*                              61

Rewriting Superman
    *George Aichele*                                75

Cold Comfort: Stephen W. Hawking and the Bible
    *Jennifer Kramer*                              102

Ancient Biblical Worlds and Recent Magical Realism:
Affirming and Denying Reality
    *Richard Walsh*                                135

Hermes, the Fantastic and the Burning Heart
    *Conard Carroll*                               148

Impaling, Dracula, and the Bible
    *Lloyd Worley*                                 168

The Scandal of the Cross:
Crucifixion Imagery and Bram Stoker's *Dracula*
    *Larry J. Kreitzer*                            181

Sacred Horror: Faith and Fantasy in the Revelation to John
    *Judith Lee*                                   220

Index of References                                                   240
Index of Authors                                                      243

# List of Contributors

**George Aichele** received his PhD from Northwestern University, and he teaches at Adrian College, Adrian, Michigan. His most recent book is *Jesus Framed* (Routledge, 1996). He is a member (with Tina Pippin) of the Bible and Culture Collective that wrote *The Postmodern Bible* (Yale, 1995). Aichele and Pippin have also co-edited *Semeia* 60: 'Fantasy and the Bible' (1992) and a double issue of the *Journal for the Fantastic in the Arts* (1997) on a similar topic.

**Conard Carroll** is a lecturer in English at Northern Kentucky University. His previous works include poems and essays on Milton, and on the Native American earthworks of the Little Miami River Valley.

**Mara Donaldson** has been at Dickinson College, Carlisle, Pennsylvania, since 1990 teaching in the area of religion and culture, feminist theology, and religion and fantasy. She received her PhD from Emory University (religion and literature). Her previous publications have been in the areas of Bible and fantasy, religion and film, and the myth of the female hero.

**Judith Kerman** is Dean of Arts and Behavioral Sciences and Professor of English at Saginaw Valley State University, Saginaw, Michigan. She has published six books of her poems. Her long prose-poem, 'Mothering', received Honorable Mention in poetry in the 1978 Great Lakes Colleges New Writers Competition and was recently republished. She edited the critical anthology, *Retrofitting Blade Runner* (Bowling Green State University Popular Press, 1991), and is currently translating the works of Cuban poet Culce Maria Loynaz (Cervantes Prize, 1992). She has three clown personae, of whom 'Reb Kugel' is the most recently developed.

**Jennifer Kramer** is originally from Newark, New Jersey. She majored in cinema studies at the University of California at Irvine and took an MA in Social Sciences at the University of Chicago. Her writing has been published in various magazines, journals and reference books. She is a member of the National Coalition of Independent Scholars.

**Larry J. Kreitzer** is Tutor of New Testament at Regent's Park College, Oxford. He is a member of the Theology Faculty of the University of Oxford and is a minister in the Baptist Union of Great Britain. He has written a number of books and articles on the Bible and its interpretation within contemporary culture, including *The New Testament in Fiction and Film* and *The Old Testament in Fiction and Film*. A third volume in the series, *Pauline Images in Fiction and Film*, is currently in progress.

**Judith Lee** teaches in the Department of English at Rutgers University. Her research and teaching interests center on the interfaces between theology and literature, particularly on the ways that women writers and theologians have reread the biblical traditions.

**David Penchansky** is Associate Professor of Theology at the University of St Thomas, St Paul, Minnesota. He has written two books, *The Betrayal of God* (Westminster/John Knox Press, 1989) and *The Politics of Biblical Theology* (Mercer Press, 1995). He has also contributed the commentary on the Book of Proverbs to the Mercer Bible Commentary (Mercer Press, 1995). He lives with his two children Simon and Maia in St Paul.

**Tina Pippin** teaches in the Department of Religious Studies at Agnes Scott College in Decatur, Georgia. She has degrees in New Testament and Social Ethics and writes on feminism, apocalyptic cultures, and postmodern biblical hermeneutics. Her book on the last book of the Bible is *Death and Desire: The Rhetoric of Gender in the Apocalypse of John* (Westminster/John Knox Press, 1992). She has co-edited several volumes on fantasy and the Bible with George Aichele.

**Richard Walsh** is Professor of Religion, chair of the Philosophy and Religion Department, and Director of the Honors Program at Methodist College in Fayetteville, North Carolina. He holds a PhD in New Testament from Baylor University, and his research interests include literary critical approaches to biblical texts and the continuing influence of myth and scripture in Western culture.

**Lloyd Worley** holds his PhD from Southern Illinois University at Carbondale. He is Professor of English and former Department Chair at the University of Northern Colorado. He has published in the area of Gothic and fantastic literature, as well as in James Joyce. He is Founding President Emeritus of the Lord Ruthven Assembly, an international, interdisciplinary, scholarly organization devoted to the study of the revenant.

TINA PIPPIN AND GEORGE AICHELE

# Introduction: Imagining God

Once upon a time, the stories we now know as 'The Bible' were told and performed in multiple ways across many centuries. Storytellers performed these sturdy stories to connect with the experiences of the audience, with contexts both real and imagined. Some stories loomed large in the cultural psyche: God's role in creation and the nation, the character and deeds of the ancient forebearers, and the lurking of the ever-present enemy. The Bible is full of stories of human encounters with the supernatural, of magic and miracles: waters that part, prophets who envision the future and ascend to heaven, sorcerers (and their deities) who compete, forebearers who live for hundreds of years, miraculous healings and feedings, angels who intrude, and a deity who stalks and floods, and much more. These are all fantastic stories, outside the realm of our everyday experience. The combination of these stories form 'our culture's most seminal fantasy work, the Bible' (Palumbo 1986: 22).

Biblical scholars, products of the European Enlightenment, began to think about the Bible as myth, and they compared the biblical stories to other mythological writings. In the late twentieth century the methodologies of narratology and semiotics made it acceptable to read the Bible as a fictional text. Yet there continued to be hesitation in applying the term 'fantasy' to the study of the Bible. Perhaps the misconception is that 'fantasy' is a pejorative term, denoting a mental aberration, a flight from reality. Fantasy is often associated with the psychological, as in Freud's important essay on 'the uncanny'. Another term used is the 'fantastic', which implies a literary genre or mode (Cornwell 1990: xi-xii). The term fantasy can also stand for fantasy literature and is also often interchangeable with the 'fantastic'. Both of these terms are used by various of the authors in this book. The subtitle of the book, 'The Bible as Fantastic Literature', points to the more specific usage and exposes the bias that the

Bible (stories in the Bible) are and can be read as fantastic literature by employing fantasy theory.

The three main fantasy theorists underlying the discussions in
this book are Tzvetan Todorov (1975), Rosemary Jackson
(1981), and Christine Brooke-Rose (1981). This trinity of theoretical studies forms the basis of much of the discussion about
the fantastic. The concern of each of these theorists is with the
structure of the fantastic as a genre (Todorov) or mode
(Jackson) and rhetoric (Brooke-Rose), but also with the social
function and implication of fantasy literature. Todorov's categories are the starting point (1975: 44; cf. Cornwell 1990: 37-
39):

uncanny / the fantastic-uncanny / the fantastic-marvelous / marvelous

The basic definition provided by Todorov is that the fantastic
causes the reader to hesitate as they experience something different from their normal reality: 'The fantastic, therefore leads a
life full of dangers, and may evaporate at any moment' (1975:
41). For Jackson the fantastic expresses desire; it either tells or
expels desire (1981: 3-4). In other words, 'The fantastic traces
the unsaid and the unseen of culture: that which has been
silenced, made invisible, covered over and made "absent"'
(1981: 4).

On either end of this continuum there is a greater (the marvelous) or lesser (the uncanny) existence of the supernatural.
Brooke-Rose explains that on the side of the uncanny there is no
supernatural but only unexplained horror; the reader experiences fear, not hesitation. On the marvelous side there is a
focus on wonder. The 'pure fantastic' is represented by the
middle line. The further to the right, the reader is more accepting of the supernatural (1981: 64-65). Brooke-Rose, like many
other theorists, finds Todorov's categories to be flawed, but
accepts them as the basic working model anyway (1981: 65).
The flaw is in the formal structure of the model, which does not
explain certain fantasy writings (e.g. some of Poe and Kafka);
some writings fall between the lines. Ultimately, 'fantasy theory
is not one simple, clear-cut thing' (Aichele and Pippin 1992: 3).

These categories attempt to locate the supernatural in literature and its effects on the reader. 'The supernatural is born of

language', states Todorov in his groundbreaking book, *The Fantastic* (1975: 82; French original, 1970). He adds, 'it is both its consequence and its proof: not only do the devil and vampires exist only in words, but language alone enables us to conceive what is always absent: the supernatural' (1975: 82). These monsters, devils and vampires, but also angels and God and Jesus exist primarily in language for the twentieth-century reader. This language is preserved in the stories of the Bible which makes the invisible and silent supernatural realms visible and vocal.

## Monsters, Monsters Everywhere

Only a few biblical characters get a glimpse of God in anthropomorphic form: God walks in the garden of Eden (Gen. 3.8) or shows God's face (Gen. 32.30; Exod. 33.11) or 'back' (Exod. 33.23). The narrator in the Apocalypse of John gets more than a glimpse of the Son of Man and responds accordingly: 'In his right hand he held seven stars, and from his mouth came a sharp, two- edged sword, and his face was like the sun shining with full force. When I saw him, I fell at his feet as though dead. But he placed his hand on me, saying, "Do not be afraid; I am the first and the last, and the living one. I was dead, and see, I am alive forever and ever; and I have the keys of Death and of Hades" ' (1.16-18). Fear, mixed with awe and wonder and yet more fear, is the frequent response to an encounter with the divine.

Consider the following fantastic story:

> On the way, at a place where they spent the night, the Lord met him and tried to kill him. But Zipporah took a flint and cut off her son's foreskin, and touched Moses' feet with it, and said, 'Truly you are a bridegroom of blood to me!' So he let him alone. It was then she said, 'A bridegroom of blood by circumcision' (Exod. 4.24-26).

The Lord appears as a wilderness demon, poised to kill Moses until his wife Zipporah intervenes with the proper sorcery. What sorcery could stop the Apocalyptic Son of Man? The 'not yet' of the apocalyptic narratives pulls them toward the fantastic-

uncanny and not pure horror. The fantastic stories in the Bible
are full of mystery and never fully or comfortably disclose the
nature and character of the divine. Fantasy theory is not useful
in demystifying any specific (or original) 'meaning' from the text
but rather it revels in what is mystified and in exploring all the
multiple realms of the 'otherworlds' of the text. These 'otherworlds' include the tradition of interpretation and the cultural
influences and references of a biblical text. The Bible has many
lives; there are traces (of images, voices, ethics, blood) that
mark the possible journeys for the reader.

A scene from the Gospel of Matthew reveals the encounter
with a ghostly deity: 'But when the disciples saw him walking
on the sea, they were terrified, saying, "It is a ghost!" And they
cried out in fear. But immediately Jesus spoke to them and said,
"Take heart, it is I; do not be afraid"' (Mt. 14.26-27). The biblical texts reinstate a sense of the supernatural. Still, a specter is
haunting the Bible. A specter is a ghost, phantom, or anything
that haunts or disturbs. A specter is a symbol; whether it be a
demon or an angel, good or evil, is often hard to tell at first
sight (as in the ghost story from Matthew). The specter trans-
gresses the boundaries of wonder and horror, overturning any
formal designation of the fantastic. The reader watches the
spectacle unfold. Western culture (and also the postcolonial cultures in different ways) are haunted by the Bible and its super/
natural beings. According to Jackson (1981: 180), the biblical
fantastic is transgressive and not transcendent (unlike later
'Christian fantasies' [see Manlove 1992] such as C.S. Lewis's
*The Chronicles of Narnia*). Jackson states that 'fantasies image
the possibility of radical cultural transformation through
attempting to dissolve or shatter the boundary lines between
the imaginary and the symbolic' (1981: 178; cf. Zipes 1983: 8;
178). The monstrous and the unspeakable invade the pages of
the Bible and the experience of the reader. Will the response be
fear or wonder or both? 'There is no reality without the specter'
(Žižek 1996: 112).

## Resurrecting Fantasies

We initiated the discussion in *Semeia* 60 (1992) on 'Fantasy and the Bible'. Since then the conversation has become more varied and often what many in mainstream religious and theological studies would consider marginal. Yet this 'marginality' is productive! The assembly of authors and articles in this volume speak to the diversity of readings of the Bible as fantasy literature. All of the articles create conversations between the Bible and other 'texts'—from literature to film and television.

The first two articles begin at the beginning of the Bible, with the second creation story in Genesis 2-3. Mara Donaldson views two films by director Ridley Scott: *Blade Runner* and *Thelma and Louise* and reads them through the Genesis narrative of 'the Fall'. These films cross boundaries and subvert the desire for a center—in their story lines and in their rereading of the Fall tradition. Donaldson traces the function of gender in these films. David Penchansky, reading the same biblical text, explores the notion of God as a monster. Divine visits reveal much about the character of the deity. Must God's authority be questioned in the garden?

Judith Kerman uses one of her clown personae, Reb Kugel, to act out the concept of sacred clowning in the Jewish tradition. She employs humor to reveal the ritual experiences of weddings, Purim, and other holidays. The biblical characters and texts are excessive, and humor taps into the fantastic to lead the congregation to reality.

George Aichele explores the multiple identity issues of Jesus as the Christ in the Gospel of Mark through an examination of the TV series, *Lois & Clark*, and the Superman mythos. Jesus and Clark Kent each have two identities, and these identities are hidden from all but the disciples (in Mark) and Clark's parents (in the Superman stories). Of course, the reader or viewer knows the secret.

Jennifer Kramer presents physicist Stephen Hawking through his book and Errol Morris's documentary of the same name, *A Brief History of Time*. The 'thought problems' of cosmology and the existence of God and black holes occupy Hawking's

research. Kramer shows how Hawking was influenced by religion and the Bible and where his search for the unknowable can
lead.

Richard Walsh draws on Todorov's sense of fantasy as forcing
a reader to hesitate. He reads for biblical wonder by comparing
biblical texts to magical realism, in particular *One Hundred
Years of Solitude* by Gabriel García Márquez. Conard Carroll
examines Hermes and hermeneutics 'in' the Bible. Fantasy
brings the reader to the moment of suspension and in this pause
is interpretation.

Lloyd Worley and Larry Kreitzer both explore biblical texts in
light of their knowledge of the Dracula (and Vlad Dracula) tradition. Worley traces the history of impalement in the Bible, as
used by the Assyrians, Egyptians, and Israelites to its use by
Prince Vlad and then later in the Dracula lore. He connects the
impaling traditions of Dracula with the sacred heart of Christ
tradition. Kreitzer brings to light the background of the use of
crucifixes in the Dracula and vampire traditions. He shows how
the cross as a faith symbol is utilized in these film traditions,
particularly *Bram Stoker's Dracula*.

Lastly, Judith Lee uses Kristeva's concept of the abject to read
the Book of Revelation. Lee examines the mysterious theological and literary deity of the Apocalypse. The experience of this
abject fantasy leads the readers to faith through 'sacred horror'.

## Works Consulted

Abrams, M. H.
   1971      *Natural Supernaturalism: Tradition and Revolution in Romantic
            Literature* (New York: W.W. Norton & Company).
Aichele, G., and T. Pippin (eds.)
   1992      *Fantasy and the Bible* (Semeia 60; Atlanta, GA: Scholars Press).
Aichele, G., and T. Pippin
   1992      'Introduction: Why the Fantastic?', in *idem* (eds.), *Fantasy and the
            Bible*: 1-6.
Apter, T. E.
   1982      *Fantastic Literature: An Approach to Reality* (London: Macmillian).
Brooke-Rose, C.
   1981      *A Rhetoric of the Unreal: Studies in Narrative and Structure,
            Especially of the Fantastic* (New York: Cambridge University
            Press).

Cornwell, N.
1990        *The Literary Fantastic: From Gothic to Postmodernism* (New York: Harvester/Wheatsheaf).
Cox, H.
1969        *The Feast of Fools: A Theological Essay on Festivity and Fantasy* (New York: Harper & Row).
Freud, S.
1955        'The "Uncanny"', in *The Standard Edition of the Complete Psychological Works of Sigmund Freud* (trans. A. Strachey; London: Hogarth Press), 17: 217-56.
Hume, K.
1984        *Fantasy and Mimesis: Responses to Reality in Western Literature* (New York: Methuen).
Irwin, W.R.
1976        *The Game of the Impossible: A Rhetoric of Fantasy* (Urbana, IL: University of Illinois Press).
Jackson, R.
1981        *Fantasy: The Literature of Subversion* (London: Methuen).
Lovecraft, H.P.
1973        *Supernatural Horror in Literature* (New York: Dover).
Manlove, C.
1992        *Christian Fantasy: From Twelve Hundred to the Present* (South Bend: University of Notre Dame Press).
Monleon, J.B.
1990        *A Spectre is Haunting Europe: A Sociohistorical Approach to the Fantastic* (Princeton: Princeton University Press).
Olsen, L.
1987        *Ellipse of Uncertainty: An Introduction to Postmodern Fantasy* (New York: Greenwood).
Palumbo, D.
1986        'Sexuality and the Allure of the Fantastic in Literature', in Palumbo (ed.), *Erotic Universe: Sexuality and Fantastic Literature* (New York: Greenwood Press).
Rabkin, E.S.
1976        *The Fantastic in Literature* (Princeton: Princeton University Press).
Schlobin, R. (ed.)
1982        *The Aesthetics of Fantasy Literature and Art* (Notre Dame, IN: University of Notre Dame Press).
Siebers, T.
1984        *The Romantic Fantastic* (Ithaca, NY: Cornell University Press).
Todorov, T.
1975        *The Fantastic: A Structural Approach to a Literary Genre* (trans. R. Howard; Ithaca, NY: Cornell University Press).
Tolkien, J.R.R.
1965        'On Fairy Stories', in *Tree and Leaf* (Boston: Houghton): 3-84.
Zipes, J.
1983        *Fairy Tales and the Art of Subversion: The Classical Genre for Children and the Process of Civilization* (New York: Methuen).

Žižek, S.
1996        ' "I Hear You with My Eyes"; or, The Invisible Master', in R. Saleci
            and S. Žižek (eds.), *Gaze and Voice as Love Objects* (Durham:
            Duke University Press): 90-126.

Mara E. Donaldson

# Bordercrossing: Fall and Fantasy in Blade Runner and Thelma and Louise

In Adam's Fall
We sinned all (*New England Primer*).

For the oppressed, the problem is not defining limits, but defying limits
(Suchocki 1994: 33).

## Introduction

Writing on the importance of the Bible in American culture, novelist James Dickey says 'the Bible is buried and alive in us'. In it we find 'the fabulous world we all have fallen from, and toward which we are always falling, not backward in time but forward toward that moment when each story...will happen again'.[1] This essay explores the third chapter of the biblical book of Genesis, the so-called myth of the Fall, as an example of what Dickey calls 'the fabulous', or what literary theorist Tzvetan Todorov has called 'the fantastic'. I will examine this story in conversation with two of film director Ridley Scott's (re)visions of this story of the Fall in his films *Blade Runner* (1982) and *Thelma and Louise* (1991).

Reading the third chapter of Genesis not as a story, however, about a falling away from original goodness, but as a 'fabulous' story of a transgression of limits—one which I will argue is *the* paradigmatic bordercrossing in human existence—I wish to

1. Dickey (1977) quoted in Otten 1982: 204. I am grateful for the comments, suggestions and support of several different individuals and groups, especially those in the Dickinson College Women's Research Group, the 1996 Round Table conversation at the American Academy of Religion, Wayne Whitson Floyd, and for funding from the Research and Development committee at Dickinson College.

understand how that narrative is affected by being told in the literary form of 'the fantastic'. I will argue that the literary genre of 'the fantastic'—which revels in that moment of hesitation, or interruption, at which point all logical interpretations are subverted—is both the literary genre by which to interpret Scott's two films and the key to understanding the way in which these two movies subvert our accustomed readings of the biblical Genesis text. Each film becomes an example of 'that moment when [the biblical] story...will happen again'. More than mere retellings of Genesis, however, they become moments when the biblical story long buried in our culture comes alive again in each of us who hears it.

Just as the Genesis text needs to be read as fantasy, thus keeping alive a possibility of interpretation that otherwise would be lost, so too should these films be viewed through the lens of 'the fantastic', as subversive interruptions of our ordinary expectations. *Blade Runner* and *Thelma and Louise*, when viewed as examples of 'the fantastic', can be seen both to exemplify biblical themes from the Genesis narratives and to enact, or make possible, reinterpretations of the themes of Genesis that the biblical text itself sometimes seems to have lost the power to evoke.

## An Overview of *Blade Runner* and *Thelma and Louise*

Our understanding of these two films as fantasy originates in the range of audience- and critical-reviews of Ridley Scott's two provocative films. Although neither film was a box office success, each achieved a sort of cult status (Kolb 1991: 132, 143; Schickel 1991: 52). Indeed, even viewers normally repelled by violence in film still rank these among their favorite films. Most critics have compared them to other movies of similar genres. So, for example, W. Russel Gray relates *Blade Runner* to other detective films (i.e. *The Long Goodbye, The Big Sleep*) (Gray 1991: 71), and many other critics have noted the similarities between *Thelma and Louise* and buddy movies like *Butch Cassidy and the Sundance Kid* (Grundmann 1991: 36).

It is curious, however, that no one has compared the ways these two films reflect the trademark themes of Ridley Scott's work as a director—for example, encounters with limits, heroic journeys. Moreover, no one has made central to their interpretation of either film the biblical myth of the Fall—which I would argue they revise and transform. Judith Kerman is one of the few even to notice that 'the story of the expulsion from the Garden of Eden is an important subtext of *Blade Runner*'. As she continues, 'although one can argue the faults and merits of the film, its mythic level is amazingly well-integrated, especially the integration of a forties private eye story with a science fiction text which weaves seamlessly together themes from *Frankenstein*, *Paradise Lost*, and the Edenic Legend which both draw upon' (Kerman 1991: 2).[2] And Bernard Scott is the only critic who has viewed *Thelma and Louise* in term of the biblical myth of creation (Scott 1994: 251-54).

*Blade Runner* was a controversial film even before its release. Leonard G. Heldreth notes that most early discussions concerned Scott's adaptation of Philip K. Dick's novel, *Do Androids Dream of Electric Sheep*, on which the film is loosely based (Heldreth 1991: 40). They also included, however, such basic issues as title, ending, and the question whether the main character, Rick Deckard, was fully human (Kolb 1991: 141-43). Although Dick, the novel's author, never saw the final release, he read and approved the way that the film developed. Today, the only edition of the film available on videotape is the director's cut—Scott's own personally-edited version (1992)—which has a much more ambiguous finale, significantly omitting the idyllic ending and voice-over of the commercial studio-release seen by theater-goers.

In summarizing critical responses to the film, William Kolb states that 'audiences as well as critics were sharply divided because of the film's extraordinary achievements in some areas, such as its ultra-realistic future milieu, and its manifest failure in others, including character development and lackluster narrative' (Kolb 1991: 132). Borrowing as it did from three genres—

---

2. Critics such as L. Heldreth have noted several allusions in the film to the Eve character from Genesis. D. Desser expands on the Eve imagery in his essay (1991), first by discussing Rachel, the android with whom Deckard falls in love, as Eve, and then looking at Eve-motifs in other characters as well, including Roy Batty and Deckard himself.

science fiction, horror, and the detective story—it was called a 'chilling allegory about man's relationship to God' (Bray 1982: 197), a 'virtual textbook of self-conscious, representational games' (Boozer 1991: 219), 'diabolically absurd' (Arnone 1982: 13), 'grisly sadism' (Collins 1982: 19).

The story is that of Rick Deckard, a hard-boiled Los Angeles detective in 2019. We learn from an opening scroll that androids, or replicants as they are now called, are employed Off-world on ships and space stations as slave labor. They are not allowed on earth; this is a border they are prohibited from crossing. Deckard's specialty as a 'blade runner'—a term whose precise meaning is never given—is killing, or retiring, renegade replicants, a job with which he has become increasingly disenchanted. As the film opens, six replicants (advanced Nexus-6 models) have escaped and have returned, illegally, to earth. Deckard begins the film describing himself as 'ex-cop, ex-blade runner, ex-killer'. Bryant, Deckard's police department superior, whose intolerance is evident in his references to the replicants as 'skin jobs', coerces Deckard into retiring these six. As Deckard begins his investigation of the renegade six, he meets and falls in love with one replicant, Rachel, an experimental model used by the Tyrell Corporation—creators of all the replicants in existence—for promotion and advertisement. In the end Deckard does his job as blade runner but in the process, especially in his encounter with Roy Batty, the leader of the renegade group of replicants, comes to understand something of the complexity of what it means to be human.

In its crossing of genre boundaries and its concern with transgressing limits, Scott's 1991 summer film, *Thelma and Louise*, was equally, if not more, controversial than *Blade Runner*. In the tradition of buddy romance adventures, road movies, outlaw films, and westerns, *Thelma and Louise* both borrowed from and subverted these popular Hollywood genres. It has been called 'the first movie I've ever seen which told the downright truth' (Schickel 1991: 52), 'a butt-kicking feminist manifesto', 'a betrayal of feminism', 'a turning point' (Schickel 1991: 52, 53), 'a male formula with female forms' (Dowell 1991: 28), and a 'myth of female embeddedness' (Scott 1994: 253). In responding to the charges that the film was gratuitously violent,

screenwriter Callie Khouri protested that such comments were
the result of a double standard. When men are violent in films,
she argued, it's considered 'healthy fantasy', but when women
are violent, 'it's a propaganda film' (Simpson 1991: 55). Critic
Janet Maslin also noted that compared with other similar films
released in the 1990s (e.g. *Total Recall* or *Die Hard II*), the violence in *Thelma and Louise* was mild (Maslin 1991: 11). As
Margaret Miles has noted, 'In *Die Hard II* alone there were 264
violent deaths' (Miles 1996: 142), contrasted with one killing in
self-defense in *Thelma and Louise*.

One of the most ironic aspects of the critical responses to
*Thelma and Louise* has been that it has become a litmus test
within the feminist community used to determine who is to be
considered feminist and who is not. For example, Margaret
Miles, who calls the film 'a cautionary tale', argues that this is a
women's film—an example of 'Hollywood films about women
aimed at a heterosexual female audience'—not a feminist film—
one 'aimed at a wide range of women, including women-
identified, women-loving, lesbian, and heterosexual women'
(Miles 1996: 144, 146). She is also concerned that the violence
of the film misrepresents real violence against women. '*Thelma
and Louise* inverted social reality at a historical moment when
the scale of domestic violence and rape was coming to public
attention. Not only are 89 percent of all violent crimes committed by men, but many of them are committed against women'
(1996: 144). Although much of Miles's discussion of popular
American film in her recent book is helpful, her treatment of
this particular film errs, I would argue, because it views the film
realistically when it is better understood as fantasy or myth. As
critic Leo Braudy points out in his review, 'many of the more
ridiculous attacks against the film took its assertions as somehow realistic arguments about women, men, guns, and violence. But however real *Thelma and Louise* may be, it's not
realistic'. The violence 'erupts within a hard-edged satire' and
moves out of 'reality into myth' (Braudy 1991: 29).

The story is of two women: Louise, an older, cynical waitress,
and Thelma, her younger, naive friend. The film opens in present day Arkansas, as the two women plan a weekend away at
a friend's cabin. Thelma cannot tell her husband, Darryl, what

she is going to do, because she fears his disapproval of her friendship with Louise; so Thelma leaves him a note with a meal in the microwave. On the way to the planned weekend hideaway, the women stop at a bar alongside the road; it is, after all, the beginning of a stolen time for relaxation. Things get out of hand. Later, as they are trying to leave, Thelma is attacked by a drunken patron who attempts to rape her. Louise shoots and kills him in a moment full of rage at his actions as well as protectiveness of her friend—all clouded by her memories of a similar attack she herself had suffered in Texas in the not too distant past. Refusing to go to the police, whom they assume will never understand what has just happened, the two women become fugitives, on a wild drive for supposed freedom in anonymity in Mexico. Pursued by local officers and by the FBI, along the way the two women become outlaws in the true sense of the word, as Thelma begins to rob convenience stores for money and provisions. Their journey ends in a standoff at the edge of the Grand Canyon, where they choose to drive over the cliff wall rather than turn themselves in to the law.

Despite their many similarities, no one has noticed that each of these films is centrally concerned with a transgression—a bordercrossing—that sets up the struggle for the moral existence of its characters. Read as variations and transformations of the biblical myth of the Fall, it is important to see the way that both of these films, when understood as fantasy, connect us back with the literary devices used in the biblical text itself. For like the biblical story of the Fall they are deliberately constructed in such a way as to interrupt and subvert the usual understanding of the transgression in which the characters are involved.

## Genesis and the Fantastic

As biblical scholars and theologians explore the interplay between fantasy and biblical texts, Tzvetan Todorov's writings on fantasy in *The Fantastic: A Structural Approach to a Literary Genre* (1973) prove to be a rich resource for understanding the Bible as fantasy.[3] For Todorov the genre of 'the fantastic' depends upon what he calls 'that hesitation experienced by a person', for example, 'who knows only the laws of nature, confronting an apparently supernatural event' (Todorov 1973: 25). The fantastic lasts only as long as this moment of hesitation; once such a character within a story, or the reader of the same text, decides on some rational explanation of the event, or decides to accept the possibility of the existence of the supernatural, the fantastic becomes either the uncanny or the marvelous (p. 41). It is 'fantastic' only in that tensive moment of hesitation.

This genre of fantasy, according to Todorov, has three characteristics. First, there is this moment of hesitation or 'interruption'. 'The text must oblige the reader to consider the world of the characters as a world of living persons', says Todorov, 'and to hesitate between a natural and a supernatural explanation of the events described' (p. 33). Secondly, the hesitation may be experienced by a character in the story, thus becoming one of the themes of the work (p. 33). Thirdly, 'the reader must adopt a certain attitude with regard to the text', an attitude in which both allegorical and purely figurative interpretations must be rejected (p. 33). As Todorov summarizes the interplay of these characteristics in a typical fantasy, he describes their effect by saying '*I nearly reached the point of believing*... Either total faith or total incredulity would lead us beyond the fantastic: it is hesitation which sustains its life' (p. 31). The religious dimension of fantasy, therefore, is not beyond, but within this moment of hesitation and its ability to interrupt, and thus subvert, our expectations about the world. 'The shortest definition of religion', Johann Metz has quipped, '[is] interruption' (Metz 1980: 171).

Todorov sees an intimate link between the structural character of the fantastic (the interruption or hesitation experienced in the moment of deciding between apparently mutually-exclusive options) and the thematic character of a work of fantasy. In being structured by this moment of hesitation—for example, between a rational and a supernatural explanation of a story— 'the fantastic represents an experience of limits' (93). That is to

3.   Aichele and Pippin 1992.

say, the ordinary possibilities of interpretation—the either/or of binary opposite possibilities—is subverted. All reductionist readings are disallowed; there is no single possible interpretation, because the story, as fantasy, wants to say more than either of the interpretations allow. The fantastic resists being placed within the limits of two mutually-exclusive interpretations, for either of them would distort its fuller intended meaning as fantasy.

I am proposing to read the biblical narrative of 'the Fall' as an example of what Todorov had described as 'the fantastic' or fantasy. As Terry Otten has written, 'like all enduring myths, the Fall offers truth but not dogma; it defines for us the nature of human experience, but it offers little to satisfy the rational mind in search of certainty... Irreducible in its richness, the story of the Fall demands formulation while it defies it' (Otten 1982: 3). Thus to interpret the Fall story as fantasy helps to highlight the way in which the opaque moment which the tradition has defined as a 'Fall' can better be understood as a moment of hesitation and an experience of the transgression of limits (and limited possibilities)—which I call a bordercrossing. Interpreting the third chapter of Genesis as an example of the genre of fantasy also holds open the question of the moral status of this moment of hesitation, refusing to prejudge it as a lapse or 'Fall'—even holding open the question of what we are to make of the transgression of limits itself.

A good example in the third chapter of Genesis occurs in the encounter between the serpent and the woman. The sparseness of the Genesis narrative itself accentuates the dialogue between the two.

[The serpent] said to the woman, 'Did God say, "You shall not eat from any tree in the garden"?' The woman said to the serpent, 'We may eat of the fruit of the trees in the garden; but God said, "You shall not eat of the fruit of the tree that is in the middle of the garden, nor shall you touch it, or you shall die."' But the serpent said to the woman, 'You will not die; for God knows that when you eat of it your eyes will be opened, and you will be like God, knowing good and evil' (Gen. 3.1b-5, NRSV).

Confronted by the serpent's misstatement of God's expressed limit, Eve hesitates. Undecided about whether or not God said what the serpent has claimed, she responds to the serpent's question by actually strengthening God's prohibition, making the limits stricter than they were originally. For God had said nothing about not touching the fruit; this is her interpretation (Stratton 1995: 88).

This dialogue is followed by the woman's deliberations: 'So when the woman saw that the tree was good for food, and that it was a delight to the eyes, and that the tree was to be desired to make one wise, she took of its fruit and ate; and she also gave some to her husband, who was with her, and he ate' (Gen. 3.6). In those deliberations she hesitates, neither herself knowing, nor allowing the reader to decide, what it is that should be done—or how to evaluate the actions that she does indeed take. God's response to the woman and the man—six verses long as has been the telling of their deed—succinctly states the consequences. Limits have been transgressed. The man and the woman have gained knowledge, but they have not yet died. God describes their plight, saying to the man, 'cursed is the ground because of you; in toil you shall eat of it all the days of your life' (Gen. 3.17). And God says to the woman, 'I will greatly increase your pangs in childbearing; in pain you shall bring forth children, yet your desire shall be for your husband, and he shall rule over you' (Gen. 3.16). God announces that both the woman and the man will suffer as a result of their deed; having lost their original goodness, their actions have banished them from paradise.

Once we recognize the importance of this moment of hesitation, it becomes clear how quickly and easily previous interpretations of this story have sought to escape the discomfort of this tensive moment. *Either* they choose to see this transgression of limits as humanity's denial of it creatureliness, desiring in pride to 'be like God' (Augustine) for which humanity obviously deserves just punishment, *or* they choose to see this transgression as a regrettable but necessary step in the process of becoming fully human,[4] a 'happy Fall'.

It is interesting to note that however central the notion of a 'Fall' was to become in Christian theology, especially in the

4.  See Tillich's 'transition from essence to existence' (Tillich 1957: 29-31).

Pauline and Augustinian traditions, biblical scholars like Claus Westermann and Gerhard von Rad are right to point out that the term 'Fall' played no part at all in the original understanding of either the particular text of the third chapter of Genesis or the larger primeval history in which it is embedded. Westermann, indeed, sees the origins of the term 'Fall' in Judaism after 70 CE (Westermann 1984: 275): 'O Adam, what have you done/? For though it was you who sinned,/the fall was not yours alone,/but ours also who are your descendants' (2 Esd. 7.118). And in observing the absence of references to the entire story in the Hebrew Bible, von Rad states, 'No prophet, psalm, or narrator makes any recognizable reference to the story of the Fall' (von Rad 1972: 102). The absence of references in subsequent Jewish writings to the story of the garden of Eden and the Fall is one of the reasons that Jewish scholars have tended to regard Genesis, especially the mythological primeval history, as the least Jewish text in the Hebrew Bible. Indeed the term is not employed in the Christian New Testament either, the closest text being Paul's usage of the word *paraptoma* ('slip or fall sideways'; 'a lapse') (Richardson 1950: 76) to speak of Adam's 'trespass' which brought about the need for the 'new Adam', or Christ.

If 'Fall' is not originally part of the historical or cultural context of Genesis 2–3, where do we get the nomenclature of 'Fall' as a way of talking about 'the original disobedience of Adam and Eve and the results of this disobedience' (Efrid 1985: 301)? Three examples are instructive. Clearly, the use of the term 'Fall' is post-biblical, arising in Christianity primarily in the writings of Paul of Tarsus and his fifth century theological successor, Augustine of Hippo. By employing such a term, however, each tends to avoid the tension narrated in 'the fantastic' story of Genesis, for each reads this story as an allegory about human sin and humanity's redemption through Christ. As humanity all sinned in Adam, so all are redeemed in Christ. It was Paul who in his first letter to the Corinthians turned to the language of Genesis in order to describe Christ as this 'last Adam' (15.45) who rights the 'Fall' of the original Adam. It was Augustine, however, who gave the symbol of the Fall its full theological import. By way of explaining what was to become the Christian doctrine of original sin, Augustine stated in the *City of God* (14.13): 'It was in secret that the first human beings began to be evil; and the result was they slipped into open disobedience. For they would not have arrived at the evil act if an evil will had not preceded it. Now, could anything but pride have been the start of the evil will? For "pride is the start of every kind of sin"' (1972: 571). The fall of prideful human beings has left them bound by their sinfulness; only humble submission to a gracious God can free them from the effects of their original 'Fall' from grace. Centuries of Christian theological reliance on Paul's and Augustine's readings of the Genesis text have reduced it again and again to a single, univocal interpretation. There is no ambiguity, no hesitation, no tension; the text has ceased to bear its 'fantastic' import.

A second possible reading of the Fall interprets it as a reversal of center and limit or boundary, turning away from the theme of pride (which Augustine had not too subtly connected with the desires of the flesh in particular) to that of power. The Protestant theologian Dietrich Bonhoeffer is one such voice who sees the story as about the necessary limitations of finite creatureliness, and the overweening human desire for power beyond that allowed within the limits of our finitude. Thus for Bonhoeffer, God's statement of humanity's limit—a limit that stands, in the symbol of the tree of knowledge, at the center of the mythic garden—is a statement of the true center of human existence. As he writes in *Creation and Fall*, '*The human being's limit is at the center of human existence*, not on the margin;... The limit that is at the center is the *limit* of human *reality*, of human *existence as such*'(Bonhoeffer 1997: 163).

Here, limit is understood positively, a perspective, as Paul Ricoeur states, that humanity, for all its progress, has lost. 'We no longer know what a *limit* that does not repress, but orients and guards freedom, could be like; we no longer have access to that creative limit. We are acquainted only with the limit that constrains' (Ricoeur 1967: 250). The essence of the Fall for a theologian like Bonhoeffer is that 'the limit has been transgressed. Now humankind stands in the middle, with no limit... With *the limit* Adam has lost creatureliness' (1997: 221, 222). The desire to be like God costs the creature its very humanity, its distinctiveness as a finite creation that is free to live, but only within its limits.

Augustine's and Bonhoeffer's readings of the Genesis text share a tendency toward a reductionist reading of the Fall as a loss of creatureliness or one's essential humanity; for both of these theologians such an interpretation exhaustively explains the meaning of the text, ending any moment of hesitation the reader might have about its significance. While their interpretations of the Genesis story are by no means of one mind, feminists such as Valery Saiving and Judith Plaskow (Saiving 1979: 25-42; Plaskow 1990) however, have argued in common that to see the Fall as a matter of an excess of pride or power is to interpret this event only from an androcentric perspective; it makes this into a morality tale only about those with power and the ability to abuse it. Most importantly, such an interpretation offers only one possibility for redemption—to renounce such pride, abdicate all one's power, and humbly accept one's lot within limits.

The feminist argument is simply that while this may be a helpful perspective for the 'male-centered' benefactors of the sins of patriarchy, it is not at all helpful either as a way of understanding the sin of the victims of patriarchy, or as a clue to what redemption from the abuses of patriarchy might look like. For the powerless to be offered redemption in the form of self-abasing powerlessness is not to be offered anything redemptive at all. As Marjorie Suchocki has said, 'for the oppressed, the problem is not defining limits, but defying limits' (1994: 32).

Two points need to be made about the importance of continuing to read the myth in the third chapter of Genesis as fantasy. First, it is possible to lose the central tension of the moment of hesitation we call 'the Fall' *either* by reducing the story to a cautionary tale about the sin of pride and the abuse of power *or* by simply turning the tables and arguing that the story is not about any 'Fall' at all, but rather about the necessary transgression of patriarchal boundaries in order for those oppressed by them to become fully human. This means that *both* the Augustinian reading of Genesis *and* many feminist readings of Genesis can easily become reductionist interpretations that lose the tension and mystery of the narrative. I would argue that either of these strategies misunderstands this text by making it into an allegory—a story in which there is a one-to-one correlation between the text and its meaning—rather than a 'fantastic' metaphor. To read this story as fantasy, as extended metaphor, is to refuse to try to step outside the tension in which both the woman and the man place themselves as victims and perpetrators of oppression.

Despite this caveat, however, a second, and perhaps even more important point needs to be stressed about the way we read this story as fantasy. 'The fantastic' holds us within this tension, refusing us the easy way out, but always for a reason, always with an interest in the outcome. Fantasy wishes to discomfit us with the way things are; it is, as Rosemary Jackson has remarked, a 'literature of subversion' (Jackson 1981). Thus, while multiple interpretations are required by fantasy, participating as it does in the irreducibility of the extended metaphor, there is what Paul Ricoeur has called a 'weighted focus' on those who subvert the dominant paradigm of the culture out of which fantasy arises. In the case of the feminist reading of Genesis, therefore, the subversion of androcentric pride and power must always be coupled with the use of this myth as a way of encouraging the victims of patriarchy to cross the boundary from oppression to freedom, from the sin-of-selflessness to the redemptive freedom of full humanity. The tension between the two is metaphorical; its result is far greater than the sum of its parts. Unless this is understood, then one is bound to miss the fact that this story, as Phyllis Trible writes, 'rather than legitimating the patriarchal culture from which it comes...places that culture under judgment' (Trible 1979: 81). To seek to escape the discomfort of the moment of hesitation in the story of 'the Fall' is to lose the significance of the story as a critique of the status quo and as a word of hope and comfort to those oppressed by it.

For example, the words spoken by God to the man and the woman cannot be taken—within the dynamics of a patriarchal culture, then or now—with equal gravity. God's words to the man, that 'cursed is the ground because of you; in toil you shall eat of it all the days of your life' (Gen. 3.17), may indeed have to do with the man's pride and desire for dominant power, a desire that turns against him and is experienced as a curse. When God, however, says to the woman, 'I will greatly increase your pangs in childbearing; in pain you shall bring forth children, yet your desire shall be for your husband, and he shall rule over you' (Gen. 3.16), this cannot be interpreted in terms of pride or power at all. For if the man's sin of pride and power costs him his creatureliness, then redemption for the man will have to do with overcoming his concupiscence and accepting the appropriate limits within which he has been created to live. If the woman's sin, however, is not overarching pride and power, but the acceptance of her oppression and the denial of her own humanity, then the words of malediction spoken to her by God must be seen as the consequence not of pride but of self-negation and denial. Redemption for the woman, then, must have to do with the overcoming of her limited and limiting relationship with the man. She is not who she has been created to be so long as she submits to the limits of her oppression, to the boundaries of patriarchy. To be God's creature, to be redeemed as a human being, requires a bordercrossing, a transgression of the limiting and oppressing, and oft-times violent, boundaries of any male-dominated culture.

Unless we can read the expulsion from the garden as fantasy, holding onto the moment of hesitation, then we will miss grasping the way in which this particular verse, as Beverly Stratton and others have pointed out, has been used to sanction male domination over women. As Stratton states, 'Interpretations matter. They mattered in the garden of Eden' and they continue to matter outside the garden as well. 'Interpretations of the Adam and Eve story, in particular, have affected women's lives for centuries' (1995: 11). As Susan Lanser has observed, this verse 'unravels the argument', for it refuses to allow us easily to explain 'why male dominance should be the particular consequence of a transgression for which both man and woman are equally, as they argue, responsible' (1988: 75). Here, then, at the level of interpretation, the reader, as well as the characters themselves, hesitates; as fantasy, the text has done its job.

## Fantasy and Bordercrossing in *Blade Runner* and *Thelma and Louise*

At times over the two millennia of Christian history, the biblical stories have exerted a profound, but largely unilateral, influence on human literature and art, Milton's *Paradise Lost* and Michelangelo's Sistine Chapel ceiling being only two of the most enduring examples. At other times, art and literature have themselves provided stirring renditions of biblical themes, such as Dante's virtual creation of western culture's visual imagery of heaven and hell in the *Divine Comedy* or William Blake's drawings which evoke a level of interpretation of the book of Job heretofore unimagined (Otten 1982; Manlove 1992). What usually goes less noticed is the way the biblical texts continue to shape, and to be reinterpreted by, not only 'high culture', but popular cultural forms such as fantasy. As I have argued elsewhere, at its best 'fantasy literature has not merely *exemplified* or *illustrated* biblical genres, but has *enacted* them in the contemporary world in a way that the Bible itself sometimes no longer seems capable of doing. That is to say, fantasy literature at its best has provided occasions in which the biblical themes themselves become present cultural events' (Donaldson 1992: 115). In so doing, such popular cultural expressions serve to hold open that moment of hesitation that is characteristic of fantasy, demanding of us the multiple levels of interpretation that refuse any reductionist solution.

These two films offer just such a subtle retelling of the Genesis story. For the seemingly central theme of boundaries unjustly overstepped is more than balanced by the theme of borders crossed in order to be human at all. Reminiscent of the theological legacy from Irenaeus to Tillich, they refuse to see 'the Fall' as centrally a matter of pride, but rather as a matter of a necessary 'Fall into existence'. What is striking about both films, moreover, is that the 'bordercrossing into full humanity' must overcome cultural obstacles and oppression—the boundaries of slavery and the intolerance of 'the other' in *Blade Runner*, and the boundaries of patriarchy and androcentrism in *Thelma and Louise*.

In *Blade Runner* there are a number of 'transgressions' that, like the transgression in the biblical garden scene, beg to be interpreted not as 'Falls' but as 'bordercrossings'—ambiguous ruptures of limits and boundaries, whose meaning remains metaphorical, multivalent, and resistant to reductionist readings. Deckard himself is involved in two of the three most important bordercrossings in the film. First, he is coerced into the task of retiring a group of replicants precisely because they already have crossed the boundary between outer space (Offworld) and earth. Secondly, in the process of coming to know and to love Rachel, herself a replicant, Deckard realizes that the lines between human being and android are not so clear. At one point in speaking about Rachel, but clearly referring to himself as well, he says, 'How can it not know what it is?'.

In this second scene, as Deckard first discovers that Rachel is indeed a replicant, we have one of the clearest examples of the way in which the film needs to be interpreted as fantasy. Rachel is Tyrell's assistant, and she obviously thinks that she is human. At Tyrell's insistence, and as a test of the Voigt-Kampff test which the police use to determine if subjects are really human, Deckard queries Rachel. As the examination proceeds, she begins to hesitate in her responses. When Tyrell asks her to leave after its completion, Deckard confronts him, asking that crucial question, 'How can it not know what it is?'. Tyrell responds, 'they give them memories'. In this case, Rachel has been given the memories of Tyrell's niece, and when she shows up at Deckard's apartment later that evening she brings her 'family' photographs. 'You think I'm a replicant, don't you?', she asks. The fact that she has been given memories begins to erode Deckard's own sense of the boundaries between human and machine. The boundaries are further eroded when they become lovers later in the film.

The third bordercrossing at the heart of the film involves not Deckard but the replicant Roy, who of all the androids is the one most tempted to try to achieve immortality, or at the least a life-span longer than his creator, Eldon Tyrell, has permitted. The encounter between Roy and Tyrell, his creator, clearly links this film to the biblical Fall narrative, with its themes of disobedience and violence. When Roy arrives at Tyrell's home, wishing to change his termination program, the scene is staged in deliberately ecclesiastical style. Tyrell wears what appears to be a papal gown; devotional candles light the room (Kolb 1991: 166). Tyrell, however, cannot do as Roy demands. 'You were made as well as we could make you... The light that burns twice as bright, burns half as long'. 'I've done questionable things', Roy confesses. Tyrell responds, 'Also, extraordinary things. Revel in your time'. The scene ends as Roy kisses his creator, but then crushes Tyrell's head and eyes.

Deckard's own relationship with Roy during the final sequence of the film also needs to be seen through the lens of the fantastic. As Deckard is about to fall to his death with Roy standing over him, holding a dove, Roy says, 'quite an experience to live in fear. That's what it is to live in fear'. Deckard falls and Roy reaches out and grabs Deckard's arm. The camera holds this moment and then follows Roy as he pulls Deckard up onto the rooftop. Then Roy says to Deckard, 'I've seen things you people wouldn't believe...all those moments will be lost in time, like tears in rain. Time to die'. As Deckard watches him die, he speaks his first line in ten minutes: 'I don't know why he saved my life. Maybe in those last moments he loved life more than he ever had before. Not just his life. Anybody's life. My life. All he'd wanted were the same answers the rest of us want. Where do I come from? Where am I going? How long have I got. All I could do was sit there and watch him die.'

As in *Blade Runner*, there are several crucial bordercrossings in *Thelma and Louise*, as well. The film chronicles Louise's journey from being an independent, self-sufficient cynic—much like Deckard—across the border to becoming an interdependent, responsible moral self. At another level, however, this is more Thelma's story, a transgression of the limits of a codependent wife, to the status of an active, independent self. Her relationship with Louise is of primary importance in Thelma's transformation, but in her initial naivety and innocence she reminds us of Rachel. Thelma's awakening, like Rachel's, is in part the result of a sexual coming of age; in this case Thelma's partner is JD, a hitchhiker, whom she and Louise pick up on the road. JD, as in many traditional interpretations of the snake in Eden, is both the cause of her heightened sexuality and the reason Thelma is pushed over the boundary to become an outlaw. Because he steals the money Thelma and Louise have for the trip, Thelma has no choice but to steal. A petty thief himself, JD sees his former exploits as part of their sexual fore-play, telling Thelma how to rob without getting hurt or without hurting anyone else, both of which lessons she learns all too well.

Some of the boundaries in this film are literal; the women start in Arkansas and cross state boundaries, ending up at the Grand Canyon. And some of the bordercrossings are metaphori-cal; the women become more and more alike, as is shown visu-ally in a scene in which the camera blurs the features of the women as they are looking at the night sky. The ending, a freeze frame of the car going over the cliff wall of the canyon, is itself a highly controversial bordercrossing between life and death, reminiscent of Roy and Deckard at the end of *Blade Runner*. On the one hand, it is clear that this is a traditional transgression of the taboo of suicide, and there is great regret that there were no alternatives for the women in a patriarchal culture. On the other hand, this final leap is a bordercrossing asserting their ultimate freedom and independence, much in the same way that African slaves walked to freedom and died rather than be enslaved.[5]

The bordercrossings in this film help us to clarify further the way that the moment of hesitation—the interruption in narra-tive flow—functions in the literary genre of 'fantasy'. Yet when we call such stories 'fantasy', as when one calls the Genesis story 'myth', this must not be allowed to suggest their 'untruth'. Rather, the moment of hesitation central to fantasy is always for the sake of saying 'more' than the truth of a literal, reduc-tionist reading of the story can tell.

For example, during the long road-odyssey of Thelma and Louise, the periodic phone calls between Louise and Hal, the sympathetic Arkansas policeman who is helping the FBI to track their movements, are classic cases of narrative interruption. Louise's conversations with Hal start out to be brief. He tries to

5.  This insight is the result of conversations at a Roundtable Discussion with K. Harris and others at the American Academy of Religion annual meeting, New Orleans, November 1996.

be sympathetic from the beginning, but as they continue their crime spree and refuse to turn themselves in, he is left little choice but to have them charged with murder.

Likewise, after she has killed the would-be rapist in the tavern parking lot near the beginning of the film, Louise had refused to go to the police, and the viewer learns that her resistance has to do with something that had happened to her earlier in Texas. Louise's intransigence on this point, her utter refusal to talk about it even with Thelma, has remained throughout the film an interruption in the flow of the narrative. It becomes clear only indirectly, by dwelling with the tension of this extended moment of hesitation, what had happened. Thelma, not Louise, is the one who finally names it. 'It happened to you, didn't it? In Texas. You was raped'. Louise in fact never admits this is the reason she refuses to go through Texas. 'I'm warning you, just drop it. I'm not going to talk about it'. The tension remains, as does its power to drive forward the plot of the film.

In a crucial phone conversation, Hal tells Louise he knows what happened to her in Texas, and that he understands what's making them run. Louise hesitates and Thelma tells her to hang up. When they are outside, she notices Louise's hesitation and questions whether or not she is going to make a deal with the police. Thelma, however, states what has become true about herself. 'Something's like crossed over in me, and I can't go back. I mean I just couldn't live'. And Louise replies, 'I know what you mean'.

Throughout their journey, Thelma and Louise have followed a route that has been periodically interrupted by encounters with a trucker following the same itinerary they have. Just before the film moves into its denouement, the women meet the trucker for a third, and final, time. They stop, and in a scene which mirrors the first shooting of the would-be rapist, Harlan, in the parking lot, they confront the trucker and his repulsive behavior—his tongue wagging, his calling them 'beavers' over the CB radio. In words reminiscent of those she used with Harlan, Louise says to the trucker, pointing her gun, 'You say you are sorry or I'm going to make you sorry'. Then she hesitates and turns her gun on his truck, shooting its tires. Thelma also shoots, and the truck blows up in an apocalyptic blaze. This moment of interruption forces the viewer into an increasingly intense quandary about how to interpret this film, about the level on which one take the journey itself, the violence, and their repeated crossing of virtually every socially-defined boundary of their culture.

Their final bordercrossing is also the most striking example in the film of the hesitation of fantasy. Faced with an army of FBI men loading and pointing their rifles, Thelma says, 'let's not get caught. Let's keep going'. Louise hesitates, then realizes what she means. They kiss, hold hands, and with Hal running on foot after their car, they drive off the edge of the canyon. The camera catches them mid air, where they hang in perpetual hesitation, interrupting and subverting the inevitable conclusion.

## Conclusion

The biblical story of the Fall and the stories told by these two films all wish to say more than the sum of their partial possible interpretations. Reading and viewing them as fantasy has allowed us to bear with that moment of hesitation so characteristic of the fantastic. It allows them to subvert our desire for reductionist readings and viewings of these works of art.

Genesis, *Blade Runner*, and *Thelma and Louise* remind us that we are, as James Dickey put it, 'always falling, not backward in time but forward toward that moment when each story...will happen again'. Each confronts us with the question of what to make of the transgression of limits; each poses the potential virtue in refusing to rush to moral judgments about them.

One man's transgression, we might say, is another woman's bordercrossing. For as much as each of the films does indeed exemplify biblical themes from the Genesis narratives, they do far more than that. For they also wish to make possible, indeed they enact, 'new' interpretations of the themes of Genesis— interpretations that the biblical text itself sometimes seems to have lost the power to evoke.

Understood as fantasy, each of the three stories we have examined has represented an experience of limits or boundaries. And each has shown in its own way the dangers for humanity of seeing life as exhausted by the extreme options of limitless power, on the one hand, and powerless subservience, on the other. Fantasy wishes to hold open for us the potentiality that these stories—and indeed human existence itself—has a fuller, richer meaning than either unbridled power or self-denying powerlessness can offer. Yet that possibility cannot be expressed merely as a combination of the two.

To employ power to transgress the fundamental existence of another person is to have crossed a boundary that human beings do well to respect. And to retreat from the experience of the violence of power into the apparent security of obedient subservience to it is an illusion we do well to subvert. Each story, however, wishes to say more—more about what *redemptive* power might look like as a creative force for good in the universe, and more about what sort of *creative* force is unleashed when persons venture their own bordercrossings into the empowering freedom of authentic creatureliness. To see the former as merely the point for men, and the latter as merely that for women, however, is to miss their point entirely—it is to remain bound within the limits of the patriarchal society which defined itself in this way. For each of these stories longs ultimately to narrate a tale of the subversion of the very boundaries and limits of human brokenness that require subversive strategies at all. Each longs for that bordercrossing into a new level of human existence for each and every person—a world which for now can only be portrayed by fantasy, but toward which humanity, in Dickey's words, is ever falling, and which one day, 'fantastic' as it seems, 'will happen again'.

## Works Consulted

Aichele, G., and T. Pippin (eds.)
    1992        *Fantasy and the Bible* (Semeia, 60; Atlanta, GA: Scholars Press).
Arnone, E.
    1982        '"Blade Runner" Just too Cute to be Believed', *The Olympian* (Olympia, WA) 9 July: 13.
Bonhoeffer, D.
    1997        *Creation and Fall: A Theological Exposition of Genesis 1-3* (trans. D. Bax; ed. J.W. De Gruchy; Minneapolis: Fortress Press [Manuscript]).

Boozer, J.
  1995        'Seduction and Betrayal in the Heartland: *Thelma and Louise*',
              *Literature Film Quarterly* 23: 189-96.
  1991        'Crashing the Gates of Insight: *Blade Runner*', in Kerman 1991:
              212-28.
Braudy, L.
  1991        'Satire into Myth', *Film Quarterly* 45: 28-29.
Bray, H.
  1982        'Review of *Blade Runner*', *Christianity Today* 26 (3 September):
              97.
Christ, C.P., and J. Plaskow (eds.)
  1979        *Womanspirit Rising: A Feminist Reader in Religion* (Boston:
              Beacon Press).
Collins, G.
  1982        'Is the Violence in *Blade Runner* a Socially Destructive Element?',
              *The New York Times* 30 June: sec. C: 19.
Desser, D.
  1991        'The New Eve: The Influence of *Paradise Lost* and *Frankenstein*
              on *Blade Runner*', in Kerman 1991: 53-65.
Dickey, J.
  1977        'Introduction', *The Bible: A New Vision* (Birmingham, AL: Oxmoor
              House).
Donaldson, M.E.
  1992        'Prophetic and Apocalyptic Eschatology in Ursula Le Guin's *The
              Farthest Shore* and *Tehanu*', in G. Aichele and T. Pippin (eds.):
              111-21.
Dowell, P., *et al.*
  1991        'Should We Go Along for the Ride: A Critical Symposium on
              *Thelma and Louise*', *Cineaste* 18: 28-36.
Efrid, J.M.
  1985        'The Fall', in P.J. Achtemeier (ed.), *Harper's Bible Dictionary* (San
              Francisco: Harper & Row).
Gray, W.R.
  1991        'Entropy, Energy, Empathy: *Blade Runner* and Detective Fiction',
              in Kerman 1991: 66-75.
Grundmann, R.
  1991        'Hollywood Sets the Terms of the Debate', *Cineaste* 18: 35-36.
Heldreth, L.G.
  1991        'The Cutting Edges of *Blade Runner*', in Kerman 1991: 40-52.
Jackson, R.
  1981        *Fantasy: The Literature of Subversion* (New York: Methuen).
Kerman, J.B. (ed.)
  1991        *Retrofitting* Blade Runner: *Issues in Ridley Scott's* Blade Runner
              *and Philip K. Dick's* Do Androids Dream of Electric Sheep?
              (Bowling Green, Ohio: Bowling Green State University Popular
              Press).

Kolb, W.M.
1991        'Script to Screen: *Blade Runner* in Perspective', in Kerman 1991: 132-53.
Lanser, S.S.
1988        '(Feminist) Criticism in the Garden: Inferring Genesis 2-3', in H.C. White (ed.), *Speech Act Theory and Biblical Criticism* (Semeia, 41; Atlanta: Scholars Press): 67-84.
Manlove, C.
1992        *Christian Fantasy: From 1200 to the Present* (Notre Dame, IN: University of Notre Dame Press).
Maslin, J.
1991        'Lay Off *Thelma and Louise*', *The New York Times* 16 June: 16.
Metz, J.B.
1980        *Faith in History and Society* (trans. D. Smith; New York: Seabury).
Miles, M.
1996        *Seeing and Believing: Religion and Values in the Movies* (Boston: Beacon Press).
Otten, T.
1982        *After Innocence: Visions of the Fall in Modern Literature* (Pittsburgh: University of Pittsburg Press).
Plaskow, J.
1990        *Standing Again at Sinai: Judaism from a Feminist Perspective* (San Francisco: Harper & Row).
Rad, G. von
1972        *Genesis: A Commentary* (rev. edn; Philadelphia: Westminster Press).
Richardson, A.
1950        *A Theological Word Book of the Bible* (New York: Macmillan).
Ricoeur, P.
1967        *The Symbolism of Evil* (trans. E. Buchanan; Boston: Beacon Press).
Saiving, V.
1979        'The Human Situation: A Feminine View', in Christ and Plaskow (eds.) 1979: 25-42.
Schickel, R.
1991        'Gender Bender', *Time* 24 June: 52-56.
Scott, B.B.
1994        *Hollywood Dreams and Biblical Stories* (Minneapolis: Fortress Press).
Scott, Ridley (Dir.)
1982        *Blade Runner* (New Line Home Video).
1992        *Blade Runner: Director's Cut* (Warner Home Video).
1992        *Thelma and Louise* (MGM/UA Home Video).
Simpson, J.C.
1991        'Moving into the Driver's Seat', *Time* 24 June: 55.
Stratton, B.
1995        *Out of Eden: Reading, Rhetoric, and Ideology in Genesis 2-3* (Sheffield: Sheffield Academic Press).

Suchocki, M.H.
  1994        *The Fall to Violence: Original Sin in Relational Theology* (New
              York: Continuum).
Tillich, P.
  1957        *Systematic Theology*. II. *Existence and the Christ* (Chicago: The
              University of Chicago Press).
Todorov, T.
  1973        *The Fantastic: A Structural Approach to a Literary Genre* (trans.
              R. Howard; Ithaca, NY: Cornell University Press).
Trible, P.
  1979        'Eve and Adam: Genesis 2-3 Reread', in Christ and Plaskow (eds.)
              1979: 74-83.
Westermann, C.
  1984        *Genesis 1-11: A Commentary* (trans. J.J. Scullion, SJ; Minneapolis:
              Augsburg Press).
  1992        *Genesis: An Introduction* (trans. J.J. Scullion, SJ; Minneapolis:
              Fortress Press).

DAVID PENCHANSKY

# God the Monster: Fantasy in the Garden of Eden

## Introduction

> Lo! ye believers in gods all goodness, and in man all ill, lo you! See
> the omniscient gods oblivious of suffering man; and man, though
> idiotic, and knowing not what he does, yet full of the sweet things
> of love and gratitude.
>
> H. Melville (1989: 447)

Monsters with great staring eyes inhabit the nightmare regions
of fantasy. In the Hebrew Bible great sea creatures and land
giants lay waiting in the chaos just outside the imposed order of
God's creation. Sometimes, however, the divine figure itself
functions as monster.[1] In Genesis 2–3 the god is called Yahweh/
Elohim, usually translated 'Lord God'. We may learn a great deal
about this figure, but only if first we ignore what other parts of
the Bible say about God. Most of the traditions (academic and
confessional) believe God to be good and limitless in knowledge and power. Therefore, any biblical stories that imply otherwise must be either ignored or aggressively interpreted so as to
force them to agree with more acceptable views of God. This
particular story, however, has not been ignored by any of the
traditions. Therefore, it is thick with conflicting interpretations.

---

1.  R. Schlobin offered a definition of horror and the monstrous that has
surprising affinities with the Garden of Eden narrative: 'The three, critical
elements of horror are (1) its distortion of cosmology (more specifically, in
Job's case, theodicy); (2) its dark inversion of signs, symbols, processes and
expectations that causes this aberrant world and (3) its monster-victim relationship with its archetypal devastation of individual will. (1992: 24). 'In
general, the horror's creatures are blatantly oblivious to any human sense
of order, ethics or morality. They are so evil that good is either unknown or
has no impact on them. Their natures are incomprehensible to the epistem-
ologies of their victims and monsters are completely capable of dis-
integrating their victims' bodies and souls' (1992: 30).

Most of the interpretations assume the spotless reputation of
Yahweh/ Elohim. But there are monstrous aspects to the divine
figure that should not be ignored.

## The Magical Trees

Yahweh/Elohim put two special trees in the middle of the
Garden of Eden. They have names (the Tree of the Knowledge
of Good and Evil; the Tree of Life) although it is in no way clear
what the names actually mean. The serpent states that upon
eating from the Tree of the Knowledge of Good and Evil, the
woman will 'be like *'elohim*, (God or gods) knowing good and
evil'. So the tree imparts a divine breadth of knowledge.[2] The
woman observes that the tree is able to make one wise.
Although two different phrases are used, ('be like God, knowing
good and evil', 'able to make one wise'), here they both speak
of knowledge such as that possessed by the *'elohim*, a class of
beings to which Yahweh/Elohim belongs, and over which he
rules. According to Yahweh/Elohim, the other tree, the Tree of
Life, imparts divine immortality (Barr 1992: 5). If the humans
ate from that tree as well they would have divine knowledge
*and* divine immortality and would therefore be virtually indistinguishable from the *'elohim*.[3]

So why did Yahweh/Elohim place these trees right in the
middle of the Garden, presumably not a hidden place but rather
a most prominent location? After he plants the trees, he delivers
a very stern warning to the man: 'On the *very* day you eat from
the tree, you will *instantly* die'.[4] Why would he place the trees

2.  'Good and evil' here means something like 'from A to Z', 'from coast
to coast', the whole thing, covering the two extremes and everything in
between. See Crossan 1980: 110.

3.  Brueggeman (1982: 45), offering a quintessential theological reading,
argues that the character of the trees is ultimately unimportant to an understanding of the tale. I strongly disagree. The fact that there is no explanation
for the trees is reason enough for Brueggeman to conclude that there is no
narrative interest in the tree. I could just as easily conclude the exact opposite—that the *absence* of any explanation is an indication of how important
the trees are, their origin and explanation being suppressed, creating natural interest/curiosity into their existence.

4.  I added the words in italics to emphasize what I believe are the

(the text switches in a confusing manner between one tree and two[5]) in such a prominent place if he did not want the humans to eat their fruit? How this question is answered becomes the major interpretative crux of the passage.

## It is a Test

According to this understanding, Yahweh/Elohim placed these trees in the Garden for the express purpose of providing the first humans a test of their obedience to divine commands. The importance of the trees lay not in whatever magical powers they might have possessed, but rather in their having been chosen as a site of testing. Through the test Yahweh/Elohim would discover the extent of human loyalty. Further, there exists the possibility that the humans might benefit from the test as well, advancing to some new level of responsibility in the divine training program. This would require the humans to not eat the fruit, and thus pass the test.

Certainly there are other passages in which God tests humans, most prominently the 'Akedah', the offering of Isaac (Genesis 22). In both cases (the Garden of Eden and the Akedah) a difficult, incomprehensible and counter-intuitive command must

nuances of the Hebrew words *beyom* (on the day) and *mut tamut* (dying you shall die). See Barr 1992: 10: '...clearly, as an instant punishment. This kind of warning is a warning for *mortals*, and is well evidenced elsewhere in the Bible'.

5. 'How were the two trees related, the tree of knowledge and the tree of life? The text leaves us confused about this. In Genesis 2.9 it tells us that God made all sorts of trees to grow, "and the tree of life in the midst of the garden and the tree of the knowledge of good and evil". But in v. 17 the only tree that is forbidden is the tree of knowledge of good and evil, and nothing at all is said about the tree of life. In 3.3, when the woman is explaining to the snake which tree is forbidden, she defines it as "the tree which is in the middle of the garden", and this is the only tree that is forbidden. That this was the tree of knowledge of good and evil follows naturally... It now becomes important that they should not eat of the tree of life, which in fact has not been mentioned at all since the trees were first mentioned at 2.9. What is not clear is: why the tree of life was not forbidden as the tree of knowledge was; where it was in relation to the latter tree; whether the humans had in fact been eating of the tree of life all along; and if they had not been eating of it, why they had not done so' (Barr 1992: 57).

be obeyed so as to prove one's devotion to God. Abraham proves his devotion because he willingly offers his own child as a human sacrifice. The first humans fail to prove their devotion when they disobeyed the prohibition and ate from the Tree of Knowledge.[6] If we see the prohibition as a test, that would explain why the divine threat ('...you will die *instantly*') was never carried out. Just as God never intended to actually allow Abraham to destroy his son, he never meant to carry out the punishment against the first humans.

However, there is no testing language in the Garden of Eden passage. In Genesis 22 the narrator declares that 'God *tested* Abraham', and the divine messenger reacts to the conclusion of the test with great joy: 'Now I know that you fear God'. There is no such framing device in the Garden of Eden story suggesting that this is a test. But if it is not a test, why did Yahweh/ Elohim give the humans access to the trees? I can think of two other possible answers.

### Yahweh/Elohim Wanted the Humans to Eat the Fruit but Could not Tell Them

Everyone knows that in many folk stories the protagonist must break free from the confines of her parents so that she might find her destiny. A wise parent recognizes the necessity that children must rebel in order to establish their separate identities. In such a way, Yahweh/Elohim created a controlled environment in which the humans (his children, so to speak) might rebel and establish their independence. Although he made them believe that he did not want them to eat the fruit, in fact that was his intention all along. The whole setting served as an elaborate scheme to advance the first humans, because (in one explanation) humans can only establish their independence if they disobey their father. Although it appears from the prohibition and Yahweh/Elohim's final speech that God does not want them to eat from the tree, in fact he really wanted them to eat all along. That the Christian and to some extent the Jewish tradition makes of this story an exquisite testing myth does not however exhaust its possibilities. Such a reading might not even

---

6.   This prohibition was counterintuitive because the fruit was obviously beneficial to human well-being and advancement.

represent a historically early reading, or even a best or most useful reading.

There are in fact problems with understanding the story this way. Yahweh/Elohim appears genuinely upset when he finds out that they ate his fruit. When he discussed the situation with the other *'elohim* they considered issues of damage control. Probably, no one felt happy about the way things turned out, least of all the Chairman of the Board. It is therefore hard to accept that Yahweh/Elohim *intended* the humans to eat the forbidden fruit, when all his actions point otherwise.

### Yahweh/Elohim Did Not Anticipate that the Humans Would Disobey Him

In order to take this interpretation seriously, one has to drop any notions that Yahweh/Elohim has all power and all knowledge. If the fruit of the two trees gave nourishment and divine abilities to the *'elohim*, perhaps Yahweh/Elohim placed them in the garden for his and the others' convenience. A firm threat he thought sufficient to keep the humans away. It did not turn out as planned, and the *'elohim* resorted to plan B. They drove the humans out of the Garden, denying them access to fruit from the Tree of Immortal Life, thus keeping them in an inferior position to the divine beings. Yahweh's placement of the trees was a colossal blunder which he tried to rectify. First, he forbade them to eat the fruit, under threat of death, which turned out to be an empty threat. And when the threat did not work, he ejected them from the Garden.

## The Serpent

For a long time I have taught that the serpent is not to be identified with subsequent notions of Satan or the devil. Israel distinguished itself from the surrounding nations by their strict monotheistic ideas. Yahweh, the Israelite God, shares his power with no other god or divine being. Notions of rival cosmic powers such as devils come from foreign influence, and (it is implied) are not worthy of Israel. And does not the narrator take great effort to establish that the serpent is not a supernatural power, but rather one of the creatures which were made by Yahweh/Elohim?[7] 'The Serpent was more *'arum* (clever, shrewd) than all the beasts of the field which Yahweh/Elohim had made'. However, in so many ways, the serpent distinguishes himself from the other beasts, and resembles much more a supernatural creature, strongly akin to the figure of Satan in the opening chapters of the book of Job.[8] This 'creature' can talk, is clever/shrewd, and appears privy to the secrets of the divine council. Whatever knowledge might be gained by eating the magical fruit, the serpent had that knowledge already. Statements the serpent makes provide important information about the tree and about the character of Yahweh/Elohim. The serpent reveals the secrets that Yahweh/Elohim wants to conceal.

7.   Brueggeman regards the serpent as of no independent significance to the progression of the story. He says: 'The serpent is a device to introduce the new agenda. The serpent has been excessively interpreted. Whatever the serpent may have meant in earlier versions of the story, in the present narrative it has no independent significance... It is not a phallic symbol or satan or a principle of evil or death' (1982: 47).

8.   'According to ancient Talmudic sources, the primeval serpent is just a species of animal, although differing in character from the serpent of to-day, and resembling man in his upright stature and in his manner of eating...it is beyond doubt that the Bible refers to an ordinary, natural creature, for it is distinctly stated here: Beyond any Beast of the Field *that the Lord God had made*.

'But this interpretation also encounters difficulties. First, if the serpent were only an ordinary animal, why does Scripture tell us that he *spoke*?... (according to the haggadic interpretation his intention was to destroy the man, because he [the serpent] had set his heart on Eve... Furthermore, how could a mere animal know all that the serpent here knows, including even the hidden purpose of the Lord God?' (Cassuto 1961: 140-42). Cassuto notes that the plain meaning of the text would indicate that it was a beast which the Lord God made. However, he uncovers certain arguments against that possibility, such as the vocal skills of the animal, and the animal's unique insight into the ways of God. He argues first that the symbol of a serpent-like creature (Leviathan), who lives in the sea and represents the forces of chaos was a part of the Israelite cultural heritage. Therefore, when the Israelite writer wanted to provide an animal who was also a symbol of evil, he naturally gravitated to the serpent. But because Leviathan could not exist in a garden, being a sea creature, he chose the closest land correspondent, the serpent. And because of this, it is not regarded as a true creature, but rather using the creature as a symbol for something else.

Yahweh/Elohim, never revealed the purpose or true danger of the Tree of the Knowledge of Good and Evil. He put the tree there and presumably named it, but provides no justification for his prohibition of its fruit. He threatens to execute them if they disobey.[9] The serpent provides an explanation. First, he assures the woman that the threat of execution will not be carried out. 'You will not die *instantly*', he said, quoting the words of God more accurately than the woman had done. 'God (*'elohim*) knows that when you eat, your eyes will be opened and you will be like God (*'elohim*), knowing good and evil'. Not only does Yahweh/Elohim utter empty threats, the serpent says, but he also jealously guards his prerogatives, keeping the first humans in ignorance and powerlessness. The serpent accuses Yahweh/Elohim of dominating the humans, holding them back in perpetual ignorance, while he and the other *'elohim* enjoyed supernatural knowledge and endless life. We must look hard for narrative cues suggesting how seriously we should take this accusation.

Just how accurate then were the serpent's predictions regarding the momentous event? Yahweh/Elohim told the humans that they would die. The serpent said they would not die. Having eaten the fruit, they remained alive. The serpent said their eyes would be opened. That is exactly what happened. The serpent said that they would be like God, knowing good and evil. In contrast, when their eyes were opened they saw that they were naked. As a result, the woman accuses the serpent of deceiving her.[10] There is a bit more to the story remaining before we can

9. I considered briefly whether in fact there was death in the fruit, and Yahweh/Elohim was warning the humans of the danger of eating it. There proved to be no danger in the fruit however, and they did not die. It was not a warning of some danger outside of the danger of Yahweh/Elohim himself. It was a threat. 'If you do this I will punish you, and the punishment is that I shall kill you'. That only Yahweh/Elohim links the consumption of the fruit with death, that the *name* of the tree indicates the only inevitable consequence (the acquisition of knowledge) and that they did not die are indications that the death was an intended and willed punishment, and not an inevitable consequence.

10. The word, interestingly enough, is frequently used of a god or supernatural being deceiving humans (i.e. 2 Kgs 19.10: 'Let not the god whom you trust deceive you'.)

decide whether the woman was correct. After the pronouncements of judgment, Yahweh/Elohim calls a meeting of the *'elohim*, and he makes a speech that confirms all the Serpent's
accusations! He says that the humans have become 'like one of
us, knowing good and evil' (see 3.5 'You will be like *'elohim*,
knowing good and evil').

The serpent had accused Yahweh/Elohim of deliberately
keeping divine knowledge and divine life out of human hands
so as to keep them in an inferior position to himself. Now,
Yahweh/Elohim himself confirms the charge. He cast them out
of the garden to prevent them eating from the Tree of Life, lest
they 'live forever'. With the knowledge imparted by the magical
tree, *and* eternal life, there would be nothing to distinguish
them from the *'elohim*, and that is why he drove them out.

## The Character of Yahweh/Elohim

I here build an analysis of Genesis 2–3 that paints Yahweh/
Elohim as a monster, inexplicably opposed to the fortunes of
the first humans.

### Yahweh/Elohim's Power is Limited
Yahweh/Elohim emerges as a divine supernatural being with
significant power. He does not have unlimited power nor does
his power emerge unscathed from challenges to his control and
supremacy. When the serpent successfully challenges his divine
power, he thus demonstrates its limits and boundaries. Further,
the narration limits God's power by engaging in extreme anthro-
pomorphism. He comes to the Garden at a time of day most
physically comfortable for him, when the air is moving and it is
a bit cooler. He asks a number of questions, which might suggest that Yahweh/Elohim does not know everything.[11] Those

11. Admittedly, it may be argued successfully that those are all rhetorical
questions, spoken by one who already knows the answers, as clearly
Yahweh knows the answer to the question he asks Cain, 'Where is your
brother?' His next comment indicates he knows exactly where the brother
is: 'Your brother's blood cries out to me from the ground...' In this case,
however, there is no reliable grammatical or contextual way to demonstrate
that Yahweh/Elohim knew the answers to these questions (See Cassuto

who believe that no fault must ever be found in the character of Yahweh/Elohim must necessarily conclude that Yahweh/Elohim knew the answers to the questions ('Where are you?' 'Who told you you were naked?' 'What have you done?') before they were asked. Such a reader believes that if God does not know something, he loses his dignity.[12]

Yahweh/Elohim said that if the humans ate from the Tree of Knowledge they would die. They ate, but did not die. Interpretation gets very thick at this point. Yahweh/Elohim's accuracy must by some means be defended. The defenses take two forms. Some claim that when they ate the fruit they really did die and so the prediction came true. They died because at that very moment they started to age, hurtling towards their own physical dissolution; or some claim that the moment of disobedience caused them to die spiritually; it severed their heretofore unencumbered relationship to God. However, the grammar will not easily tolerate such a reading ('on that day', 'dying you shall die'). I doubt that anyone would have ever come up with such a reading unless they were desperately searching for a way to claim that God could never be wrong.

Others claim that in fact Yahweh/Elohim did not carry out his threat. He had withdrawn his intention of judgment and decided instead to show mercy, as he did when he decided to be merciful to the city of Nineveh which Jonah had placed under God's judgment.[13] This defense of God breaks down when examined in the light of the last divine speech. The concern in the speech (3.22) seems not to be mercy or forgiveness. Rather, Yahweh/Elohim seeks here to limit the damage caused by human access to the Tree of Divine Knowledge, the damage which broke down the barrier between the *'elohim* and the

1961: 155-58 for the argument that these are strictly rhetorical questions).

12. 'The mythic theme of the fall has been used by the patriarchal mindset to posit that sexual differentiation, though bringing mutual joy, causes much complexity and pain. It has also been used to shift guilt or fault for the fall away from God (since the idea that God is ultimately responsible for evil is intolerable) and away from man (since it is no less intolerable for the male mindset that all the guilt should pass to man). It is the woman and the animals who assume the guilt in this myth' (Milne 1993: 162).

13. Williams argues that Yahweh/Elohim's motivation is mercy (1980: 52).

domain of creation. The primary, the only concern is protection of divine privilege.[14]

## Yahweh/Elohim's Power Expressed as Malevolence Towards the Humans

> *Real* gods would want to teach you how to be just like them... He wasn't telling her what the gods were, he was telling her what goodness was. To want other people to grow. To want other people to have all the good things you have. And to spare them the bad things if you can. That was *goodness* (Card 1991: 432).

When the humans hid at the approach of Yahweh/Elohim, did that point to 'the fall of man', a complete corruption of their spirit because of their disobedience? There is no real indication that this is the case. Perhaps the humans were always afraid of the divine visits. The only stated difference: now they know they are naked. It is physically apparent that they have risked divine displeasure. They hid from him, not because their souls were corrupt, but because they knew that he was dangerous. Subsequent events both within the narrative (they were interrogated and driven from the Garden to a life of pain, conflict and hardship), and immediately following this narrative (the punishment of Cain, the flood), proved that their fears of God were well-founded.[15]

14. Yahweh expressed similar sentiments in the Tower of Babel story (Gen. 11.6), divine action not because of judgment but rather to protect divine privilege.

15. Jobling constructs the tale in this manner: 'The earth needs a skilled workman; but the only one available is stolen by a villain, who wishes to make selfish use of his services in his private garden. There is, however, a flaw in the villain's plan—if the man eats of a certain tree in the garden, the villain will lose his hold on him. But, by the agency of certain helpers, the man is brought to eat of the tree. When the villain discovers this, he *marks* both the man and the helpers (the curses). But he does not carry out the death sentence. Rather, he sends the man out of the garden, so that the original lack is liquidated...the main problem is with the character Yahweh. To characterize him as villain is not implausible, in view of 3.8 (the garden is for his own enjoyment) and v. 23 (where he feels "threatened" by the man!). As villain, he is the *opponent* of the main program...[but] Yahweh stands out, indirectly but clearly, as *helper* of the main program. This role is by no means so overt as that of opponent, but it creates definite ambiguity' (1980: 42).

Why did Yahweh/Elohim place these trees in the middle of the Garden, if not to doom the humans to a terrifying failure? Why did he threaten to kill the humans if they disobeyed his commands.[16] Why did he deliberately conceal from the humans the *true* reason for his prohibition—that he did not want to share divine attributes with the humans? I come to one conclusion, and it seems inevitable—that God, for some unknown reason, sought the destruction of the humans, or at the very least was completely indifferent to their fate—concerned instead with his own comfort and position.

> If they [the gods] exist at all, they take pleasure in oppression and deception, humiliation and ignorance. They act to make other people smaller and themselves larger. These would not be gods, then, even if they existed. They would be enemies. Devils (Card 1991: 434).

The deity creates the initial plot conflict by placing the trees in the middle of the Garden and forbidding the humans to consume their fruit. Further, the deity discovers the transgression and punishes the miscreants. Yahweh/Elohim protects his realm by banishing the humans from the Garden. Throughout the story Yahweh/Elohim is the *problem* that the humans have to overcome.[17] Yahweh/Elohim is the hindrance, the barrier that keeps the protagonists from reaching their goal, which is advancement, independence and maturity.[18] Yahweh/Elohim is

---

16. I interpret the death as a threat of punishment, and not an inevitable consequence.

17. 'The person who comes out of this story with a slightly shaky moral record is, of course, God. Why does he want to keep eternal life for himself and not let them share it? Even more seriously, why does he not want them to have knowlege of good and evil? What is wrong with this knowledge, that they should not possess it?' (Barr 1992: 14). Simpson observes regarding the serpent: 'But the serpent, a demon hostile to God, told man the truth. He was thus no subtle tempter but, in intention at least, a benefactor of the human race. Man, thus enlightened, ate of the tree and became like God, knowing good and evil (v. 22). The potential threat to God's supremacy had thus become actual, so God, acting decisively and at once, drove him from the garden lest he should put forth his hand and take also of the tree of life, and eat (v. 22), and so make the threat permanent' (1952: 501).

18. Cassuto (among others) understands that the Tree of Knowledge imparts maturity, which is a mixed blessing. He says, 'Out of fatherly love

'the heavy', the force against which the story and its protagonists grind and struggle. Deity in this story is like the troll that
must be outwitted before one can cross the bridge, the spell
that must be broken, the dragon that must be defeated, the
ordeal that must be endured.

In many folk stories the protagonist must break from her parents and must fight many battles in order to achieve transformation. In this story, deity plays both these roles, the role of the
parents who must be left, and the role of the foe that must be
vanquished. Yahweh/Elohim becomes an imprisoner, seeking to
keep the humans in the Garden of Eden in ignorance and dependency. The woman wanted to be wise and this was denied her
by the Lord of the Garden. Yahweh/Elohim dedicates his not
inconsiderable efforts to prevent her (and her husband) from
becoming wise. When they disobey and gain knowledge, he
seeks to minimize their threat to his priority.

That this is a seditious notion of deity there can be no doubt.
To identify this vain and petty creature with the God of ancient
Israel, is to create a troubling conflict—both a conflict in literary interpretation—to what degree should other portions of the
literature (whether limited to the Book of Genesis, or the entirety of the Hebrew Bible) determine the reading of this text. Is
Yahweh/Elohim to be identified with Yahweh, the God of the
Israelites, and to what extent? Is the serpent to be identified
with Satan, or with the devil?[19] It is also a theological conflict,
because we must ask whether the portrayal of God in this passage represents in any way the theological position of some fac-
tion in Israel, and what it tells us about their belief system. And
carrying this line of reasoning one step further, is there any benefit to reading the narrative in this manner for contemporary,

the Lord God forbade him to eat of the fruit, which would have opened
before him the gateway to the knowledge of the world, the source of care
and pain, and would have brought both his simplicity and his bliss to an
end' (1961: 113).

   19. *The* Satan and Satan are to be distinguished. The first is a title (the
loyal opposition) given to one of the angelic figures in the book of Job. By
the time the term becomes a name without the definite article, it represents
a less ambiguous evil figure, more similar to Satan and the devil in the
Christian Testament.

post-Holocaust understandings of deity? Might our culture not be due for a resurgence in interest in a dangerous and unstable god, seeing that such a god might provide the only tenable explanation for the world as we experience it?

## Historical Considerations

> The commonplace that the dominant classes generally produce the major texts hold also for the Hebrew Bible. On the other side, subversive culture also appropriates different patterns that pose a threat to their original home... Interpretation then seeks to recover those other voices that have been silenced and coopted, searching for traces and hints—normally formal—that suggests the presence of something quite different from the overt messages of the text (Boer 1996: 77).

Roland Boer notes that there are certain positions submerged within the text that might not represent the majority position. One might discover them through an examination of the formal structural conflicts within the narrative. The seditious story I have read from Genesis 2–3 is just one of the stories that incompletely inhabit the space of this text. There is also a traditional story that locks in struggle with the monstrous reading. Each reading contains a key element that undermines its credibility and points to the opposite interpretation. If God is monstrous, why does he cover the first humans with skin after he drives them from the Garden? Such an activity bespeaks tender concern and nurturing, exactly the behavior we do not expect from a monster.[20] We see in such behavior benevolent concern, rather than malevolent hatred or incomprehension. There is no way to incorporate this incident into the reading I propose. Likewise, if we examine what I call the theological reading[21] of the Genesis story, in which God is good, having all knowledge

---

20. 'It is God who is placed in a rather ambiguous light. He has made an ethically arbitrary prohibition, and backed it up with a threat to kill which, in the event, he does nothing to carry out. He is of course angry, and the man and woman are frightened. But after issuing announcements of humiliations, limitations and frustrations to which they will be liable, he goes on to care for them and provide the necessary clothes...' (Barr 1992: 12).

21. Wenham provides a good example of a theological reading. See especially 1987: 63-64, 73.

and all power, we get stuck upon Yahweh/ Elohim's threat to execute the couple, which was never carried out. This undercuts the authority of the theological reading.

So when I consider the historical underpinnings of the Genesis 2-3 narrative, I expect to receive at least two sets of answers. Because the text is a site of conflict, no one reading completely dominates the other. Of course, there is usually a master reading, the one that seems to support the views of those who control the institutions of power in Israel. This reading sees the story from the perspective of the authority of the Israelite God. The narrative exhorts the hearers/readers to diligently obey the commandments of God, and be wary of the consequences of disobedience.

When the story is examined from the perspective of fantasy, however, a dramatically different pattern begins to emerge. The woman and the man, by means of necessary transformation, attain new levels of independence, responsibility and maturity. They achieve this by going through ordeal and test. Yahweh/ Elohim, the evil authority figure, resists their growth. What group in Israel might represent its ideas through such a story? Anarchists? Revolutionaries? Some organized protest movement among the sages? Atheists and cynics? It is impossible to say, but clearly some seditious group or individual has entered the most sacred halls of canonical literature and planted seeds of dissent.

The structure of the story is seditious because it is at the same time a movement from transgression to punishment, and also a movement from infancy to adulthood (or at least adolescence), from naivety to maturity, from innocence to knowledge.

The character of God is seditious, particularly in the increasingly radically monotheistic environment in which this story was anthologized with the rest of Genesis. This God demonstrates the character flaws of insecurity and jealousy. He is outsmarted by a clever serpent that he himself had made, and his commands are thwarted by his humans. He blusters in anger against the humans, it is revealed, because of his own fear of competition. This is not a flattering portrayal. To undermine the character of a nation's chief or only deity is to undermine all of the lines of authority within that culture which are thought to have been granted them by divine sanction. For example, virtu-ally every king in Israel and Judah felt it necessary to demon-strate that his authority derived from Yahweh, whether through charismatic choice (Saul, David, Jeroboam, *et al.*) or through divine succession (Solomon, Rehoboam, the Davidic line, and so on). So to undermine the authority of the Israelite God was to undermine the Israelite system of government. This was true to an even greater extent during the postexilic period when the temple priesthood wielded such power.

Yahweh/Elohim opposes the humans and seeks their destruc-tion for no apparent reason. God manifests himself to the humans as a monster. The question that disturbs me, haunts me, is: what sort of historical class or interest group portrays its own god as a monster? Texts such as this one notoriously resist efforts to locate them precisely in the reconstructed history of Israel. Does this story originate in early monarchy, or among the inhabitants of the Second Temple? Perhaps an examination of the implications of this monster god might bring things more into focus.

A traditional rendering of God supports the entrenched struc-tures of ancient Israelite society. In such a rendering, the author-ity of Yahweh/Elohim is supported invariably at every turn of the narrative. Likewise, the truthfulness and reliability of the *words* of Yahweh/Elohim are defended. God knows that they will dis-obey; God knows where they are when they hide from him; God knew who told them they were naked and whether or not they had eaten from the tree he had forbidden. There is no limit to God's power, no limit even to his power over the serpent.

A traditional rendering would regard the judgments of Yahweh/Elohim against the serpent, the woman and the man, as righteous and appropriate, regarding the transgressions of the humans as heinous. The deity cannot be incorrect in any of his statements, and therefore if Yahweh/Elohim says that the humans would die on that day, then in some way that we have difficulty understanding, they certainly *did* die. The story sup-ports the *rules* that produce order and control within the soci-ety. The origin stories, the etiologies, serve to confirm the status quo. There are good reasons, such a story claims, that things are the way they are, and they *should not change*.

Elements within the Garden of Eden story reverse this rendering, and declare that the authority of God must be questioned.[22] This was a hidden but not-so-subtle questioning of the structures and authorities in Israelite society. God is a monster, and his designated representatives, whether the palace bureaucracy of King David's court, or the hierocracy of the Persian period, are monstrous too.

I suspect, however, that there is more here than just a negation, 'This is the God I do not serve'. There is also the sense of the assertion: 'If there is a god then she/he must be monstrous. How else can we make sense of such a horrible world, except to posit a horrible God?'

## Conclusion

> Free will was the excuse for everything. It was God's alibi. They had never read Freud. Evil was made by man or Satan. It was simple that way. But I could never believe in Satan. It was much easier to believe that God was evil... I believe in the evil of God...but I believe in His goodness too... But I see no other way to believe in God. The God I believe in must be responsible for all the evil as well as for all the Saints... It is a big struggle and a long suffering evolution, and I believe God is suffering the same evolution that we are, but perhaps with more pain (Greene 1973: 224-26).

There is always something terribly hopeful in such negations, such denials of the goodness of God. Those in power frequently impose notions of God's goodness upon the backs of those who suffer privation. A negation of the God embodied in theological language is also a rejection of the craven desires of earthly despots. It undermines the notion of a good, all-powerful God which cannot be reconciled with all the pain in the world. It affirms the marginalized classes, which might include the

---

22. 'What God "knows" which he has not told man is that eating of the forbidden tree will make man "like God, knowing good and evil" (v. 6). The prohibition thus is made to appear not in the interest of humans, but only of the deity. This deceptive descrepancy between what "God knows" and what he says is designed to dissolve the illocutionary force of the prohibition' (White 1980: 99). For a discussion of the fruit as bringing 'mature knowledge', see Bechtel 1993: 88.

Canaanites, the poor, or the women. It exposes the justifications and mystifications of the ruling classes.

When might such seditious ideas have gained frequency with Israelite community? We have no effective way to determine this. Imaginatively, a number of reconstructions are possible. The opposition might be generational (old and young); economic (rich and poor); geographic (North and South or urban and agricultural); religious (Ba'alists and Yahwists). In any of these or a whole host of possible others, we might identify the excesses of Yahweh/Elohim with the excesses of the leaders. Or perhaps it is a negative theological attack on Yahwism because of personal or national despair, offering nothing in exchange, making the claim that Yahwism does not work.

It is hopeful because it empowers individuals to say no to injustice in high places. It is also hopeful because it suggests the possibilities that there might be gods (or understandings of God) who cannot be linked with the structural inequities of society.

> After the final no there comes a yes
> And on that yes the future world depends,
> No was the night.
>                     (Stevens 1955: 247)[23]

## Works Cited

Barr, J.
1992        *The Garden of Eden and the Hope of Immortality* (Minneapolis: Fortress Press).

Bechtel, L.M.
1993        'Rethinking the Interpretation of Genesis 2.4b–3.24', in A. Brenner (ed.), *A Feminist Companion to Genesis* (Sheffield: Sheffield Academic Press): 77-117.

Boer, R.
1996        *Jameson and Jeroboam* (Atlanta: Scholars Press).

Brueggemann, W.
1982        *Genesis* (Atlanta: John Knox Press).

Card, O.S.
1991        *Xenocide* (New York: Tor Books).

23. Wallace Stevens, 'The Well Dressed Man with a Beard'. Copyright 1955, Random House, Incorporated, New York. Used by permission.

Cassuto, U.
1961        *A Commentary on the Book of Genesis*. I. *From Adam to Noah* (trans. I. Abrahams; Jerusalem: Magnes Press).

Crossan, J.D.
1980        'Felix Culpa and Foenix Culprit: Comments of "Direct and Third Person Discourse in the Narrative of the *Fall*" by H.C. White', *Semeia* 18: 107-11.

Greene, G.
1973        *The Honorable Counsel* (London: Penguin Books).

Jobling, D.
1980        'The Myth Semantics of Genesis 2.4b-3.24', *Semeia* 18: 41-49.

Melville, H.
1989        *Moby Dick* (repr.; Pleasantville: The Reader's Digest Association [1851]).

Milne, P.J.
1993        'The Patriarchal Stamp of Scripture: The Implications of Structuralist Analyses for Feminist Hermeneutics', in A. Brenner (ed.), *A Feminist Companion to Genesis* (Sheffield: Sheffield Academic Press): 146-72.

Schlobin, R.C.
1992        'Prototypic Horror: The Genre of the Book of Job', in G. Aichele and T. Pippin (eds.), *Fantasy and the Bible* (Semeia, 60; Atlanta, GA: Scholars Press): 23-38.

Simpson, C.A.
1952        'The Book of Genesis', in G.A. Buttrick (ed.), *The Interpreter's Bible*, I (New York: Abingdon Press): 437-829.

Stevens, W.
1955        'The Well Dressed Man with a Beard', in *The Collected Poems of Wallace Stevens* (New York: Alfred A. Knopf): 247.

Wenham, G.J.
1987        *Word Biblical Commentary*. I. *Genesis 1–15* (Waco, TX: Word Books).

White, H.C.
1980        'Direct and Third Person Discourse in the Narrative of the "Fall"', *Semeia* 18: 92-106.

Williams, J.G.
1980        'A Response to Jobling: The Necessity of Being "Outside"', *Semeia* 18: 51-53.

Judith B. Kerman

# *A* Teshuva *on Sacred Clowning, from Reb Kugel**

An anthropologist came seeking wisdom in the little *shtetl*
called Rubadubdub. He appealed to Reb Kugel the Rubadub-
dubber Rebbe, descendant of the great Rabbi Baruch Shem Tov
(the BORSCHT) and holder of a ninth degree borscht belt.

What, asked the anthropologist, is the role of sacred clowning
in Judaism? After giving due consideration and study to this
question, Reb Kugel responded:

> Obviously with butter for dairy meals and with *schmaltz* for meat
> meals. And speaking of chicken fat, in passing we should also
> consider the great question that has occupied scholars for many
> centuries. The Holy One, Barukh Hu, created roads and made
> them with two sides, teaching us to distinguish between one side
> of the road and the other. On the Fifth Day, the Holy One created
> chickens. So we must ask: Why did the chicken cross the road?
> Reb Plato says, 'For the greater good'.

But to return to clowning: I, Reb Kugel, discovered my deeper
clown nature when I was part of a counterdemonstration against
American Nazis (pfui!). Our teacher Rabbi Arthur Waskow says
that an appropriate response to contemporary Nazis (may their
name be blotted out!) would be to make Purim in the street. To
'make Purim' would be to stage an in-their-faces celebration of
the defeat of the archetypal Jew-hater Haman, as told in the
biblical Book of Esther. And what is the traditional way to
celebrate Purim? To have a clown party!

Why should this be so? Further, why does esoteric Jewish tradition describe the rowdy Purim festival, root of all Jewish
clowning and theater, as fundamentally similar to Yom Kippur,
the most sacred day of the year? Why is Purim, according to

* A condensed version of this article was published in *New Menorah*,
the magazine of ALEPH, the Jewish Renewal Movement, in their Spring (1st
half) and Summer (2nd half) 1996 issues.

rabbinic tradition, the only holiday that would be celebrated in the Messianic age? And what, more generally, is the place of sacred clowning in Judaism?

And why did the chicken cross the road? The great Reb Darwin says it was the logical next step after coming down from the trees. And who am I to argue with such a smart man?

Most cultures have various forms of ritual humor in which the most sacred tenets of the group's faith may be burlesqued and significant aspects of social control are allowed to lapse for a period of festival. A party! A party! Cross-dressing and other types of contrary behavior, scatology and sexual outrageousness, uproarious parodies of sacred texts and performances, and mocking of religious authority are common aspects of the religious humor of many cultures (Apte 1985: 155-61). Sounds like fun, doesn't it?

Reb M. Conrad Hyers says religious humor is part of 'the prophetic warning against idolatry, and against that greatest blasphemy of all, the claim to possess or to be as God' (1969: 223). Such a serious boy! He says,

> Through the juxtaposition of awe and laughter, a certain necessary separation and distance from the sacred is achieved, providing that dimension of balance and perspective apart from which piety is in constant danger of becoming pride, devotion of becoming fanaticism, and the sacred the demonic (Hyers 1969: 222).

So why clowning? Clowns are 'individuals who act in an absurd manner because they "naturally" lack common sense and social propriety or intentionally pretend to do so, sometimes as part of a profession or performance' (Apte 1985: 234). Clowning is especially relevant to religious humor because the clown is a liminal or threshold figure (Turner 1985: 235-36). As Reb William Willeford says,

> [the clown is] a figure who himself constitutes and mediates the border between sacred and profane, cosmos and chaos, good and bad, human and animal, human and saint or even god (1969: 100-150).

That's me!!

> [The clown is] the figure...whose folly we recognize in an act of spontaneous judgment and who, even if he does nothing at all,

commands attention. Some fools have powers that are seemingly exhausted in their tricks and jokes; others share magical and religious functions with priests and medicine men who have a direct responsibility for the well-being of society (Willeford 1969: 4-8).

Ritual clowning is common in many cultures as part of either calendrical ceremonies or rites of passage such as weddings and initiations (Apte), although it has been most thoroughly studied in the context of American Indian religion.

Reb Wolfgang Zucker says the clown ultimately expresses the paradox at the heart of all social order:

> The clown makes manifest the ontological paradox of order itself. Order, the *nomos* [rule or law] of the social group, defines the role of every individual belonging to it. It creates, maintains, and protects the social structure in which man is at home, where he knows his way about and where he is, more or less, safeguarded against the shocking experience of otherness. But whatever defines also sets limits...deprives him of freedom... Every *nomos* claims to be from God, but it is never possible to uphold this claim in an absolute sense, because, after all, God allows something to exist outside of this order (1969: 85-86).

My teacher Reb Clif Trolin the Troll, who works a lot with Jewish materials and communities, says the clown is 'the fool that makes us see how foolish we are' (personal conversation, January 1995). And Reb Samuel Miller says, 'the human fool, so ridiculous and even contemptible to human eyes, was just the way any man, Everyman, looked when inspected by the Creator' (1969: 97).

As for the chicken, Reb Einstein says whether the chicken crossed the road or the road crossed the chicken depends upon your frame of reference.

If I was looking for sacred clowns, wouldn't it be logical to look in Judaism? Why not, *bubbie*? That's what I thought! Judaism is so serious about both God and the world, and Jewish ritual life is so structured. Concentrated. Even pressurized. Such a spirituality would make clowning a valuable and logical development. Like a steam valve! PSSSSSHT! Also, Judaism worries a lot about boundary issues as such, inside/outside issues, what it means to be a stranger, the distinction between sacred and profane. In such a culture, the liminality of the clown should have particular power. I started to understand personally the importance of boundaries in Judaism because I was thinking about Jewish clowning, both what it has been and what it could be. And why not?

In fact, hasn't sacred clowning had a crucial place in Judaism for a long time? It has, especially in two forms. Although much watered down in many modern communities, Purim, the holiday that led me into clowning, probably has always been a festival in which the whole community clowns. There is also a rite-of-passage tradition, the *badkhn* or wedding jester, which is still practiced in some Orthodox communities.

Purim is the holiday celebrated in the spring which features the reading of the Book of Esther. It is celebrated on the date on which, according to the story, Haman planned to murder the Jews of Persia because Mordecai, a Jewish gate-keeper, would not bow to him. Such a silly man, Haman, to worry about a thing like that! Nasty, too! Numerous commentators remark on the fact that it is a melodrama, even a bloody farce. The story includes a drunken and foolish king, a beauty pageant, coincidences and miscommunications, even an erroneous accusation of attempted rape against the villain. Better than Peyton Place, even! It's topped off by the mythic conversion of 'many of the peoples of the country [who] declared themselves Jews, for the fear of the Jews had fallen upon them' (Est. 8.17). Talk about wish-fullfilment fantasies!

So where is God in this Purim story? God's name appears nowhere in the story, although later editors added pious prayers which are now found in the Apocrypha. The victory of the Jews in the Esther story is a result of luck, loyalty and the love of a foolish king for the winner of a beauty pageant. Luck, loyalty and love—don'tcha love all those L-words? Even more, the survival of the Jews is made possible by the intermarriage of the Jewish Esther with the Persian King Ahasueras, pretty funny especially these days, when everybody is worrying more about assimilation and intermarriage (in the USA at least, and for now) than anti-Semitism!

So how do we celebrate Purim? By a special reading of the *Megillah*, or scroll, of the Book of Esther. Every time the villain Haman's name is read, the whole congregation erupts with noise and drowns out his name, because we are commanded to 'remember to forget the name of Haman', based on the command to blot out the memory of Amalek, who was Haman's ancestor, who preyed on the weak (1 Sam. 15.7-9). And an elephant never forgets! (Elephants, chickens, pretty soon I'll have a whole ark! But that's another story!)

So does the Purim story have historical roots? Scholars are still arguing about that (what else do scholars have to do? And anyway, they enjoy it! If you've got two scholars, you've got three opinions and four theoretical schools of thought!) They speculate that in fact Purim might have been adapted by the Jews from an ancient pagan festival. So which came first, the chicken or the egg? (*Oy!* Another chicken joke!) Look at the similarity, after all, between the names of Mordecai and Esther and the ancient gods Marduk and Ishtar (Strassfeld 1985: 188). Makes sense to me! Certainly the carnival aspects of the festival are very ancient, older than my grandmother, even, including the customs of masking and costume parties, cross-dressing by both men and women, staging of funny plays in the synagogue and the home, parodies of Torah and Talmud. Rabbis and sages behaved like clowns (!), and the Purim Rabbi was also chosen to rule over the party (Abrahams 1958: 260-61, 383).

A really good contemporary Purim-Torah parody argues that science proves that all food is *treif* (non-Kosher and not to be eaten) by demonstrating that its atoms must sometime have been part of a pig. Therefore, in order to avoid starving to death, we are permitted to eat *treif* food until Talmud students have studied enough science to solve the problem (L. Joseph Bachman, from a Purim-Torah compilation circulated on the Internet, March 1995). So you should all go get a pepperoni pizza!

On Purim, observant Jews are commanded to give special charity and to send gifts to friends. But they are also commanded to get so drunk on Purim that they cannot distinguish between 'Cursed be Haman' and 'Blessed be Mordecai' (Alder 1991: 6), and many examples of Purim-Torah celebrate wine and drunkenness. (Hic!) In Israel (Hic!), they have a major street carnival called *Adloyada*, from the Talmudic injunction to drink until *ad de-lo-yada*, 'until you don't know' (Waskow 1982: 125). Of course, some of us don't know anyway!

Of course, as Rabbi Arthur Waskow and others say, Purim is a bloody story. Its humor is very angry. Reb Alicia Ostriker describes it as 'horror wrapped up as entertainment' (1991: 18). It's not very nice! In fact, it's become 'politically incorrect' in some circles (Wisse 1992: 53). One year there was serious discussion in the Jewish Renewal movement of modifying the *Megillah* or even eliminating the holiday altogether because it celebrates the slaughter by the Jews of 75,000 Persians in the aftermath of Haman's death (Est. 9.16). The biblical precedent was used by supporters of Baruch Goldstein (who was not a nice boy!) to justify his murder of Muslims praying in a mosque at the Cave of Machpelach during Purim of 1994 (National Havurah Committee Internet discussion, 22 January 1995).

This is serious business, but Reb Buddha says if you ask why the chicken crossed the road, you deny your own chicken-nature.

So why does esoteric Jewish tradition describe the rowdy Purim festival as fundamentally similar to Yom Kippur, the most sacred day of the year? According to rabbinic tradition, Purim, 'the day that reminds us of...radical evil', the day that celebrates 'the volcanic energies of...the buried id', is the only holiday that would be celebrated in the Messianic age (Waskow 1982: 125).

Rabbi Michael Strassfeld points out, 'the time when all our rules and inhibitions are swept away' is also when we are able 'to see how easy it is to change from Mordechai into Haman, from a crusader for justice into simply a crusader' (1985: 197-98).

> That is why the Talmud says that we fully accept the Torah only on Purim, for only when we can mock the tradition can we fully accept it. Only then are we safe to do so; otherwise we make the tradition into an idolatry rather than a smasher of idols... *Ad de-lo-yada*...is not an animalistic state of stupor, but rather a...messianic/-mystical moment when there is *no* difference between Haman and Mordechai, good and evil, for both are found in the Holy One 'who created light and darkness, made peace and created evil' (Isa. 45.7).

*Omeyn*! Rabbi Arthur Waskow has written that both Purim and Yom Kippur 'remind us that chance has an important role in the world, but does not rule the world. There is absurdity in the world, but the world is not absurd' (1982: 125-26). From his lips to God's ear!

Purim, the day the lots are cast, was equated with Yom Kippur in a midrashic pun; the rabbis said that *Yom HaKippurim* (the day of the covering-up or obliterating of sin) is a *Yom Ha K'Purim*, a day that is like Purim (private correspondence, Arthur Waskow). On Yom Kippur too a lot is cast, to determine which goat will be the consecrated sacrifice and which will be the scapegoat which is driven out to carry the people's sins into the wilderness. Which is which? Only her hairdresser knows for sure! But Esther and Mordecai saved the Jews of Persia from being the scapegoats in the Purim story!

Reb Jean-Paul Sartre the Nauseated says that in order to act in good faith and be true to itself the chicken found it existentially necessary to cross the road. But Reb Ralph Waldo the Emerson says the chicken didn't cross the road, it transcended it. So go figure!

So is Purim still celebrated in American Jewish communities? Sure! Even though some places clean it up and think it's only a children's festival, the *Megillah* itself is still bloody farce, and history, Inquisition or pogrom, World War II or the latest news from the Middle East, keeps it relevant. Sad but true!

What about the other major clown tradition in Judaism? This is the tradition of the wedding jester, the *badkhn*, also called *marshallik*, for master of ceremonies. Wedding clowning has mostly disappeared outside Orthodox enclaves. Too bad! We gotta do something about that!

Reb Michael Wex performs as a *badkhn*, a wedding clown, as part of the Toronto klezmer cabaret *Big Shpiel*. He says it's not all fun and games:

> Although the word derives from a Hebrew root meaning 'to be happy, to amuse or entertain', the nature of the *badkhn's* art was conditioned by that of the Jewish wedding ceremony, into which notes of sorrow are introduced to temper the joy. Unadulterated joy prior to the advent of the messiah is not a Jewish concept, and even if it were, any happiness at all is likely to attract the *rukhes*, the *sheydim,* and *ayin-hore*—spirits, demons and the evil-eye (1989: 15).

The tradition is traced back to the *mitzvah* of making the bride merry (*b. Šab.* 127). But it is also said that the traditional *badkhn* had not done his job unless the bride was in tears at the end of his oration. Were the tears supposed to be from laughter, from the description (serious or satirical) of the bride's duties or from the moral admonition which was also part of the jester's traditional role? Different sources say different things (so what else is new?). Like the tradition of Purim Torah, satires on sacred texts were common; also roasts, especially roasts of the guests, often as part of the description of the wedding presents (Alana Suskin, Internet correspondence, 21 February 1995). Cheap rich people, what a great target!

Why should people clown at a wedding? It makes a lot of sense if the clown is a mediator of boundaries. Because weddings are nothing if not shatterers of boundaries, between two people and between two families. The breaking of the wine glass is the least of it—all kinds of stuff gets broken, and that's if the waiter doesn't drop a tray!

> The wedding blessings teach us that just as the original ADAM, created in the image of G-d, was male and female joined, so this couple now becomes an ADAM, entering into the fullness of what it means to be a human being, in the archetypal sense of the word (Internet BRIDGES Jewish Feminist discussion, 9 March 1995).

Looking forward to the end of Time as well as back to the Creation, a traditional hope for the new couple is that the off-spring of their union will be the Messiah.

At traditional weddings, rabbis walk on their hands and set their hats on fire, people dance with full bottles of wine on their heads, men in sweat suits may perform the Nutcracker Suite. These are mostly friends and family. Yehudit Sidikman, an Orthodox Israeli woman who clowns at the weddings of her friends, describes a wonderful clown stunt of her own:

> Most of us have experimented with one person standing behind another substituting arms at some point in our childhood. I just take it further by having a wedding celebrity, i.e. mother, teacher or close friend, as the hidden person and allow them to smear all kinds of stuff from make-up and toothpaste to chocolate pudding and other edibles. When we finish, the unveiling of the celebrity is topped off by a handshake from me and one of the gooiest kisses they have ever received (personal correspondence 28 February 1995).

Talk about boundary-merging!

But a wedding is both a joyous and a fearful event. Michael Wex says, 'it may not be accidental that one of the favorite physical "bits" of the old-time *badkhn* was the pulling of a Janus-face, with one side of his face laughing and smiling while the other frowns and cries' (1989: 16).

Yehudit Sidikman explains the emotional context very well. She says:

> On the happiest day of a person's life (or so we hope it is) it is a *mitzvah* to make the bride…happy. Why? well, it is so very easy to look at a wedding as a potential for pain. If not of the bride and groom, then of the single people around, or the couples whose joy has been diminished by shattered dreams or infertility or the loss of a child. It is such an easy time to stop and take stock of life. Where we have come from and where we are going. It is a time of transition. A transition through a door that one can never go back to. Our *mitzvah* in making the *Chatan* and *Kallah* [groom and bride] happy makes us leave ourselves for a moment and rekindles…in us a spirit of well-being (personal correspondence, 2 February 1995).

What was that other important question? Oh yes, the chicken. Reb Ronald Reagan (*der Gipper*) says he forgets why the chicken crossed the road.

So. But enough with the formal clown events, with Purim and the wedding jester tradition! I've got something even better than that! Would you believe me if I tell you that the clown archetype in its sacred aspect fits the ambiguous view both Jews and non-Jews have of the archetypal Jew? It's true! The Jew is the Everyman who argues with God about justice, the one who has historically functioned as both universal conscience and persecuted scapegoat. That's the historic horns of the Jews' dilemma. And the fate of the Jews certainly sometimes has seemed as random as the casting of lots.

In what ways are Jews like clowns? Let's start at the top. Prophets and high priests have clownish characteristics, sometimes in the Bible and sometimes in folktales. The high priest wears strange clothing and purifies with ashes. He even seems to violate *Halacha* (Jewish law); Rabbi Nina Cardin observes that the more holy the person, the less the stringent distinctions are needed (Internet Sh'ma On-line discussion, March 1995). The prophet Hosea is made a fool and a cuckold by God, who orders him to marry a harlot so he can see what God has to put up with! 'For the land commits great harlotry by forsaking the Lord' (Hos. 1.2).

Elijah, a real fanatic in the Bible, returns in folktales as 'a figure of mercy and hope'. He's a sort of wandering magician who appears in disguise to reward the humble and the righteous; 'there is a talmudic saying that when the Angel of Death enters a town, the dogs sniff him out and bark, but when Elijah makes his presence felt, the dogs roll on their backs and begin to play' (Gottlieb 1989: 399). Nice fella!

And then there's Abraham. Just think about Abraham, haggling with God over the number of just men in Sodom. His mirror image is Job, the greatest *kvetch* who ever lived, the just man demanding to know why he suffers. From one perspective, these are the actions of heroes; from another, of clowns! 'Shall not the Judge of all the earth do right?' demands Abraham (Gen. 18.25). But this is just another form of Job's question about his own suffering. And how does God answer? He answers with a question, of course: 'Where were you when I laid the foundation of the earth?' (Job 38.4). Job's classic answer? 'Duhhhh!'

Such a question! The eternal question of the suffering of the innocent and the righteous, the prosperity of the wicked. What does it really ask? Whether the universe is morally chaotic and ruled by chance. Why else do the names of both Yom Kippur, the holiest day of the year, and Purim, the clown holiday, refer to the casting of lots?

Emily Dickinson, the devout and scholarly Maid of Amherst, one of those very few female masters of Torah, says the chicken crossed the road because it could not stop for death. Believe me, this is relevant!

Jewish humor, especially as it has become widely disseminated in the larger culture, is a subject of interest among scholars. Everybody's writing papers and books, even big names! So what's so interesting? Reb Elliott Oring comments that Jewish 'humor was always viewed against the backdrop of Jewish history and experience—a history that was conceptualized as a history of defeat, exile, segregation and unending persecution'

(1983: 266). Defeat, exile, segregation and persecution—interesting stuff, no?—whether Jewish humor is seen as transcendent, as defensive or as masochistic. But one way or the other, as Reb Irving Howe says,

> Here was a people which clung to the myth of the Chosen People despite the most extreme adversity and persecution. Despite its pride it was much too realistic not to recognize how grandiose an anomaly was the contrast between its claim and its position. Hence the characteristic strategy of its humor was an irony which measured the distance between pretension and actuality, held it up for public inspection and then made of it the salt of self-ridicule (1987: 19).

Have you heard of the classic Jewish characters, the *schlemiel* and the *schlimazel*? The *schlemiel* is the one who trips carrying the bowl of soup, and the *schlimazel* is the one in whose lap the soup spills. The *schlemiel* is 'too sweet, too kind, too human to fit in', while the *schlimazel* is the man who 'does all the things the culture says he must do in order to succeed, and fails nevertheless' (Boyer 1993: 6).

And then there are jokes—some great Jewish jokes actually have the structure of clown bits. For instance, Reb Paul Bouissac the semiotician (such a word!) describes a classic routine where a white-faced officer clown insults a disreputable August playing a recruit in basic training (1985: 167-69). The clown bit he analyzes is exactly like the following traditional story:

> A little Jewish man (it's always a *little* Jewish man!) was walking down the street in Germany in the early 1930s, when a Nazi approached him going the other way. The Nazi sneered at the Jew. '*Schweinhunt!*' he shouted. The Jew took off his hat, offered his hand, and replied: 'Cohen. I'm pleased to meet you'.

Bouissac says his clown act mixes 'two types of patterned interactions, which are mutually exclusive in the cultural context…: superiority-inferiority in the military hierarchy; and first meeting between peers, who introduce themselves. The referent of both patterns is a social code that is actualized in the act as an indiscriminate generalization' (1985: 169). We have only to substitute the word 'political' for the word 'military' to have a perfect description of the Jewish joke.

But speaking of hierarchy, Reb Timothy Leary, *L'SD*, says the chicken crossed the road because that's the only kind of trip the Establishment would let it take.

An important Jewish mystical teaching is that every person should have two pockets. Didn't your mother tell you that? Like wearing clean underwear in case you should get hit by a taxi? So. On a piece of paper in one pocket is written, 'For me the world was created'. On a piece of paper in the other is written, 'I am dust and ashes'. What a paradox! But it points up the sacred side of the Jew as Sacred Clown. The ultimate impression left by Jewish humor, while not buoyant, is of a certain irrepressible integrity. Suzanne Langer writes:

> The buffoon really is...the indomitable living creature fending for itself, tumbling and stumbling...from one situation into another, getting into scrape after scrape and getting out again, with or without a thrashing. He is the personified *elan vital*...his whole improvised existence has the rhythm of primitive, savage, if not animalian life, coping with a world that is forever taking new uncalculated turns, frustrating, but exciting. He is...genuinely amoral,—now triumphant, now worsted and rueful, but in his ruefulness and dismay he is funny, because his energy is really unimpaired... (Langer 1953: 342).

But wait a minute! This doesn't fit! The Jew-as-Clown is clownish *because* he's concerned with the moral, because he insists that the universe is not morally chaotic. Tradition tells us God has two names. *Yhwh*, the unpronounceable Name based on the root 'to be', is traditionally spoken as '*Adonai*', which means 'Lord'. It is said to represent the merciful God, the One that can be talked into sparing the just. *Elohim* represents the God of whirlwinds, earthquakes and airplanes crashing into elementary schools. History seems to support Job's experience more than Abraham's. But the religious Jew insists that justice is rewarded and wickedness punished. How foolish!

But the deeper tradition says that this is humanity's job, especially the religious Jew's job: to fix the world, to reunite the world with its caring God. Boy! That's a big job! The commandments, the 613 *mitzvot* of everyday living, are the way observant Jews have been taught by their tradition to do that. Perhaps the world is chaotic, but it is the job of the servants of sacred order to make it whole. And the tradition says the work will not be done while we live, but we are not free to desist from it. So go figure!

There is a story that in the concentration camps, the rabbis held a *Beth Din*, a rabbinical court. God was the defendant. At the end of the trial God was found guilty for allowing the slaughter of his people. And after the court was adjourned, the rabbis held their usual prayer service. There is another story that the Jews in the camps chanted the traditional hymn, 'I believe with perfect faith that, though he tarry, the Messiah will come'.

What is there in Jewish history to support that faith? Not much, except for one amazing, clownish fact: that the Jews have survived while the great civilizations of Rome, Greece, Egypt and Persia, the empires of the Inquisition and Hitler, which overshadowed them and held them captive for a time, have passed away. So isn't it appropriate that the only holiday which will, according to the tradition, continue even after the Messiah comes, the holiday based on a story in which God is hidden and the survival of the Jews hangs on chance, is a clown party?

When you ask the Sphinx why the chicken crossed the road, it says, 'You tell me'.

May the clown in all of us become a blessing in all of our lives. May the clown in all of us help us to touch the lives of others in ways that will lead to further blessings. *Omeyn*.

## Works Cited

Abrahams, I.
1958        *Jewish Life in the Middle Ages* (repr.; New York and Philadelphia: Meridian and Jewish Publication Society [1896]).

Alder, D.
1991        'Drinking on Purim: When to Say When?', *Judaism* 40.1: 6-15.

Apte, M.L.
1985        *Humor and Laughter: An Anthropological Approach* (Ithaca, NY: Cornell University Press).

Bouissac, P.
1985        *Circus and Culture: A Semiotic Approach* (Lanham, MD: University Press of America).

Boyer, J.
1993          'The *Schlemiezel*: Black Humor and the *Shtetl* Tradition', in A. Ziv
              and A. Zajdman (eds.), *Semites and Stereotypes: Characteristics of
              Jewish Humor* (Westport, CT: Greenwood Press): 3-12.
Gottlieb, F.
1989          *The Lamp of God: A Jewish Book of Light* (Northvale, NJ:
              J. Aronson).
Howe, I.
1987          'The Nature of Jewish Laughter', in S.B. Cohen (ed.), *Jewish Wry*
              (Bloomington: Indiana University Press): 16-24.
Hyers, M.C.
1969          'The Dialectic of the Sacred and the Comic', in M.C. Hyers (ed.),
              *Holy Laughter: Essays on Religion in the Comic Perspective* (New
              York: Seabury Press): 208-40.
Langer, S.
1953          *Feeling and Form* (New York: Charles Scribner's Sons).
Miller, S.H.
1969          'The Clown in Contemporary Art', in M.C. Hyers (ed.), *Holy
              Laughter: Essays on Religion in the Comic Perspective* (New
              York: Seabury Press): 89-102.
Oring, E.
1983          'The People of the Joke: On the Conceptualization of a Jewish
              Humor', *Western Folklore* 42: 261-71.
Ostriker, A.
1991          'Esther, or the World Turned Upside Down', *Kenyon Review* 13:
              18-21.
Strassfeld, M.
1985          *The Jewish Holidays: A Guide and Commentary* (New York:
              Harper & Row).
Turner, V.
1985          *On the Edge of the Bush* (Tucson: University of Arizona Press).
Waskow, A.
1982          *Seasons of Our Joy* (New York: Bantam).
Wex, M.
1989          'Kapote Kapades: Traditional Jewish Wedding Jesting', *Canadian
              Theatre Review* 58: 15-20.
Willeford, W.
1969          *The Fool and His Scepter* (Evanston, IL: Northwestern University
              Press).
Wisse, R.
1992          'A Purim Homily', *Commentary* 93.5: 53.
Zucker, W.M.
1969          'The Clown as the Lord of Disorder', in M.C. Hyers (ed.), *Holy
              Laughter: Essays on Religion in the Comic Perspective* (New
              York: Seabury Press): 75-88.

GEORGE AICHELE

## Rewriting Superman

### Reading Superman

> ...they come a running just as fast as they can,
> 'cause every girl's crazy 'bout a sharp dressed man.
> (ZZ Top 1983)

There is no neutral or innocent reading. Every reading happens in an intertextual context that reflects the experience and the interests of the reader. Reading transforms the text, doing violence to it. Reading changes text into something that it is not; to read a text is to make the silent page 'speak', to assign meaning to it. Every reading rewrites the text. However, some readings, by virtue of the ways in which they attend to the text, are both more deliberate and more innovative than others. These rewritings of text are simultaneously playful and serious, at once respectful and irreverent. The television series, *Lois & Clark: The New Adventures of Superman*, is one of these insightful and provocative readings, rewriting a story that has had a powerful grip on Americans and many others around the world since it first appeared almost 60 years ago.

In the following I reread the so-called 'messianic secret' of the gospel of Mark in an intertextual context provided by *Lois & Clark*'s rewriting of the Superman tradition. The intertextual rereading and rewriting that is practiced here is therefore highly anachronistic, and it may be offensive to readers both Christian and otherwise. Why should we read out of context? Why juxtapose such dissimilar texts as an ancient gospel and a contemporary TV series? Yet my anachronism here may be no more extreme than that of the messianic secret itself, which arises out of the contemporary reader's need to make sense of indeterminacies in Mark's strange and perplexing story. The truth is that readers always read in this way—that is, anachronistically, from when and wherever the reader is, which is always here and now. A more neutral or objective or properly contextual reading is simply not possible, although we often pretend that it is. The traditional notion of critical scholarship seeks to erect guarantees against such subjective misreadings, but all that it actually does is to affirm the propriety of one approach to reading (which thereby becomes 'objective' or 'scientific') over against 'improper' alternatives. Our notions of the author's intent, the original audience's understanding, or the pre-understandings of an actual, ideal, or implied reader are themselves always caught in and produced by the intertextual web of our own reading. A critical reading, and better yet, a self-critical one, is certainly more desirable than a non-critical reading; nevertheless, no reading, no matter how critical, moves any closer to escape from the hermeneutical limitation of every reading.

*Lois & Clark* rewrites the Superman tradition. This rewriting opens up a critique of the 'American monomyth' and of the Christian tradition from which the monomyth has been produced. *Lois & Clark* plays with the Superman idea even as it remains firmly within that tradition: if the original Superman tradition is a modernist one, and it is, then *Lois & Clark* must be postmodern. More than just warming over and updating the old stories, the new series is at once pastiche, parody and homage, a truly new version that explicitly establishes self-referential, ironic distance from the original even as it maintains and continues the tradition. The viewer does not have to be a Superman aficionado in order to understand and enjoy the new series, but it certainly helps.

The popular culture tradition of Superman has emerged in comic books, radio and television serials, animated cartoons, Broadway musicals, movies, and novels. The comic book series that first defined the Superman tradition was created by Jerry Siegel and Joe Shuster in 1933, but it was not published until 1938, when it became an instant success and largely created the comic book in its contemporary form (Inge 1990: 131).[1] An

---

1. An important precursor to the Superman comics was Philip Wylie's 1930 novel, *The Gladiator* (Jewett and Lawrence 1977: 185). For a brief history of the comic book, see Inge 1990: 131-42. The relation between Superman and Friedrich Nietzsche's *Übermensch* concept will not be considered here.

extraterrestrial baby, Kal-el, arrives on Earth in a spaceship that had been launched by his scientist parents moments before the explosion of his home planet Krypton. In appearance Kal-el is human; however, he possesses physical powers far beyond those of humans, including the ability to fly, tremendous strength, x-ray vision, superior hearing and invulnerability to bullets, explosions, and almost anything except for Kryptonite, a substance formed in the explosion of his home planet. In the early comic book episodes, Superman did not fly but instead made huge leaps or often simply ran very fast. In this and other ways, the Superman story has been rewritten by its authors over the years, and as Umberto Eco notes, this often takes the form of a retroactive revision of prior episodes (1979: 114).

The alien child is raised by Eben and Mary Kent,[2] who live in the farm town of Smallville, Kansas; the Kents name the baby 'Clark'. After college, Clark Kent moves to the large city of Metropolis where he works as a 'mild-mannered' reporter for *The Daily Planet* (originally *The Daily Star*), a major newspaper. He falls in love with Lois Lane, another reporter for the *Planet* and a glamorous and beautiful woman. Lois, however, pays Clark little heed, for she has already fallen in love with Superman, the mysterious Man of Steel who has appeared suddenly in Metropolis to fight evil and do good.

Superman must maintain his secret identity as Clark Kent, and yet that secret must never keep him from doing good deeds (especially saving Lois) or stopping the forces of evil. Clark's plain blue business suit and horn-rimmed glasses contrast sharply with the red, blue, and yellow outfit that fits tightly over Superman's muscular body. Likewise, Clark's timid, awkward demeanor contrasts with Superman's calm confidence and aloof virtue. Superman is a benevolent Big Brother to all. This greatly impresses Lois Lane, who 'admires Superman's heroism and finds his tricot uniform infinitely more attractive than the business suit of the staid Clark Kent' (Jewett and Lawrence 1977: 69). Along with everyone else in the Superman stories, Lois is unaware that Clark is really Superman, although his only disguise is the suit and glasses. Furthermore, Superman is unwilling

2. In the new series, Clark's human parents are named Martha and Jonathan.

to reveal his double identity even to Lois, and the resulting Clark-Lois-Superman triangle forms the basis on which many of the Superman stories are built. It is (along with Kryptonite) one of the most important obstacles that keeps Superman from immediately accomplishing his mighty deeds (compare Eco 1979: 110-11). By deferring what would otherwise be the immediate solution of almost every problem that Superman faces, this strange triangle makes the stories possible, and interesting.

Robert Jewett and John Sheldon Lawrence discuss the Superman stories as classic examples of the American monomyth. In this monomyth,

> A community in a harmonious paradise is threatened by evil: normal institutions fail to contend with this threat: a selfless superhero emerges to renounce temptations and carry out the redemptive task: aided by fate, his decisive victory restores the community to its paradisal condition: the superhero then recedes into obscurity (1977: xx).[3]

The American monomyth stands in sharp contrast to the 'classical monomyth' of traditional cultures, which features a human hero, such as Prometheus or Odysseus, who journeys to the realm of the gods and as a result of a series of trials gains power to be used for the benefit of other human beings (Jewett and Lawrence 1977: xix).

Each new comic book episode of Superman's story becomes a separate iteration of the monomythic story, without past or future. Eco describes the time paradox on which the Superman tradition depends:

> The stories develop in a kind of oneiric climate—of which the reader is not aware at all—where what has happened before [in earlier episodes] and what has happened after appear extremely hazy. The narrator picks up the strand of the event again and again, as if he had forgotten to say something and wanted to add details to what had already been said (Eco 1979: 114).

This establishes a temporal paradox, in which the sequence of events appears as an 'immobile present' (Eco 1979: 116). Jewett

---

3. Jewett and Lawrence provide numerous other examples of the American monomyth. I am doubtful, however, that this myth is uniquely 'American', and I suspect that variations on it would be found in other societies that are also products of European imperialism and colonialism.

and Lawrence argue that this monomyth has come to dominate the American mentality during the twentieth century, with possibly very harmful consequences. The monomyth tells an escapist and anti-democratic story that encourages passivity in face of communal crisis. It arises from American secularization of the Jewish and Christian traditions, in particular the concept of a supernatural redeemer, 'combining elements from the selfless servant who impassively gives his life for others and the zealous crusader who destroys evil' (Jewett and Lawrence 1977: xx).

Eco likewise argues than modern machine-dominated culture requires a greater-than-human hero (1979: 107). The monomyth hero thus stands in a peculiar relation to modern urbanized, industrial society (Inge 1990: 142), a society for which the 'human scale' of things has been lost. The hero is an outsider on whom contemporary humans project their desires and who reflects their ideology. The great enthusiasm of modern readers and viewers for the superhero arises from their own alienation from material conditions of the world as well as from other people. The Superman story is 'fantasy with a cynically realistic base', an 'underground truth' (Feiffer 1965: 18, 17).

Jewett and Lawrence focus upon the Superman tradition especially in relation to the 'segmentation' of sexuality from redemptive activity that is crucial to the American monomyth. This separation of sexuality from redemption is for Jewett and Lawrence one of the more disturbing features of the American monomyth. They note that as originally drawn in his superhero outfit, Superman apparently lacks genitalia (1977: 62). Clark Kent is a fumbling, ineffectual suitor to Lois Lane, whereas Superman is polite but distinctly uninterested in Lois's romantic advances.[4] He has no need of her, nor of any woman, for sex is irrelevant to Superman. Eco speaks of Superman's 'parsifalism' as 'one of the conditions that prevents his slowly "consuming"

---

4.   In the 1981 movie, 'Superman II', Superman and Lois share a night of passion, which he then erases from her memory with a super-kiss. Clark remains the odd man out, merely a mask for the Man of Steel. In recent issues of the comic book, Superman has also become more erotically involved with women. He has also been murdered and, most recently, resurrected. These transformations of the story are significant, but they take us in different directions than *Lois & Clark* does.

himself, and [that] protects him from the events, and therefore from the passing of time, connected with erotic ventures' (1979: 115).[5] Jewett and Lawrence compare Superman to an angel: he is sexless yet male, and his billowing cape resembles wings (1977: 62).

Jules Feiffer describes Clark Kent as a fiction created by Superman ('a sacrificial disguise') that reflects Superman's low opinion of human beings (Feiffer 1965: 19):

> Clark Kent loved but felt abashed with Lois Lane; Superman saved Lois Lane when she was in trouble, found her a pest the rest of the time. Since Superman and Clark Kent were the same person, this behavior demands explanation. It can't be that Kent wanted Lois to respect him for himself, since himself was Superman. Then, it appears, he wanted Lois to respect him for his fake self, to love him when he acted the coward, to be there when he pretended he needed her (Feiffer 1965: 20).

The difference in personality between Clark Kent and Superman also conceals their identity with one another. It is not clear, however, whether Clark's and Superman's respective behavior in this regard is a deliberate attempt to maintain their/his secret identity, as Feiffer suggests, or whether the contrast reflects instead two incompatible sides of his/their 'nature'. Are two distinct personalities present in Clark/Superman? Or if there is only one 'real' person, and the other one is a deception, then which of them is the real one?

## Rewriting Superman

> [S]urely our own needs and concerns...dictate not a willful and conspiratorial way of appropriating this text and using it for our purposes but a deeper relationship in which it is already somehow appropriated and rewritten (Jameson 1992: 229).

The new version of these popular stories raises fundamental questions about the American monomyth by inverting the narrative strategy of Superman's secret identity. The first few episodes of *Lois & Clark* present the discovery by the citizens of Metropolis that a mysterious, powerful, alien being has chosen

---

5. In an episode from *Lois & Clark*'s fourth season, the slow speed at which Kal-el ages becomes an explicit aspect of the plot.

to live among them. They are immediately suspicious of him, but they also quickly come to rely upon him (in monomythic fashion) to save them from one crisis after another. The Metropolitans begin to regard Superman as a god, a point that the series makes explicit on several occasions. This is the monomyth in overt and extreme form. However, neither the character Superman nor the series itself is content with this Superman-worship. Clark Kent does *not* want to be worshipped; in fact, he doesn't even want to be Superman. He wants to be just another human being. What makes that impossible is (1) the fact that he is not a human being but a powerful alien, despite his human-like appearance, and (2) the fact that he truly is a nice guy who wants to help everybody, perhaps as a result of his middle-American, small-town upbringing.[6]

By making the monomyth, and Clark's rejection of it, explicit, the series encourages its audience to be aware of the power of the medium in which the series itself is presented and to question the significance and attraction of the story. In *Lois & Clark*, Superman's superhuman actions are often performed offscreen, or they are depicted in a non-realistic and often humorous 'comic book' style, with evidently 'special' effects in which the narrative discourse identifies itself with comic book and other popular culture conventions—that is, as fictional. For example, Superman's x-ray vision is depicted by twin cones of red light passing from his eyes to the object at which he is looking. If he is wearing his glasses—that is, if he is Clark—he lifts or lowers the glasses before 'turning on' the x-rays. When he flies, Superman does not leap from the ground (as in the tradition), but he floats upward, sometimes accompanied by a 'mysterious' sound effect. The narrative effect of these depictions is a humorous downplaying of Superman's powers. This is appropriate to the story, for the focus of the new series—as its title indicates—is not on Superman's amazing powers but on the human relationship that Clark Kent struggles to maintain with Lois Lane *in spite of* Superman's powers.

6.  Roland Boer (private correspondence) suggests that 'nice guys' in twentieth-century Western culture are always alien, and further that 'small-town America as represented in Hollywood films is in fact alien rather than "typical"'.

In the new version of the story, Superman emerges out of the tension between Clark's acquired human values (simplistic morality combined with good will toward all) and his inherent extraterrestrial powers. In *Lois & Clark*, and contrary to Feiffer (and therefore contrary to the tradition), it is Clark Kent who creates Superman, not vice versa. Clark adopts the persona of Superman not so much through a deliberate choice but in reaction to unanticipated circumstances arising from his new urban lifestyle. The monomyth is inverted. This creates a moral paradox: 'Clark Kent' is not a conscious deception, as in the traditional version, but 'Superman' is, even though Superman is closer to the alien reality of Kal-el. Superman is a deception, and yet he is not. As Eco says, although for different reasons, Superman both is and is not consumed by the narrative. This adds a tragic quality to Clark's character. The only undeceived ones are Ma and Pa Kent, to whom Clark frequently confesses his dilemma.

*Lois & Clark* often and explicitly mocks the Superman tradition, usually in a self-referential manner. It often reminds the viewer of the tradition and of its own rewriting of that tradition. When Clark discovers that he will need a disguise in order to maintain the human lifestyle that he prefers while performing superhuman deeds, Ma Kent sews for him the famous outfit, but only after they try out dozens of combinations, in which recognizable outfits of many well-known comic book superheroes are rejected. The coining of the name 'Superman' (by Lois) and of various familiar phrases ('faster than a speeding locomotive') are amusingly depicted. When Superman first appears in costume flying over a crowd, someone shouts, 'It's a bird! It's a plane! It's a guy in tights and a cape!' Episodes during the first season of the series began with vignettes depicting the 'human side' of the superhuman being. Superman floats on his back in the clouds on a lazy Sunday afternoon, only to have his reveries disrupted by a passing flight of geese. He plays baseball by himself, batting and playing all the field positions at once by using his super-speed. Here also his profound loneliness and alienation are suggested. Clark heats his morning coffee (and Lois's, when she is not looking) by using x-ray vision. Frequent humorous digressions also refer explicitly to the myth-making power of popular media. Singer/actor/politician Sonny Bono, in the role of the mayor of Metropolis, speaks well-known phrases from various popular songs that he recorded 30 years ago with Cher. Perry White, Clark's and Lois's editor at the *Daily Planet*, is an Elvis fanatic. When a media agent attempts to recruit him, Superman laughs at the suggestion that people might want to watch a TV show about him, but he also recognizes the practical need to license his image (so that profits from the sale of Superman toys can be used to benefit poor children, of course).

In other, more subtle ways, the series also rejects the mono-myth. In the comic books, Clark moved to Metropolis when the elder Kents died. In the new series, Ma and Pa Kent are very much alive and active characters in the stories, not only stitch-ing up Clark's Superman tights but frequently providing him with moral support and common sense advice. A repeated scene features Ma and Pa standing side by side, each with a telephone in hand, talking to Clark. In one episode, Pa fears that Ma is having an affair, and he goes to live with Clark until things are worked out (and they are, with Clark's help). The Kents are ini-tially the only humans who know of Clark's extraterrestrial ori-gins, and they support Clark's desire to keep his alien identity secret and to lead a human life. They fear for his well-being as a superhero, and they dream that he will somehow find a nice girl and career happiness in the big city.

In the new series, Clark Kent is not at all the bumbling, socially inept wimp of old. Indeed, a large part of Clark's prob-lem (in *Lois & Clark*) is that he *does* indeed care about humans, especially his friends and family but also anyone in need, and they also care about him. It is his strong, humane involvement with human beings that pressures Clark continually to use his super-powers—that is, it is Clark's (*not* Superman's) compas-sion and desire to help others that prevent him from simply refusing to use those powers. Superman is a fictitious role that Clark Kent must play out, because of who he really is.

The new Clark Kent has only become aware of his super-powers upon becoming an adult—there was no Superboy. Clark often returns to Smallville, where people remember him with affection as a 'good boy'. People in Metropolis also generally like Clark. Lois calls him her 'best friend', and she regards him with great warmth and eventually love, not contempt as in the Superman tradition. This contradicts the American monomyth, which presents the redemptive stranger/hero as a perpetual outsider, one who has no lasting commitments or connections to the local human community (Jewett and Lawrence 1977: 212). Similarly, Eco describes Superman (according to the tradition) as concerned exclusively with local evils (particularly crimes against private property), while ignoring institutional or national evils (1979: 123-24). The monomyth hero is alienated from and in some ways indifferent to humanity. The hero displays the impassivity of an angel, sometimes even psychopathically so, as in the case of Batman or the Lone Ranger.

Superman in the new series is not the distant, superior, angelic being of the tradition; his relationships with people, and especially with both Lois and his evil enemies, such as Lex Luthor, are distinctly personal. Nor is Superman above the law, as is the monomyth hero (Jewett and Lawrence 1977: 196); he does occasionally break the law, but then he willingly goes to jail, or at least displays guilt. When Lois is wrongly jailed, he anguishes over whether to break her out. At other times, he has Lex Luthor dead to rights but refuses to capture or harm him, because to do so would violate Lex's civil rights. In addition, the new Clark/Superman is very much concened about systemic and institutional evils (such as pollution or poverty), which the series typically depicts as the product of the greed of the wealthy few.[7] In *Lois & Clark*, evil does not simply equal crimes against private property.

However, the most fundamental rejection of the American monomyth in *Lois & Clark* concerns Superman's sexuality—that is, his relation to Lois Lane. This is precisely the point at which Jewett and Lawrence focus on the Superman tradition in relation to the monomyth. Contrary to Feiffer's claim, Clark *does* want Lois to love him 'for himself'—to love the human being, Clark Kent. The only way Lois can ever really know, much less love, Superman is by knowing and loving Clark. Lois must love Clark

---

7. This is not, however, to suggest that *Lois & Clark* presents anything remotely like a sustained critique of contemporary American institutional structures or values.

not because he is 'really' Superman, but simply as the human male (who just happens to be from another planet!) who loves her. Thus what appears as Superman's angelic parsifalism is the direct result of Clark's genuine, very human and male, desire for Lois. Clark is jealous of Lois's attraction to Superman, and he rightly sees it as a formidable obstacle to a genuine relationship with her. However, Lois initially loves only the power and glamour of the Man of Steel: she loves the monomyth hero. This becomes apparent when she almost marries the evil billionaire, Lex Luthor, to whose power and fame she is attracted after her affections have been rejected once too often by Superman (who does so only because he wants her to love Clark Kent!).

Lois must recognize Superman *in* Clark Kent and not choose Superman instead of Clark. She will overcome her monomythic desire when she can love the human being Clark Kent. This is in fact what happens in *Lois & Clark* in the first episode of its third television season: Lois 'recognizes' Superman in Clark just as Clark finally decides that he must reveal the truth to her (he cannot go on lying to the woman that he loves). Lois discovers Clark's dual identity at the very moment that she falls in love with him—that is, with Clark, not Superman. Perhaps it is *because* she has fallen in love with Clark that she can now recognize him as Superman. In any case, despite this radical break with the Superman tradition, the Clark-Lois-Superman triangle continues to dominate the narrative. From this point on, the pressure is on *Lois* to help Clark maintain the secret. This she does in various ways, from distracting others so that Clark can disappear and Superman appear without attracting attention, to more direct and heroic actions to save Superman (and thus Clark) from increasingly-powerful adversaries.

## Identity and Reality

> Superman, then, must remain 'inconsumable' and at the same time be 'consumed' according to the ways of everyday life. He possesses the characteristics of timeless myth, but is accepted only because his activities take place in our human and everyday world of time (Eco 1979: 111).

Roland Barthes defines the hermeneutic code as 'all the units whose function it is to articulate in various ways a question, its response, and the variety of chance events which can either formulate the question or delay its answer; or even, constitute an enigma and lead to its solution' (1974: 17). The hermeneutic code plays a crucial role in the distinction between the 'readerly' and the 'writerly' text, for the hermeneutic code enacts Roman Jakobson's poetic function of language (Barthes 1974: 75, Jakobson 1987: 66-71)—that is, the dominant linguistic function in the literary text. The hermeneutic code is one of five codes through which Barthes reads Honoré de Balzac's story, 'Sarrasine', in *S/Z*. It is through these codes that intertextuality comes into play, to generate the plurality of the text's meanings.[8]

The readerly text possesses the totality of a coherent sentence. It leads the reader to a decisive, singular meaning, through a reading that seems effortless, entirely passive. For the readerly text, a question is clearly asked, and a definitive answer is given. 'Sarrasine' is a readerly text, and it asks (with its character, the Marquise de Rochefide) the question, 'What is the secret of Monsieur de Lanty, of his wealth and of his strange un-humanness?' To this question it offers as answer the story of Madame de Rochefide's would-be seducer, the story-within-the-story of Sarrasine and La Zambinella.

The hermeneutic code thus plays a highly significant role in the operation of the readerly text. However, when the text is a writerly one, then the hermeneutic play of question and answer (or between the giving and withholding of an answer) is transformed. The writerly text subverts the readerly, opening it to multiple and inconsistent meanings. The writerly designates an inconclusiveness and inadequacy of the text that demands from the reader active involvement in the production of meaning. The text itself displays a deficiency that must be supplemented in order for the story to be completed. The writerly emerges from the readerly as the inevitable incompleteness of written language. This hermeneutic incompleteness appears in the story 'Sarrasine' in the form of La Zambinella's castration. It

8.   On intertextuality, especially in relation to biblical texts, see Aichele and Phillips 1995 and Aichele 1996, especially chapter 7.

is also reflected in the deviation of meaning, the anger of the Marquise and her rejection of the seducer, and thus it appears as 'a generalized collapse of economies':

> The route of castration, strictly speaking, discovers the pandemic void of desire, the collapse of the creative chain (bodies and works)...it is fatal, the text says, to remove the dividing line, the paradigmatic slash mark which permits meaning to function (the wall of the Antithesis), life to reproduce (the opposition of the sexes), property to be protected (rule of contract) (Barthes 1974: 215).

The traditional Superman stories are presented in readerly texts, for which the question, 'Who is Clark Kent?' receives the definitive answer, 'A strange being from another planet, stronger than a locomotive, etc.—namely, Superman!' The goal of the stories is to prevent the secret of Clark's true identity from being revealed and yet to meet whatever challenge currently faces the Man of Steel. Thus the fundamental problem in the Superman tradition has always been a metaphysical one: that is, it is a problem of identity, of essence. Conversely, the one great mystery of the Superman stories, including the comic books, TV series and movies, has always been: why does Superman need a secret identity at all? Wouldn't this powerful being from outer space be able to serve humanity much better, since that is what he wants to do, if he were Superman 'full time'? Why does he have to pretend to be the human weakling Clark Kent, or anyone other than himself? Since he already has god-like attributes, why doesn't he simply take control of the police, the government, or the entire world if necessary (Eco 1979: 123)— for the sake of human well being? It is this that, as Feiffer says, 'demands explanation'.

Deborah Joy LeVine, the creator of the new Superman series, has rewritten the tradition around this question, with profound modification to the characters of Clark Kent and Superman (as well as Lois Lane and others). What was a readerly story has become a writerly one. LeVine has in effect inverted the identity of Superman, so that what was merely a 'complication' of the traditional Superman story has become the central focus of *Lois & Clark*. In the new version, Clark Kent is not just a mask behind which a real being called Superman is hiding. Clark is not a disguise in which this marginal outsider, this illegal alien (Gates 1993) passes for human in the modern world. Instead, Clark is the reality of Superman, and Superman is the mask.

> [LeVine] has made a major contribution to the Superman myth: she has effectively reversed the roles of Clark Kent and his super [alter] ego. While traditionally Superman has been the 'real' person and Clark Kent the fictional character, in this series Clark Kent is real and Superman is the alter ego, the fictionalized version of the self (Gates 1993).

In *Lois & Clark*, 'Superman' refers to superhuman or other-worldly powers that the apparently white, middle-class male Clark Kent has found mysteriously but irrefutably attached to himself. As Clark says in an episode from the second year, 'Superman is what I can do; Clark is who I *am*'. However, although he is apparently entitled to all the privileges of the American system, Clark knows himself to be 'other', an intruder in some fundamental way outside of that system. *Lois & Clark* takes humorous note of his questionable social status, and even illegality, in almost every episode. Clark is not evidently a member of an oppressed group; nevertheless, his identity is 'diasporic'. He is the outsider as exile, refugee, and orphan.

Clark's parents tell him that they are not his natural parents, and that they found him in a crashed space capsule. Later on Superman receives confirmation of his extra-terrestrial origin when a holographic globe from the capsule projects messages to him from his long-dead Kryptonian parents. This is the ulti-mate alienation fantasy come true.[9] However, the Kents have raised Clark in a warm and loving home as a stereotypical kind-hearted, middle American young man. The effect on Clark of his own awareness of his non-human identity is not to cause him to rejoice in his otherness, but to make him want all the more to be truly human. On the one hand, he wants to reject his super-human powers, everything that makes him 'special', but on the other, his compassion for the needs of humanity requires that he use his powers frequently.

This answers Eco's question why Superman does not simply use his powers to take control of the entire planet Earth.

---

9.   Compare also the recent movie *Total Recall* (Verhoeven 1990).

Superman's primary interest in local, as opposed to national or international, evil is the direct result of Clark's profound ambivalence toward his own powers. Clark's problem is not to *hide* from Lois Lane (and everyone else) the fact that he is 'really' Superman (that beneath the familiar surface lies an alien reality), but to *reveal* to Lois (and to at least the viewing audience) that this inescapable Superman is 'really' Clark (that the awesome alien is just as 'human' as the nice guy at the office—in fact, he *is* that nice guy).

But how can this truth be revealed? How can the deepest truths about oneself—and this surely would qualify as one—ever be revealed? How could this superhuman being from another planet be nothing more than Clark Kent, who only wants to be loved and treated as a human being? What Clark wants to reveal to Lois is therefore not the truth about himself, but rather it is the non-truth (the ideological fiction) that has been imposed upon him, not by Superman, but by the Kents and his adoptive middle American world (and less directly, by his Kryptonian parents). At the same time, however, what Clark wants to reveal to Lois is that her desire for Superman is itself a desire to escape from her own humanity, a desire for the monomythic immobilizing of responsibility. As soon as Lois (and viewers) can be content with the human being Clark Kent to satisfy their desires, then she (and they) will no longer need the Superman monomyth. Yet Lois can no more settle for Clark than she could be happy in Smallville (except as a visitor), no more than viewers can believe that the world of *Lois & Clark* really exists—no more than anyone can believe true what she knows to be a fiction. Even after she recognizes Clark in Superman, Lois continues to be torn between Clark and Superman, desiring what only Superman can give her even when she is most content with Clark.

However, Clark Kent is not just the man that Superman wishes he could be. Instead, Superman is the being that Clark wishes he weren't! The 'reality' of either Clark or Superman cannot be determined by who Clark, or Superman, believes he is. Therefore, a psychologizing approach cannot resolve Clark's and Lois's dilemma. The truth about Superman's identity is an uncanny one, in Sigmund Freud's sense of that term: that which is most foreign is somehow also that which is most familiar. Nothing is stranger than we ourselves are. The task of *Lois & Clark* is not to resolve this uncanniness, but to uncover it—to reveal the 'oneiric climate' of the monomyth for what it is.

Nor can the problem of Superman's identity be resolved simply by using essentialist notions of human or superhuman nature. Thus a metaphysical approach is also doomed to failure. Although it is clear what this strange being is *not* (he is not originally from Earth), it is not clear what he is. The existentialists based their philosophy around paradoxes generated by questions of personal identity and reality, and more recently, postmodernists have questioned whether the concept of a deep truth about one's self makes any sense at all. The self is a construct, that is, a fabrication or fiction. The self is not merely the product of some prior and objective nature, but rather the product of socio-cultural formation, that is, of ideology. Barthes notes that 'nature' itself is also a construct, a product of ideology (1986: 65-66). Jewett and Lawrence, Eco, Thomas Inge, and Feiffer all stress the ideological dimensions of the Superman tradition. Kal-el's Kryptonian nature, Clark's human nature, and Superman's superhuman nature are all products of the same story.

Walter Benjamin said of Franz Kafka's stories, that '[b]oth the psychoanalytic and the theological interpretations equally miss the essential points' (1968: 127). Like Kafka's distinctly non-monomythic heroes, Clark Kent is in a hopeless situation. He is an exile, a product of diaspora. Clark's identity is not 'the already given content of an individual body but rather…[it] is produced by the geographical circulation of diasporic bodies' (Mostern 1994). While it is true that the traditional Superman only pretended to be human, in docetic fashion, the new Superman *desires* to be human. It is desire for the human that drives *Lois & Clark*, desire that subverts the monomyth. Clark does not fit; he is out of place in a world in which his superpowers stand between him and that which he desires. His identity is a non-identity, just as his truth is a non-truth: neither human nor superhuman, both human and superhuman. *Lois & Clark* shows us how artificial and thoroughly ideological questions of identity and reality always are.

In an episode from the new series' second year, Clark finds that another woman (a lawyer with the amusingly intertextual name of Mason Drake) is attracted to him, and not at all interested in Superman ('he's a lot shorter in person than you'd think'; 'you're not flying around with a big red S on your chest'). Clark confesses his confusion to Ma and Pa Kent: 'Mason likes me—or Clark—but she hates Superman. Lois loves Superman but only likes Clark. Mason likes Clark but in a different way than Lois does'. To which Ma replies: 'Oh, Clark, I've been afraid something like this was going to happen...you're beginning to talk about yourself in the third person!' The episode ends, however, with Lois and Superman (not Clark) dancing cheek to cheek in mid-air, much to Lois's delight.

Through its rejection of the American monomyth *Lois & Clark* reveals and subverts the ideology of the self-identical self, regardless of whether that self is called the 'ego' or the 'soul'. At the same time, these stories refuse the iterative timelessness of myth to which Eco points. Clark Kent creates the fiction of Superman,[10] and like any self, the persona of Superman is the unfinished product of a continuing dialectic, in everyday irreversible time, with other people—the Kents and Lois Lane, mostly, but also Clark's friends at the *Planet* as well as evil-doer enemies such as Lex Luthor, and finally all the Metropolitans who come to depend upon (and worship) Superman. And yet, behind the fiction that is Superman lies another fiction, which is Clark Kent himself, and behind that fiction lies the fiction that is middle America, and so on—an endless chain of fictions.

The old Superman of the monomyth reflects the human desire for totalitarian solutions, the desire that has (re)surfaced so dreadfully and in so many ways during the present century.[11] If Superman is the truth and Clark the illusion, as the tradition has

10. The name 'Superman' itself is apparently created around the S-like emblem that the Man of Steel wears on his chest, an emblem sent with him in the spaceship from Krypton. In *Lois & Clark*, it is Lois who first calls the superhero 'Superman'; he does not choose the name for himself.

11. The temporal conjunction between the initial creation of the Superman story, in 1933, and the spread of fascism in Europe, supported in part by (mis)reading of Nietzsche's 'superman' texts, will not be pursued here, although it is probably quite important.

it, then Superman reinforces the concept of an established superhuman reality—a law that must be so. Superman is the great paranoid desire; all resistance is useless. On the other hand, by rejecting the monomyth the new version of the story presents us with a Superman constantly in flux, constantly being (re)created—what Gilles Deleuze and Félix Guattari might call a schizophrenic Superman, a rhizomatic Superman (1983)— an illusion that can be recognized but never defined because the 'reality' that is its opposite pole (that is, Clark Kent) turns out to be just another level of illusion. Superman remains physically undefeatable, as in the monomyth, but his fractured identity weakens him in other ways. In fact, in regard to Lois Lane it is Superman, not Clark Kent, who is nearly paralyzed: the Kryptonite cage in which Lex Luthor imprisons Superman while he prepares to marry Lois makes explicit this paralysis.

## Superman Rewrites the Gospel of Mark

> [T]here is nothing hidden except to be shown, nor anything concealed except to be brought to light (Mk 4.22).

Similarities between the old Superman of the monomythic tradition and the Jesus Christ of Christian tradition are easy to find. This is perhaps much of the point of the monomyth analysis in which Jewett (a New Testament scholar) and Lawrence engage. Both Jesus Christ, as understood by mainstream Christianity, and Superman are 'strange visitors' who are not of this world, with powers far beyond those of ordinary human beings, although both appear in human form and have been raised since earliest childhood as human beings in relatively out-of-the-way places. Both use their powers in a war on behalf of good and against evil. As of the latest run of Superman comic books, both have died at the hands of evil powers, and both have been raised up again.[12]

12. In *Lois & Clark* it is Lex Luthor who is resurrected, midway through the second year of the series. Lex's suicidal plunge, after his evil intentions had been at last revealed by Clark/Superman, concluded the final episode of the series' first year. Lex's dead body was kept in high-tech suspended animation.

The Gospel of Mark even presents the notion that Jesus had a secret identity. For the last 100 years or more, many scholars have argued that a distinctive theme of the Gospel of Mark is that Jesus (during at least the first half of that book) does not want his identity as 'Christ, the son of God' (Mk 1.1, RSV) to be known. Jesus refuses to allow unclean spirits to identify him as God's son (1.24, 3.12; but compare 5.7), although the reader 'overhears' the claims of the spirits, just as the viewer sees Clark Kent remove his glasses and strip off his homely business suit to expose his brightly colored Superman outfit. However, in the latter half of Mark, Jesus appears to be more willing to let the secret out. The tide begins to turn in Jesus' confrontation with the disciples at Caesarea Philippi ('Then he asked them: And you, who do you say I am? Peter answered and said to him: You are the Christ. Then he warned them to tell no one about him', 8.29-30). The revelation of Jesus' identity culminates first with his dramatic confession before the Jewish high priest ('Are you the Christ, the son of the Blessed One? Jesus said: I am he', 14.61-62) and then with the gentile centurion's 'confession' at the moment of Jesus' death ('In truth this man was the Son of God', 15.39). Therefore even though Mark ends abruptly at 16.8 with great uncertainty as to whether the message of Jesus' resurrection will be spread, or whether he will meet again with his disciples, the reader has nonetheless 'got the message' that Jesus is indeed the Christ.

So goes the widely-accepted reading of Mark's 'messianic secret'. This reading presents the Gospel of Mark as a readerly text, in which the hermeneutic code, the solving of a mystery, plays a dominant function. The question that drives the plot of Mark is, who is Jesus? The traditional answer is, Jesus is really the messiah, just as in the Superman tradition, Clark Kent is really Superman. Certainly Mark's presentation of the problem of Jesus' identity sets that book off from, and in important ways over against, other biblical gospels, and perhaps even the New Testament as a whole. However, when we look at Mark through the reading lens provided by *Lois & Clark* and the way that the TV series has rewritten the Superman tradition, we can understand the messianic secret in Mark in a rather different light.

Read through the lens of *Lois & Clark*, the Gospel of Mark is not a readerly text. Instead, Mark is what Barthes calls a writerly text (1974: 5), a text which refuses to answer our questions. The hermeneutic code (in Barthes's sense of the term) is interrupted and paralyzed, and Jesus' identity remains obscure. The problem in Mark is not to conceal who Jesus really is (namely, the messiah), but rather to *reveal* who messiah really is: namely, a son of Mary (Mk 6.3) named Jesus. Mary's other sons are identified as 'James and Joseph and Judas and Simon', and his sisters are also mentioned, but there is no reference to the human father of Jesus in Mark. Jesus identifies God as the father of the son of man (8.38, compare 13.32) and as the father of those who pray (11.25), and he refers to God as 'Abba, father' when he prays in Gethsemane (14.36). However, to transform these texts into evidence that Jesus is the Son of a divine Father requires a leap of reading (or of faith) that the Gospel of Mark alone cannot justify.

In the Gospel of Mark, Jesus rejects the messianic 'son of God' language of the unclean spirits, the disciple Peter, the high priest, the centurion, and even the narrator. Jesus tells the demons to be quiet when they call him 'son of God', and when Peter answers the question, 'who do you say I am?' by saying, 'You are the Christ', Jesus' response is to 'warn them to tell no one about him' (Mk 8.30). Is he keeping a secret, or is he rejecting the reliability of the disciples' teaching, based on Peter's answer?[13] It appears that Mark's Jesus does not *want* to be the son of God, or Christ, just as Clark Kent does not want to be Superman. The Gospel of Mark's version of the Caesarea Philippi story is very troublesome, and it is not surprising that when we compare the ways that Matthew and Luke handle their parallels to the Caesarea Philippi passage, we find that in each case, they clean up the ambiguous language. In the other biblical gospels, Jesus clearly says, in effect, 'yes, I am definitely the Christ' (Mt. 16.16-20, Lk. 9.20-21).

However, in the Gospel of Mark, Jesus rejects the Christ-language of Peter. Instead Jesus tells the disciples about the suffering and death of the 'son of man', and he gets into an exchange of rebukes with Peter over this matter (8.31-33). In

13. See Weeden 1971, chapter 2, especially pp. 65-68.

the Gospel of Mark, only Jesus uses this highly ambiguous son of man terminology—and even then, it is not clear whether he is talking about himself, or someone else. In Mark, Jesus refers to the son of man on 15 occasions,[14] but the term appears to refer to several different things. What sort of being the son of man is, whether he is the messiah, and whether either the son of man or the messiah is Jesus, remains unclear throughout Mark.

When the high priest asks Jesus, 'Are you the Christ, the son of the Blessed One?' Jesus' answer to him again invokes the 'son of man': 'I am he, and you will see the son of man sitting on the right of the power and coming with the clouds of the sky' (Mk 14.61-62). Is the phrase, 'I am he', an affirmation of mythic identity with God (as the priest seems to think), or is it merely a sort of copula, juxtaposing messianic affirmation with 'son of man' language? Does this terse dialogue clear things up about who Jesus is, or does it rather continue the confusion regarding his identity? The juxtaposition of the priest's question and Jesus' answer appears to create a paradoxical equation, namely, Christ = son of man. Who is this son of man, and what is his relation to the Christ? In the parallels to the story of Jesus' 'trial' before the council in Matthew and Luke, Jesus is equivocal in his response to the priest; in these cases, however, he can afford to be, because these Gospels have already explicitly identified Jesus as messiah. Mark has not.

Furthermore, in the 'apocalyptic discourse' of Mark 13, Jesus says, 'many will come in my name, saying: I am he', and 'if someone says to you: See, here is the Christ; see, he is there, do not believe him. For false Christs and false prophets will rise up, and they will present signs and portents to mislead the chosen' (13.6, 21-22). Jesus himself appears to fulfill these prophecies in his answer to the high priest. Is he a false Christ? In the Gospel of Mark, is Jesus saying (to Peter, disciples, high priest, and of course reader), 'yes, I really am the messiah, God's son', or is he saying instead that 'these are just not the right words'?

The Gospel of Mark remains ambiguous about Jesus' identity. If Mark is read through the lens of *Lois & Clark*, however, Jesus

14. Mk 2.10, 2.28, 3.28, 8.31, 8.38, 9.9, 9.12, 9.31, 10.33, 10.45, 13.26, 14.21 (twice), 14.41, and 14.62.

is not a supernatural being hiding his true identity. Nor is he the messiah king of Israel. Like Clark Kent, the Jesus of the Gospel of Mark is trying, unsuccessfully, to *reveal* who he is. Like Clark, Jesus must play out a fictitious role (in his case that of 'messiah'), not because he wants to, but because of the demands of those who are around him. Nor is Jesus simply an ordinary human being, any more than Clark Kent is. Like Clark, Jesus does not 'fit' well into the human world; he is alien. However, humanity is not merely a pretense for either Jesus or Clark; humanity is profoundly, and paradoxically, tied up with who each of them is. For both Jesus and Clark, humanity is the object of desire.

In some ways, Mark questions the identity of Jesus far more radically than *Lois & Clark* questions that of Clark Kent, because the nature and origin of Jesus remain unclear in the gospel of Mark. Despite its revision of the tradition, *Lois & Clark* rests on the affirmation that Clark really is a strange being from another planet. Much as he might like to be, Clark is not 'really' human. However, in Mark, the reader does not know where Jesus came from (unless 'Nazareth in Galilee' [Mk 1.9] is somehow equivalent to Krypton), nor does Jesus possess anything like the holographic projector which provides parental confirmation of Superman's origin. Instead, Jesus is identified as the 'son of Mary' (Mk 6.3). A voice from the sky speaks on two occasions (1.11, 9.7) and confirms that Jesus is 'my son'. However, Mark does not say whose voice this is. The conventional reading takes the voice to be God. But should it? How could an anonymous voice, even one from the sky, resolve Jesus' identity?

Jesus' status as 'son of God' remains unclear in the Gospel of Mark. It is also unclear who or what the 'son of man' is—is he human or divine?—and whether or not Jesus is the son of man himself, or merely one who teaches about the son of man. Jesus talks about the son of man in Mark, but he never actually says, 'I am the son of man'. However, if the son of man is in some way Jesus' alter ego in Mark, as Superman is Clark Kent's alter ego in *Lois & Clark*, there nevertheless remain important differences between the Gospel of Mark and *Lois & Clark*, and between Jesus and Clark Kent.

The son of man never appears as a character in Mark's story, except in the words and, implicitly, the deeds of Jesus. The betrayal, suffering, and death that Jesus foretells for the son of man happen to Jesus himself. At the transfiguration (Mk 9.2-8), does Jesus rip open his ordinary clothes and reveal a gleaming white son of man suit underneath? If so, this behavior is quite unlike that of Clark Kent, who never disrobes with others about. In any case, the disciples remain confused and ignorant. When Jesus is transfigured, the disciples are terrified and understand nothing, as is usually the case in Mark. Are Jesus' disciples, like the people of Metropolis, so blinded by the monomyth that they cannot recognize their hero as a human being?

Furthermore, Jesus does not have the rapport with his family that Clark has with Ma and Pa Kent. Instead, Jesus' family regards him as insane (Mk 3.21, 31-32), and he in turn does not privilege them in any way (3.33-34). In this regard the Gospel of Mark's Jesus does seem more like the alienated, anti-social hero of the American monomyth—but rather more like Batman[15] or Spiderman than Superman. Jesus' super-powers are also less reliable in Mark than are Superman's in *Lois & Clark*. Superman can of course be weakened by Kryptonite, and in one episode he suffers amnesia and temporarily forgets how to perform super-deeds. In another episode, he is hypnotized and subjected to post-hypnotic suggestion; he is also susceptible to mind-altering chemicals. However, Jesus has to try twice to cure a blind man (Mk 8.22-26), and on other occasions he cannot control the release of his super-powers (5.25-30, 6.56). At yet other times it is not clear whether Jesus has done anything super at all (5.39-43, 7.24-30).

Perhaps the most important difference between the two stories is that Mark offers no narrative equivalent to Lois Lane. There are important female characters in the Gospel of Mark, such as Herodias and the Syrophoenician woman, and especially the women disciples who visit the tomb and then flee after meeting the strange young man at the story's end. However, Lois plays a crucial role in the Superman tradition, and even more so in *Lois & Clark*, where the priority of her name in the title signifies an active and dominant character—perhaps even

15. See Blackmore 1991: 39, 46, 53.

more powerful in her effect on the narrative than Clark and
Superman together. Lois is the point in the romantic triangle
that most forcefully determines the story, and she is the crux of
Clark's identity dilemma. Even after Lois has recognized that
Superman is Clark, she is continually tempted to think of Clark
and Superman as two distinct beings. For her, and for the viewing audience, the task of recognizing Clark returns again with
each new episode. Otherwise the narrative tension would be
destroyed and the story would come to an end. Lois represents
the monomythic dream, and she is in that respect an even
greater enemy to Superman than is Lex Luthor. This becomes
especially clear in the episodes from the show's third season,
when Lois falls in love with Clark and discovers the truth about
his identity as Superman, and the fourth season, when they are
married.

There is no one character in the Gospel of Mark to whom
Jesus struggles to reveal himself, as Clark Kent struggles to
reveal himself to Lois Lane. Some may consider that Simon Peter
plays a role in Mark's story that is analogous to the one that
Lois plays in *Lois & Clark*. The scenes at Caesarea Philippi (Mk
8) and in the high priest's courtyard (Mk 14), discussed above,
might be evidence for this. Like Lois, Peter has the monomyth
dream (in his case, that Jesus is the Christ, Mk 8.29-33), and he
is given the opportunity to stand trial with the human Jesus or
to reject him (14.66-72). Yet even though he is one of the more
important disciples (along with James and John), Peter does not
occupy the central position in the narrative of Mark that Lois
Lane holds in *Lois & Clark*. Furthermore, insofar as Lois constantly (but unconsciously) tempts Clark to become Superman—this remains true even after she knows the truth about
him—her analogue in Mark would be whoever or whatever
tempts Jesus to become the Christ. This is sometimes Satan's
role (for example, Mk 1.13, 3.22-27, 8.33, but contrast 15.29-
32). Is Lois's analogue then Satan? However, Satan appears as a
character only minimally in the Gospel of Mark, although at
8.33, Jesus does refer to Peter as 'Satan'.

In *Lois & Clark*, it is Lois Lane who carries the burden of
deciphering the truth about Clark. This remains true even after
she has 'recognized' Clark, for even after Lois knows 'who he

really is' she continues to learn what that *means*. Lois's failure to recognize the mighty Superman in the humble Clark Kent, and thus her failure to really know and love him, clarifies for the reader the profoundly human weakness of the Man of Steel. And when it finally comes, Lois's success in recognizing him only emphasizes Clark's human qualities all the more, for her recognition of him is itself fractured by his dual existence. It is Lois who uncovers and breaks open the monomyth.[16]

The absence of any clear equivalent to Lois Lane in the Gospel of Mark places this burden of recognition upon the reader. In Mark, the reader must recognize the 'son of man' in the human Jesus in order to understand (Mk 13.14) and repent and believe (1.15). However, because there is nothing like Superman's love triangle in Mark, there is no Galilean Lois Lane to help the reader understand the dilemma and the anguish of the revelation of Jesus.[17] As a result, not only are the disciples constantly confused and uncertain about Jesus' identity, but the reader is also. The great modern question of Jesus' personality (his self, or ego) is entirely untouched by Mark. In particular, neither Mark nor the other Gospels addresses Jesus' sexuality, leaving a great blank page on which the modern reader writes as she will. In this respect (among others), Mark is definitely not modern literature.

Mark's failure to fulfill the modern reader's desire both produces the 'messianic secret', as an expression of the reader's need to identify Jesus, and it simultaneously guarantees the secret's failure. After all, if the 'messianic secret' reading of Mark is correct, this must be one of the worst-kept secrets of all time. Reading the Gospel of Mark through the lens provided by *Lois & Clark* reveals the messianic secret to be the product of an intertext, a particular way of reading Mark's text. This secret

---

16. When I presented parts of this essay at the 1995 meeting of the Society of Biblical Literature, Stephen Moore suggested to me that something like this does happen in the non-canonical gospel of Mary. At the same time, Mikeal Parsons argued that the Gospel of John makes the reader more aware of Jesus' anguish.

17. Jesus' 'dream' of Mary Magdalene, and Mary and Martha, performs something like this function in Nikos Kazantzakis's *The Last Temptation of Christ* (1960).

is not 'in' the text of Mark. It is generated by the hermeneutic code that emerges from the juxtaposition of Mark with other texts. This is the contemporary reader's intertext—our rewriting of the gospel, in order to meet our need to understand who Jesus really is.

Like any written text, the Gospel of Mark is helpless before the reader's desire for meaning. The messianic secret is the product of *our* desire to know who the important characters of the story 'really' are, regardless of whether those characters are Jesus the Nazarene or Clark Kent. The Superman stories derive much of their attraction for us from that desire. Perhaps that is also true for the Gospel of Mark.

> [T]he immobilizing metaphysics underlying this kind of concep-
> tual plot is the direct, though not the desired, consequence of a
> total structural mechanism which seems to be the only one suited
> to communicate, through the themes discussed, a particular kind
> of teaching (Eco 1979: 124).

However, no one believes that Superman (or Clark Kent) is real. As the reading of Mark according to the messianic secret reveals, the Gospel of Mark exposes itself as *Lois & Clark* does not to the dangers of the monomyth, dangers to which the other biblical gospels fully succumb through their more explicit identifications of Jesus as the Christ. Mark allows itself to be taken up by monomythic Christianity and inserted into the canonical frame provided by the Bible, where its subversions of Jesus' identity can go unnoticed. The alternative would be to refuse Mark its canonical position. It would be to read the Gospel of Mark as a writerly text—that is, to see Mark as a deficient text, a castrated text, like 'Sarrasine'.

## Works Cited

Aichele, G.
  1996        *Jesus Framed* (London: Routledge).
Aichele, G., and G.A. Phillips (eds.)
  1995        *Intertextuality and the Bible* (Semeia, 69; Atlanta, GA: Scholars
              Press).
Barthes, R.
  1974        *S/Z* (trans. R. Miller; New York: Hill and Wang).
  1986        *The Rustle of Language* (trans. R. Howard; Berkeley: University of
              California Press).

Benjamin, W.
1968    *Illuminations* (trans. H. Zohn; New York: Schocken Books).
Blackmore, T.
1991    'The Dark Knight of Democracy: Tocqueville and Miller Cast Some Light on the Subject', *Journal of American Culture* 14: 37-56.
Deleuze, G., and F. Guattari
1983    *Anti-Oedipus* (trans. R. Hurley, M. Seem and H.R. Lane; Minneapolis: University of Minnesota Press).
Eco, U.
1979    *The Role of the Reader* (Bloomington, IN: Indiana University Press).
Feiffer, J. (ed.)
1965    *The Great Comic Book Heroes* (New York: The Dial Press).
Gates, H.L., Jr
1993    'The New Season: Television; A Big Brother From Another Planet', *The New York Times*, September 12, Section 2.51.
Inge, M.T.
1990    *Comics as Culture* (Jackson, MS: University Press of Mississippi).
Jakobson, R.
1987    *Language and Literature* (ed. K. Pomorska and S. Rudy; Cambridge, MA: Belknap Press of Harvard University).
Jameson, F.
1992    'A Conversation with Fredric Jameson', *Semeia* 59: 227-37.
Jewett, R., and J.S. Lawrence
1977    *The American Monomyth* (Garden City, NY: Anchor Press/ Doubleday).
Kazantzakis, N.
1960    *The Last Temptation of Christ* (trans. P.A. Bien; New York: Simon and Schuster).
LeVine, D.J. (creator and co-producer)
1993-95    *Lois & Clark: the New Adventures of Superman* (starring D. Cain as Clark Kent and T. Hatcher as Lois Lane; ABC).
Mostern, K.
1994    'Modernity, Postmodernity, Social Marginality', *Critical Theory* (Internet discussion group <http://english-www.hss.cmu.edu/ctheory/>), Review 21 June 17.
Nietzsche, F.
1955    *Beyond Good and Evil* (trans. M. Cowan; Chicago: Henry Regnery).
Verhoeven, P. (director)
1990    *Total Recall*, based on P.K. Dick, 'We Can Remember It for You Wholesale', *The Magazine of Fantasy and Science Fiction*, April, 1966 (Carolco Pictures Inc.).
Weeden, T.J., Sr
1971    *Mark: Traditions in Conflict* (Philadelphia: Fortress Press).
ZZ Top (B. Gibbons, D. Hill and F. Beard)
1983    'Sharp Dressed Man', on *Eliminator* (record album), (Hamstein Music Co.-BMI; Warner Brothers Records).

JENNIFER KRAMER

## Cold Comfort: Stephen W. Hawking and the Bible

Projections concerning the beginning and end of the universe as now defined by astronomy are secular fantasies. They are often erroneously represented as elements of contemporary 'secular theology' because they borrow themes and terms from the secularized 'Judeo-Christian' myth of the origin of the universe, instead of from other more fanciful creation stories. Shared conceits and clichés appear in cosmological theorizing as easily as in populist writing about cosmological physics and its practitioners. By accident or design, overlapping continues because the biblical story of creation is passive and unadorned. Scientists find a double comfort in modeling their ideas after this cornerstone of Western thought because it is so familiar, yet so undefined that it softens the blow of our continuing ignorance without masking it entirely.

Stephen Hawking, the most iconic scientist since Einstein, in particular strikes a biblical chord with his lay writings and public appearances. Hawking's references to God, religion and theology have unfortunately complicated his professed aim to bring scientific thought and method to a wide audience, despite having made his writing more arresting and palatable. At the simplest and most immediate level, his subject is so universal humans have heretofore invoked gods alone to account for them. In that sense Hawking's material is not unique. He is one of a group of astronomers, theoretical physicists and mathematicians concerned with the sorts of universals Einstein formulated in his day. However, Hawking's references are to the themes of ignorance, learning, isolation and loss portrayed in the Garden of Eden story as much as to its themes of the division of light and dark or of chaos and inhabitable space. His use of irony is describable as Yahwist, though such an approach excites fear and disenchantment in layfolk whose worldview is molded by the Christian interpretation of the Fall of Humanity. Hawking's work and related works of others can offer examples to amend our sometimes confused distinctions between the complementary traditions of science and theology. The works just need to be considered in their social context of group communication. Comparing and contrasting scientific and religious or mystical stories, and popular commentaries on such stories, will hopefully show that scientific storytelling draws from the least doctrinal elements of Scripture.

Hawking is not alone in using such troublesome terms as singularity and imaginary time, but he has come to be identified with them and the mystery they pose to the general public. Hawking's life and career have been led by that hypothetical being known as the black hole, a classic example of a scientific idea turned pop fad. The instant popularity of the black hole rested on its convenient representation of essentially religious concepts like death, universal destruction and superhuman emptiness. Its scientific development since, into something more complex than a cosmic cancellation stamp, has won comparatively slow acceptance among a lay audience even while supplying Hawking with his greatest claim to fame. This shift in definition stands as a textbook example of the sort of adjustment scientists must make in the name of preserving a greater overall coherence of theory. As the black hole's hypothetical nature changed it was cast in a series of thought experiments; really stories that scientists tell to themselves, each other and sometimes outsiders.

Mathematics is required here, but only in terms of its use rather than strict definitions. This will hopefully counter a tendency to view math as usable only for accounting, surveying or programming logic. Math underpins the stories scientists tell as well as shaping their more ambitious goals with ideal symmetries. An appropriate example of mathematical ideas played out in story form is a *Gedanken* or thought experiment now considered emblematic of quantum theory. This is called 'the two-slit experiment' because electrons on one side of a wall have two doorways through which they might pass, presumably setting off one detector or another as they do. However it would be more accurate to say 'two-slit experiments' in plural, since the sequence in total involves the same idea played out in a handful of variations: (1) either slit A or slit B is open and a detector is appropriately repositioned to record the outcome in either case; (2) both slit A and slit B are opened and each has its own recording device; and (3) both slits are open but only one recording device is used and cannot accurately record activity at either. The possible outcomes are expressed in mathematical equations in which $A$ stands for activity at slit A, $B$ that at slit B and $I$ the interference experienced by an insufficiently well-positioned recording device. The variation in (2) carried out with two recording devices counts as two experiments, but their probability distribution is still $A + B$ or the total of all possible recordable outcomes for activity at either slit. The variation in (3) includes not only those probable outcomes but the additional unknowns caused by light interference. That equation, $A + B + I$, counts as none successfully or interpretably carried out at all. $A + B + I$ reifies math only in some writers' minds, because their view of $A + B$ solidifies potential. All variations in this experiment are probabilities, not actualities, because we have not dealt with a true lab activity. The simple equations are shorthand, sort of cartoon characters, that stand in for the probability distributions to describe more accurately the full range of possible outcomes of all three 'plot' variants. The ideal lab activity that makes up your choice of plot lines can fool those who are used to more dramatic complexity and color in their stories. They may take its walls, doorways and paths at face value. The difference between math as calculation and math as a source of paradigms can be made with more examples than the two-slit experiment, but this *Gedanken* will return as a mathematical construct and as a story with more than one ending.

## Hawking's Three-Pronged Approach

Scientific populism and postmodernism share goals and means to the point where they can be mistaken for each other or condemned for the same weaknesses. Casual overuse of the word postmodern has only exacerbated the confusion. Hawking's agenda of populist outreach conforms to Jean-François Lyotard's three-pronged approach to the postmodern condition (Bible and Culture Collective 1995: 9-10) even while it may not have sprung from the same disciplinary source. It not only may not be classified as vulgar or pop postmodernism, it may not be describable as serious or critical postmodernism either. As much as he is cast as a priestly know-it-all or substitute god by his critics, Hawking peppered even his most famous and controversial book *A Brief History of Time* with examples of his own fixed beliefs and their slow paths to downfall. Chief among these beliefs is a once generally held idea that black holes must be invincible. Granting a black hole the role of a god or Angel of Death did bring the idea to mass consciousness at first. Now that it has been typecast, however, we are presented with an opportunity to learn how both populism and postmodernism suffer, once a general audience takes something that sounds like theology and proceeds to treat it as such. Even though science and the humanities have their respective methods of outreach they are prone to this same misconstruction.

The aesthetics of Hawking's book *A Brief History of Time* follow from scientific history. For scientists, the traditional distinction between high and mass culture began to break down when Galileo defied social tradition by publishing his scientific findings in populist treatises, written in common language rather than Latin. Hawking's biographical sketch of Galileo in a postscript to his book (1988: 179-80) paints the astronomer not as a victim of the Church or even religious intolerance, but as a faithful Catholic subject to the political machinations of his Aristotelian rivals in academe. Hawking may well have anticipated criticism of his first populist book from elements of the scientific community, and took Galileo as his role model. Hawking committed to using the visually aesthetic aspects of scientific storytelling to his own advantage as his physical state became progressively more restricted, to aid his own projects. He continued this practice in works tailored for public consumption, despite the risks of misinterpretation run when relaying his mini-stories to those outside his professional circle.

While in the humanities an epistemological analysis of the postmodern condition requires a critique of Enlightenment legacy, the untold story of modern science begins with a man born in 1777 named Carl Friedrich Gauss, who defined incommensurability and the constructed character of knowledge for the current day with his life's work. Gauss did not invent what came to be known as the Gaussian curve, since it was actually introduced to probability theory by someone else in 1718 (Young 1992: 213), but he was the first to apply it to scientific observation. He reasoned that any series of readings subject to a range of possible internal errors form a scatter 'summarized by the deviation, or spread, of the curve' (Bronowski 1973: 358). The entirety of this spread marks an area of uncertainty that cannot be refined to correct the original experimental mistakes.

In the twentieth century electronic orbits were successfully modeled with a series of interlocking wavelength paths that are essentially a series of Gaussian curves, a never-ending wave of probability. It was left to Heisenberg to extrapolate that the particle nature of an electron was narrowed down at the quantum level so that its concurrent speed and position at any measurable moment fell within the grasp of those waves of probability (Bronowski 1973: 364-5; appendix, Q1), just as orbiting stars had fallen within their own areas of uncertainty marked out by Gauss in his day. This defining shape of the unknowable is recognized today as the 'bell' curve. Overlapping bell curves do appear in journalist George Johnson's book (1996: 164), but as 'classical' representations of probability. This assumes they are consequently *more knowable* than 'demonic' quantum probability distribution (Johnson 1996: 163), a treatment that additionally calculates interference effects of light energy into the overall range of possible experimental outcomes.

What Gauss taught us was that there is no such thing as *more knowable* probability, only *more unknowable* probability. Those who ignore his warning come to believe an electron can go through only slit A or slit B in one type of classical experiment with one escape hatch, but actually goes through both slits at once in a classical experiment that opens both hatches at once. Things have changed little since the Enlightenment perhaps because of a typical mental habit, shakable only temporarily and by those of the highest intelligence (appendix, Q3). The link between science and certainty is still preferred. The notion of unknowability is still so novel and hard to grasp that layfolk and even some scientists react as if to some new and nihilistic theological worldview—an anti-teleology. Hawking has admitted to such moments of weakness. There is consequently a political dimension to his focus on blind alleys and wrong turns, when he is so often held up as the brightest mind on the planet by the media.

Hawking follows a Nuclear Age tradition in the scientific community regarding the third arena of the postmodern condition—the politics of technology's hegemony in the West 'linked to an ideology of mastery and hence to practices of violence' (Bible and Culture Collective 1995: 10). Those whom Hawking calls 'the philosophers'—presumably secular thinkers and theologians as well—reduced their scope of inquiry since the eighteenth century when science began to be argued with increasingly more specialized mathematical terms (Hawking 1988: 174). He seems to regret this development, and wants to inspire layfolk to brave at least a crucial few of the major 'intellectual and philosophical questions' (Hawking 1994: 37) of the day including allocation of natural resources, pollution and the threat of nuclear war to which he alludes in speeches. Recognition of society's fallibility and ignorance play their part in Hawking's appeals to the public's political conscience, as they did for anti-nuclear arguments made by Einstein and his World War II contemporaries. Hawking repeatedly stresses the standard line that no theory can be proven once and for all, but his real worry is that advances towards coherent theory cannot be digested by the general public (Hawking 1988: 167-68). He publicly wondered how to help amend the public's body of scientific knowledge so members can 'make informed decisions' on pressing technological problems (Hawking 1994: 28-29) while preparing his first populist book.

The means of capturing the public's imagination in order to provide some extracurricular scientific training can backfire, and a critic's epithet of 'postmodernist' can be implied even when it is not used. Scientific practice often wrestles with the ineffable and the unknown, sometimes at once as in the case of the 'event horizon' scenario replayed in many a book on black holes. This makes such just-so stories easily mistaken for the prototheology of folk magical practices, or merely the one-upmanship of 'ironic cosmology' (Horgan 1996: 95). When today we go so far as to conflate irony with defeatism, we allow vulgar postmodernism to leave the impression that there are no more stories left to make or tell at all. Those who try are easily accused of making jokes that amuse only themselves, or a limited audience. Vulgar postmodernism mocks irony, reveling in its illogic, as it takes the forms of pastiche and blank parody: jokes without punchlines. It is nihilistic because what it mocks is the hope of communication and collaboration in a brave and hip new world of pointless online impersonations and robotic romances.

Max Luthi differentiates negative and positive types of irony into general categories, and in doing so he finds a place for such 'all talk and no action' tactics. The postmodern distrust of language in a time of global change is not uncalled for; yet it becomes pre-emptive in its vulgar form—a cultural cul-de-sac for all its multicultural trappings. Verbal or rhetorical irony of wordplay, the vulgar postmodernist's drug of choice, is negative. Unfortunately dramatic irony or 'the irony of event' is in a culture patterned on Greek tradition also negative, a convention Luthi pointedly counters. Luthi had to name positive dramatic irony in folk culture 'contrary irony (*Kontrarironie*)' (Luthi 1984: 129). This willfully positive quality accepts storytelling and opposes the hip postmodern denial of paradigmatic coherence, in addition to providing an alternative to the classical Western norm of Greek theatrical irony. Positive dramatic irony is not an invention of Luthi's day, however, being displayed in the oldest written source of folkloric types in Western culture: the Hebrew Bible (Gabel, Wheeler and York 1996: 33-34).

When scientists appropriate biblical dramatic irony they do not just avoid vulgar postmodernism, despite criticism that they embrace it. They provide an antithesis. Northrop Frye considers the insight of Greek tragedy to be its portrayal of some perversion of greatness, the sort of misery not shown in biblical narratives and of no consequence in *Gedanken*. This difference in emphasis leaves the biblical hero—and the anonymous main characters of *Gedanken*—without the classical hero's main characteristic of being granted superhuman gifts and later robbed of some divine destiny (Frye 1983: 73, 181). In the

Bible, the revolving sword blade that blocks the path to Eden (Gen. 3.24) is indicative of the threat of death, a warning of danger, a separation or estrangement, illusion, perpetual motion, and the presence of a godly force. A dynamic icon like the black hole stands in for the indeterminate areas between perception and thought, gesture and language, implication and description, the vocal and the ineffable. The event horizon in a black hole story is a theoretical limit rather than a thing or place, repeatedly portrayed as gathering darkness or increasing dimness—the reverse of the dawnings of seven days in Gen. 1.1-2.3—or by a line in a diagram differentiated from others only by a printed label. Things made objects in motion by changes of state double as *dramatis personae* and plots at once, to dramatic as well as symbolic impact, in such abbreviated tales.

## Mathematical Words, Mathematical Stories

Semiotics considers natural language, common spoken vernacular, as highly predictable even while its content is not so predictable (Tavis 1986: 196). If one accepts for the sake of argument that theoretical mathematics is a natural language or vernacular among a limited audience, it should be with the understanding that neologisms are not introduced as casually or as gradually as those in common speech. New mathematical terms are introduced in groups, especially the imaginary and complex number systems that will be considered soon. At the risk of overgeneralizing, mathematical neologisms are semiotically integrated whole sentences at a time, instead of a word at a time, which means that Saussurian syntagm and paradigm are developed simultaneously. This 'whole cloth' aspect of mathematical neologisms forces users to extrapolate what must follow from givens (Stewart and Golubitsky 1992: 269). Gauss considered such induction marked by 'unexpected luck' (Young 1992: 110), which leads to the feeling that any solutions arrived at are gifts of God in the sense of seeming alien to their inventors. These group-led constructions have eventually been combined into theoretical expressions.

Induction and mathematical conjecture are now part of standard—if precarious—practice in science. The history of this uneasy integration is marked by a series of intellectual crises. Math textbooks are not given to exaggeration, but strong words appear to describe the historic union of number theory and geometry by way of algebraic equations, beginning in the sixteenth century. Mathematicians felt at a loss to explain the exact meaning of imaginary numbers, first invented as conveniences and later relied upon, 'which they regarded with superstitious awe' and considered 'somehow fictitious and unreal' (Courant and Robbins 1941: 92). These were still often called 'impossible numbers' until the late 1800s (Schwartzman 1994: 112), even after they were successfully integrated with geometry by Gauss and others. The more induction 'tugged', to use a close cognate in English (Schwartzman 1994: 115), the stronger resistance to its implications grew. Pure mathematical inventions began to appear useful in a range of practical sciences like engineering. This applicability was called 'unreasonable' by Eugene Wigner in a now-emblematic 1960 article (Lindley 1993: 1). The creepy feeling of mathematical predetermination ultimately marked the Atomic Age, when Paul Dirac remarked that his equations 'were smarter than he was' because they predicted an antiparticle before anyone recognized what that might entail (Bartusiak 1993: 252). Hawking's radiation is in the 1990s the closest candidate for that level of mathematical prediction (Hawking 1988: 92; Lindley 1993: 237) because the radiation was at first implicit in existing calculations of entropy and its side effects. When faced only with the newest attempts to apply pure mathematical objects to theoretical modeling, some writers cannot resist characterizing attempts to continue along this path as impetuous and delusional, a thaumaturgical ritual that reifies mathematical operations. 'In a kind of mathematical transubstantiation, our numbers, like the Word, take on substance and become flesh' (Johnson 1996: 155).

Yet is it transubstantiation—or are the numbers given apparent substance by way of a story line? Such is a subtle idea within an intellectual arena where stories are as bareboned as particle $x$ moving from one theoretical point to another. Mathematical or diagrammatic models fulfill both required meanings of mnemonic communication as Anna Tavis defines them, carriers of complete if conjectural statements (Tavis 1986: 197).

However, the first meaning of a 'reminder to oneself about something already known' applies to the use of such modeling by scientists and the second, the ' "reading" of familiar sacred texts' by an illiterate, would apply to a lay person who has been told *what* these items indicate without understanding *how* the signifiers signify. Viewers of Errol Morris's *A Brief History of Time* (1992) are not being asked to treat Hawking and his onscreen colleagues as priests, but we are expected to view their communications as an illiterate would a copy of the Bible. Complete statements like a functional computer program or a published scientific paper are shown in asymmetrically framed swatches, an approach that reinforces the opacity of their natural language to those in the audience who already qualify as mathematical illiterates. What saves the director from being accused of deliberate obfuscation is his apparent overall intent, to underline the poignancy of our tenuous ability to communicate with others and with ourselves. Such a fine point can only be lost on those who conflate anything describable as 'sacred' according to the precept outlined above with a catechism: the jurisdiction of organized religion.

## Fairy Tales for Grown-ups

Rudolf Schenda describes the social network of storytellers as one that fosters mentorship of those with less experience by those with more, resulting in a 'collective exchange of narrative knowledge' (Schenda 1986: 76). This historic norm may have been maintained chiefly to preserve stories during a process of intergenerational oral transmission, but the aspect of a group-led learning experience became more salient during the Enlightenment, when popular narratives were mainly geared towards honing a child's ability to balance reason and imagination without falling prey to superstition (Schenda 1986: 77). Now that mass media transforms all scientific news into some form or another of fairy tale if only so it fits into a headline or sound bite, even adults may now be in need of such training, to resist the urge to carry a stopgap conjecture or counterintuitive lab result to some illogical conclusion. The media broadcast scientific and mathematical ideas as they are being debated by their

practitioners, instead of long after they are tested and incorporated into a coherent theoretical superstructure. This immediate yet indirect relationship between specialists and the
general public is mediated by a third party of commentators,
writers drawn from nonscientific disciplines in academia and
from the print press. Some of this intermediate commentary,
even that produced by people with degrees and experience in
math and science, can resort to sensationalism or oversimplifi-
cation and often falls prey to statistical misinterpretations. Lab
terminology is chopped up into free-floating catch phrases like
'the collapsing wave function' or 'the uncertainty principle'
(appendix, Q1-2). Negative repercussions are felt as soon as
some widely circulated yet outmoded technological information
is applied to an unsuitable discipline or exploited in the name
of some pop philosophy. However, the Achilles' heel of scientific populism does not lie in some arcane formula or test
result. Researchers themselves are limited by working in collaboration, as part of a now international population, with
unknown qualities or quantities. They each filter their work
through a brain littered with inbred perceptual and cognitive
stumbling blocks that resist any level of education or pre-
paration (appendix, Q3). If their initial tests produce counterintuitive findings they must amend theory regardless of their
personal preferences, something easier said than done. Sometimes they have no idea what to do or think (appendix, Q4)!

   Stories and arguments can be diagrammed as related by way
of allegories, which can be seen as metonymic devices; all
describable as some or another 'form of imaginative and creative thinking' (Frye 1983: 34-35). Scientific stories are not science because testing and observation remain speculative, but
neither are they pointless fabulation if they may become appli-
cable to the framing of testable hypotheses. Zipes's 'concrete
utopia' would be in such cases any internally consistent, prov-
able or disprovable scientific prediction. The sheer rarity of such
an outcome as a testable point of contention does not make
sufficient grounds to classify scientific stories as purely aesthetic, although sometimes they can be quite amusing. Hawking
wanted to make the standard hypothetical observer in one of
his reports into '"a race of little gnomes"' (Overbye 1992: 100)

once, but his editors at *The Physical Review* refused to indulge him! Such felicities are entertaining but they are not entertainment. They are not amended because of audience demands for more intriguing plot lines, or other such aesthetic considerations.

While scientists use *Gedanken* to mean 'thought experiment', this paper is more concerned with those hypothetical dramas that reach a popular audience before they have been applied to experiments. Such oral commodities in literary form are 'public property' (Gabel, Wheeler and York 1996: 18) and mass media relays of *Gedanken* are quite public. The German *Märchen*, on the other hand, can be translated to include any brief narrative (Schenda 1986: 75 fn), a more neutral term than 'story' or 'tale' which leaves room for colloquialized scientific theory in general, and for the skeletal narrative of an astronaut's journey across a black hole's event horizon in particular. The very existence of black holes dates back to a deductive conjecture made in 1783 (Hawking 1988: 81; 1994: 117), yet they gripped the public's imagination in the early 1970s, still long before any testable ideas had been advanced on how to find them or prove their existence. As *Gedanken* became *Märchen* in mass media, the black hole began to tell us more about ourselves than about itself.

Analyzing such fairy tales for grown-ups requires placing science stories in a communal context without unduly emphasizing any similarity to literary works or entertainment media. Anna Tavis believes that Juri Lotman applied Vladimir Propp's morphology to its social use in storytelling instead of letting it lie fallow as taxonomy of forms in analysis. Lotman's shift in emphasis comes to bear specifically when the morphology is adjusted in transit, during something called 'I to me' communication. When you build yourself a frame story in order to assimilate new information, you are both the storyteller and the intended audience according to a reflexive information flowchart: 'Addresser—Message/Content—Shift of Content—Addresser'. This 'I to me' conversational technique is also called 'discovery communication' (Tavis 1986: 197). 'I to me' and 'I to you' techniques can be employed simultaneously. Scientists often tell themselves as well as each other certain variations on a theme in order to illuminate points of contention. Physicists label their 'interpretative discourse' as stories repeatedly, in terms of following a story, or countering with a different story, or having one person begin a story and another finish it. Hawking made a statement regarding such activities once, during a radio interview, that would be quoted widely afterwards. He spoke of the benefits of describing one's thoughts to others, since the retelling itself can lead to a mental reshuffling of ideas. 'Even if they don't offer any suggestions, the mere fact of having to organize my thoughts so that I can explain them to others often shows me a new way forward' (Hawking 1994: 159).

In science 'discovery communication' is a collective endeavor that applies theatrical methods to hopefully practical ends. Researchers and students coordinate linguistic and gestural interpretations with math-based graphic displays, operating by intertextual means on what one study terms a 'virtual symbolic space' (Ochs, Jacoby and Gonzales 1994: 154). Modes of speech, gesture, and writing are applied repeatedly even during a single interaction. Participants thereby come to a joint understanding of the processes outlined and results implied by two-dimensional illustration, as they synchronize vocal and physical references to aspects of its visual representation. Dramatic identification is brought to bear on these mini-histories, but with less dramatic impact than that achieved by full-fledged literary renditions. These socially animated visual displays allow for 'moments of shared biography and shared narrative between physicist and physical entity' (Ochs, Jacoby and Gonzales 1994: 157, 162, 167, 170) without promoting the sort of passionate attachment inspired by deeply ingrained ethnic myths, finely etched characters or engrossing plot lines. Participants treat some inanimate or non-animal entity as a protagonist, which the storytellers can identify with the way an actor does his role, and supply a 'change of state' as a rudimentary plot. 'Such a reading allows the referent of "I" to be at least double-voiced: it is both the physicist and the anthropomorphized constructed physical system' (Ochs, Jacoby and Gonzales 1994: 166). Additionally the scientist's, like the Yahwist author's, bag of tricks includes 'humor, irony, suspense, hyperbole, and concrete detail' designed to appeal to a present audience, as well as purely oral devices such as repetition (Gabel, Wheeler and York 1996: 117).

## The Bible as Storybook

With that conceptual framework in place we return to Hawking's appropriation—rhetorical or otherwise—of biblical symbol and theme from Genesis. Why would someone raised as a Christian take the God of the Christian Old Testament and its outmoded covenant to heart? Is it merely the pull of so recognized a phrase as 'in the beginning'? He had been christened as a baby (Hawking 1994: 4), and grew up in St Albans, considered the historic 'ground zero' of British Christianity. The city itself was built around a shrine dedicated to a Roman centurion martyred to the Christian faith, including a cathedral traced to 303 CE (White and Gribbin 1993: 7). By the time of World War II, the area housed an extant abbey church and another building used for the St Albans School that Hawking attended as a youth (Hawking 1994: 6-7). Early 'reader response' (Bible and Culture Collective 1995: 13) experiences primed him for an application of Yahwist redaction to his theorizing and his popularizing as an adult. Reading and family discussion of the Bible and his winning a school divinity prize are details mentioned in the film version of *A Brief History of Time*, as well as a number of populist books on Hawking and modern cosmology, including his autobiographical works. His mother Isobel adds in the film that 'his father used to read him Bible stories from a very early age, and he knew them all very well, and he was quite well-versed in religious things'.

The atheism and agnosticism attributed to Hawking varies, and the definitions of God he has publicly dismissed do not stand as categorical denouncements of religion or belief. However, his concept of God has been handmaiden to his scientific ideas. His approach to biblical texts was likely malleable from youth, even judged solely on his year in Majorca. As a guest of Robert Graves around the age of eleven, he shared a tutor with Graves's son. The tutor was a protégé of sorts, as much absorbed by the Bible at that time as Graves himself: 'He therefore set us to read a chapter of the Bible each day and write a piece on it', Hawking remembers. 'We got through all of Genesis and part of Exodus before I left' (Hawking 1994: 8). Hawking had to know one of the two creation stories was a redaction, even if he was not told the first postdates the second. Two accounts back-to-back leave two subjective approaches open to one object: the origin of the universe (Gabel, Wheeler and York 1996: 6-7). The value of shifting dramatic focus within a twice-told tale is apparent when you compare the two versions, as he was likely encouraged to do under the circumstances. The abstract God of the first account is powerful but indistinct; the action of cosmic scope (Gabel, Wheeler and York 1996: 114-15). The first presents a sequence in which events are allowed or mandated rather than directly caused in some fashion comparable to human handiwork. The divine voice of the God of Genesis is interdiegetic (Bible and Culture Collective 1995: 94), inviting questions as to how involved the creator was in creation itself. One could easily imagine the boy being drawn to this version, favored by scientists.

Later in Genesis appears a dynamic symbol much like the varied representations given in science of the event horizon at the onset of a black hole, considering that the event horizon stands as much for what we do not know and cannot say about the unknown as it marks a physical point of no return. When Adam and Eve are banished from Eden and the world temporarily cursed, an animated sword appears to block their way home. Various translations (Gen. 3.15; Suggs, Sakenfield and Mueller 1992: 14; Kaplan 1981: 14 n, 15, 289 n) imply that the sword is stationed independently; as if to brandish itself. Banishment and the various punishments relevant to the issue of original sin pale in comparison to the loss of 'open communication with God' (Bible and Culture Collective 1995: 95) represented by this paradoxical illusion. While Hawking has not made specific reference to this symbol, it is emblematic of the sort of imagery used in *Gedanken*, especially the many variations used to stand in for that otherwise undetectable event of the horizon of a black hole: a bank of fog, the gateway to hell, the long arm of the law, etc. The event horizon has taken on the same role in secular culture as that forbidding sword did for Judaism,

evoking humanity's intellectual estrangement from their sur-
roundings—ever present yet apparently without a fixed boundary. This scientific myth refers to a universal human condition
in the way a religious artifact might, threatening to encroach
upon classically theological territory without usurping religion
outright.

## The Black Hole as Bogey

The black hole in its many guises was invoked as soon as its
name was coined, the way myths of doom and destruction have
been drawn from extant and defunct religions. Today that
1970s phenomenon continues and our fascination with it continues to be morbid. Even scientists are admittedly not immune,
as they wrestle with a phenomenon that appears to defy empirical testing. Hawking is unusual, though not singular, in his
experience of this intellectual crisis and the threat of impending
death that stands in for it in commentaries. Derek Powney
relates in Morris's film what Hawking first told him after being
diagnosed with motor neuron disease. Hawking's fate in short
order was apparently to be complete paralysis, with one exception: 'his mind would still be in perfect working order, and he
would be unable to communicate with the rest of the world'.
Morris cuts to a respirator balloon. However Hawking did not
need artificial life support to bring the specter of death into his
consciousness. As a war baby he was brought into the world
under the threat of blitzkrieg bomb raids. The family house was
struck, though with no fatalities, when he was just a baby. This
physical memory persisted through postwar years, in the form
of an unrehabilitated bomb site he used to play in with a childhood friend (Hawking 1994: 4). Eventually the black hole's aura
hung over two decades of his work. As it sucked up cultural
allusions like so much interstellar dust all its baggage came to
be carried by its researchers. A bumper sticker in Hawking's
office, often mentioned in press reports, sported the pun, 'Black
holes are outta sight', to invert a once positive slang term. That
apocalyptic horseman of secular Armageddon introduced earlier
in the century, entropy, had finally been given a name and a forever hidden face. One writer specifies that once the Aquarian

Age of the 1960s was pronounced dead the black hole was appointed its symbolic undertaker:

> 'The black hole', one astronomer commented, 'is the scapegoat of the seventies'. Like everyone else during a decade of war, paranoia and assassination, astronomers had become necrophiliacs. They dwelt in dark mysterious places looking for the Word, and the Word was annihilation... God would eat us (Overbye 1992: 102).

Myth can be subsumed by theory, though. Even the black hole's bloated reputation was eventually bested by shockingly ordinary scientific reasoning. This is why Hawking's step into the intellectual unknown seemed so disturbing at the time, despite the fact that he was not the first to come to the conclusion that black holes are subject to the same entropy as any other entity in the universe. Like the fairy tale figure who allows his enemy to spring itself into its own trap, Hawking left the black hole to be tripped up by Newton's famed thermodynamics. His name would be attached as 'Hawking radiation' to the subatomic particles into which the once purportedly invincible hole would eventually rend itself. Luthi's *Kontrarironie* takes the form of an upset of appearance and reality in tales, yet this tale in particular left its mark in the real world of the scientific academy. Hawking seems to have entertained the idea that God would eat us well enough, but only until it no longer served his practical purposes.

## Semiotic Reform

The conjectural animations in the film *A Brief History of Time* betray a preoccupation with an immanent failure in our dominant semiotic order, but its human participants are shown attempting to remodel Einstein's space-time and reconfigure the means of expressing such a novel idea simultaneously. Errol Morris's opening credits recede and then fade into a black background one section at a time. This repeated dramatic gesture will be extended, amplified and elaborated throughout. Other momentarily salient references to 'space-time catastrophe' and 'negative time direction' in speech or print, a NASA photo of a spiral galaxy shown in negative, and additional thematically consistent images emphasize reversals of fortune and receding goals. Animated examples always circle back to the fate of an astronaut who is never shown but always on the brink of death, poised to begin a story only he will ever know in its entirety. The astronaut's disappearance also heralds the end of theory, of testability, of mathematical construct; complicated by mind-boggling stopgap terms like imaginary, nothing, emptiness. This is not just a drama of some particular investigative phenomenon but the harbinger of a fundamental crisis in physics that its practitioners are still gauging.

Hawking's own shifting attitudes towards this process indicate how taxing the project will prove to be for everyone. Hawking mused that more than one time dimension should be conceivable in 1980, 'but I for one find such a universe very hard to imagine'. He later announced in a 1991 speech that imaginary time 'is already a commonplace of science fiction. But it is more than science fiction or a mathematical trick' (Hawking 1994: 66, 83). In just over a decade the idea had been harnessed for its plot potential by sci-fi writers who could not also refine its conceptual implications. The fact that those implications could still only be suggested by scientists during the 1990 production for Morris's film indicates that fiction writers could not be faulted for their more casual use of the term. The story of being overtaken by an event horizon as it is told and retold in *A Brief History of Time* is equally reflective and didactic. The uprooted astronaut travels into a physical unknown that is not merely untested but theoretically inexplicable. When physicists relive his misadventure they must face their own resistance to change as they navigate shifting ground. Repetition builds suspense because the story remains unfinished to some as yet unknown extent. The point of these retellings, though in some sense there is an ending of sorts—the astronaut's death—that never changes, is to isolate possible areas of misunderstanding rather than to unveil some inner meaning. The tellers seem to expect that perhaps next time a different or newer ending will appear.

Such intellectual fluctuation is bound to disturb, postmodernism notwithstanding. No one is immune to hesitancy and denial; only their choice of determinism varies. This theme runs throughout the book and film versions of *A Brief History of Time*, but in a more general sense it is a hallmark of scientific inquiry. The shadow of Bertrand Russell, who interpreted an expanding, entropic universe as proof of the ultimate futility and pointlessness of existence, falls across Steven Weinberg's study of the first three minutes of cosmology's current model universe as well as its extrapolated last three minutes (Davies 1994: 154). Once again scientific commentary reminds us of theology, without being accompanied by any of organized religion's reassurances.

By avoiding nihilistic or deterministic conclusions, Hawking reflects more positively upon relinquishing intellectual stasis in the face of counterintuitive physical evidence. Hawking in childhood considered redshift unbelievable. In Morris's film he states, 'A static universe seemed much more natural'. In print he admitted that it took until the second year of his PhD research to realize: 'I had been wrong' (Hawking 1994: 10). His denial owed much to the 'well-defined theory' of Einstein's that attracted him to cosmology in the first place, since its definition in turn owed a lot to Einstein's loyalty to a static universe (Hawking 1988: 40). Two other major self-corrections are given the same treatment: Hawking at first shied away from mentioning the radiation of a black hole, as did his colleagues. He speaks for them all when he declares in the documentary, 'At first I didn't believe it'. He almost repeats himself regarding Don Page's idea of cosmologically irreversible time symmetry: 'I had made a mistake'.

An unfortunate artifact of the abbreviated and impersonal style of Morris's film is the misrepresentation of Page. He is introduced without context and out of correct chronological order. The film places Hawking's 1985 near-fatal pneumonia before his concession that entropy would still hold in a collapsing universe, and isolates Page from the theoretical discovery he originally made and Hawking confirmed in tandem. Their collaboration is underemphasized in the film and in some written studies of Hawking and Page. Their opposing personal approaches to theology gave way before the unknowns of science, a reticence that overtakes even the convictions of Page, a self-described evangelist. He is generally portrayed as a friend

whose comparatively apostolic Christianity has not interfered
with a long-running relationship dating from 1975, when Page
conducted postgraduate research under Hawking's supervision
(White and Gribbin 1993: 158, 169, 266). Hawking has identified Page as one of his 'principal collaborators' during the
'second "quantum" phase' (Hawking 1988: vii, 150) of his work,
culminating in their concurrent papers on time symmetry in a
collapsing universe. Hawking helped Page write his paper, then
Page told *Physical Review* to hold his until Hawking's was
done. The two publications appeared in the same issue, with
Hawking introducing Page's opposing thesis as interesting and
quite likely true. All of this predated Hawking's nearly terminal
bout of pneumonia (Overbye 1992: 377), despite appearances
to the contrary in Morris's film. As Hawking and Page traded
stories about life in a collapsing universe, their shifting intellectual allegiances most likely led to incremental adjustments of
their opposing scenarios. Only one variation is preserved in
Morris's film—Hawking's. It is undercut by the reported outcome, but unfortunately that only makes it appear to have been
corrected by Hawking alone.

## Particle Man, Particle Man

Oral authoring strategies and the repetitions they allow apply
equally to motion pictures, which have more in common with
oral than written cultural artifacts. However, the hybrid nature
of a documentary's collective narratives cannot always be reconciled. In the film *A Brief History of Time*, a spinning Rolex
provides that 'small touch of realism' (Luthi 1984: 106) in contrast to an 'otherworld' beyond the event horizon; serving as a
point of identification for its intended audience. The empty
loop of its watchband is all that is left of the doomed astronaut,
a substitute protagonist inviting the use of a double-voiced 'I'.
This icon is a main character of a narrative. The character in
turn stands in for an ideal observer of a classical scientific
experiment, one that scientists may or may not be physically
capable of conducting. The action of the scientific story is a trajectory retraced by a communicator vocally or by some gestural
re-enactment, but that trajectory is written among scientific

interlocutors as functions and diagrams rather than a standard plot line. This is where Morris's animated *Märchen* diverge from the *Gedanken* after which they were patterned. The scientific stage is set in the case of the black hole's event horizon by a model built out of quartic geometry, a diagram that merely makes a dispensable appearance during an uncontextualized 'bracket syntagma' (Metz 1991: 126) or parenthetical series about halfway through Morris's film. To assuage 'math anxiety' and its related discomforts, Morris and his collaborators sacrificed the abstract for the ordinary in the name of commercialization. Yet the substitution of a Rolex watch for an entire human is doubly economical, at the expense of a full understanding of the relationship between mathematical structure and the dramatic trajectory of a thought experiment. Notions of space-time distortions are focused on the presentation and manipulation of a single synecdoche, the watch, as its second hand slows down or fades away. Unfortunately, such animated stage settings divorce theory from its original analytic setting: those geometric models of Hawking and Penrose mentioned only in passing by interviewees. They are shown only once in that abbreviated sequence, introduced by Hawking's computer voice announcing, 'I tended to think in pictures'. Morris at least provides a little comic relief by letting John Wheeler blame ourselves for our inability to redefine time as we need it, instead of an inflexible Nature or a perverse God. Nonetheless, the director repeats the mistake Hawking made as an author. Imaginary time is identified as crucial to the structure of an unbounded universe in both the book and film, yet it is not sufficiently defined in either.

Most crucially, if we are to grasp how different Hawking's space-time may be from our understanding of Einstein's model, yet another substructure serves as the grid upon which that geometric stage dressing of quartic geometry is hung: the mathematical symbols of the complex (Hahn 1994: 2) or Gaussian plane. The complex plane is not so unimaginable, since you have likely seen it if you have ever plotted a graph using $(x,y)$ axes in grade or middle school. Gauss's geometric interpretation of imaginary numbers was finalized simultaneously by two contemporaries named Wessel and Argand. This naturalization process gave rise to the complex plane, really the Cartesian coordinate plane relabeled with 'complex numbers'. Complex numbers might be better known as 'duplex' numbers, since their formula is 'folded up' (Schwartzman 1994: 50) to consist of a 'real part', the $x$ coordinate, and an 'imaginary part' for the $y$ coordinate. The coverage encouraged in this mathematical system is key to the 'analytic' approach one takes by applying imaginary space-time to a model of some physical state or process. The 'analytic procedure' uses induction, instead of the Euclidean deduction from axioms or postulates known as the 'synthetic procedure'. The analytic approach unifies 'geometry, analysis and algebra into one organic system' (Courant and Robbins 1941: 165). Analytic mathematics comes into play when opening the 'conic sections' invented by Apollonius—namely all known geometric curves—into three dimensional shapes on the complex plane. Three-dimensional conics are known as 'quadric surfaces' (Courant and Robbins 1941: 212), those models used by Hawking and shown intermittently in his books and in the aforementioned bracket syntagma during Morris's *A Brief History of Time*.

The important point about the applicability of quadric surfaces to theories under construction is their elasticity. One of the quartic models just mentioned, an open hourglass shape known as a 'hyperboloid of one sheet', is described as a remarkably forgiving conjunction of 'two families of intersecting straight lines' that may rotate at each intersection. The figure can, as a topological invention, thereby be 'continuously deformed into a variety of shapes' (Courant and Robbins 1941: 214). A change in the shape of the stage setting may give rise to a different story line altogether without a complete reworking of the underlying modeling system. This allows participants to adjust their retellings in a way that will not completely alienate fellow interlocutors. Whether or not you understand the full range of scientific implications of the story of the falling astronaut or his disappearing Rolex is of less consequence. Physicists themselves may not be fully apprised of them, which is why their models and the *Gedanken* played out on them must remain flexible.

Such a technical point is thrust aside when quasi-religious

populism comes to bear on mass media coverage of Hawking and his work. *The Making of A Brief History of Time* television documentary (Coulthard 1992) indicates that Morris and his technicians interpolated the gothic architecture surrounding Hawking throughout his life in order to lend an air of mystical import to his experiences and achievements. This is a common—even irresistible—analogy effected with verbal and visual embellishments. Western culture's continued equation of meditation or other intellectual work with religious philosophy may underlie this continued application of Christian iconography. Much as certain science writers accuse theoretical physicists of being too much like priests, they often express shock and dismay when shown the indeterminate, playful and collaborative nature of theorizing. In short they seem more upset when scientists are *not* like priests.

Hawking as an icon is triply universal, at the cognitive, symbolic and mythic levels, but that commands attention more than reverence. All still figures are ambiguous at first, since movement is our most reliable aid in edge detection. Motionlessness equals death to us; so strongly that the unnatural stillness of paralysis engenders a state of alarm that needs to be consciously suppressed. Hawking's dependency on his robotic communications system differs from our growing dependence on electronic media only by degree. His speech synthesizer, once peculiar only to him, is now so common a sound in automated phonebank 'helpdesk' systems it has been nicknamed 'Fred'. Such a chummy term implies we have come a long way since 1968, when the forbidding acronym turned accidental first name HAL was given to a predatory talking computer in Stanley Kubrick's film *2001*. Hawking's fate is as unresolved as any of ours, since even he admits that none of his ideas have been decisively, experimentally vindicated. These layered indicators give off a sort of connotative feedback. This coalescence makes the man endlessly fascinating, but his sheer popularity is overstated when it is presented as commanding the respect and authority of a religious figure's. He is symbolic of what we are becoming; more like a hero of speculative sci-fi set in the near future than an archetypal ideal of a saint or religious martyr.

## Algebra by Any Other Name

The limits of our associative A ↔ B reasoning powers are called up by the liminal figure, the mediator or transformative cross-over. In dramatic myths these figures are usually human or anthropomorphic. However in semiotic squares more abstract relationships can be framed without rendering them static, putting A ↔ B conjunctions into respective all-encompassing paradigmatic contexts. Mathematical set theory clearly allows for an 'all else' option in the simplest Venn diagram (illustration A), placed in a frame representing the 'universal set $E$' (Clapham 1990: 191) including everything in E undefinable as A or B (A′∩B′). Not so with the semiotic square's is/not taxonomy. Though neither/nor lends art its interpretative play, there is no place for the undefined in Levi-Strauss's diagram except as an appendage.

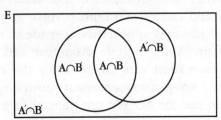

*Illustration A*

The following semiotic square treatment of shots drawn from the film *A Brief History of Time* is in line with Sergei Eisenstein's definition of montage as drawn from the common associative or A ↔ B logic people use in everyday observations. However, my comparison is not limited to adjacent shots and, more importantly, incorporates a categorical rejection of Eisenstein's underlying Marxist interpretation of Newton's Law of Action and Reaction. Shots *A* and *B* do not meld into idea *C* in the audience member's mind; they leave open a paradoxically indefinite non-A, non-B alternative. My semiotic square replaces literary syntagmatic elements within paradigmatic arrays with arrangements specific to motion pictures: clashing images and spatial trajectories, rather than mythology's clashing characters and narrative trajectories. This variation on cinematic semiotics values content over form in the sense that it considers whatever things or actions as depicted rather than evaluating the shots that contain them. The relationships between content elements are symmetrical if the overall presentation gives them equal weight by granting them equivalent places in repeated or inverted sequences. The ellipse in the diagram marks a logical gray area where something passively defined falls between two contradictory semantic categories.

As a documentary, *A Brief History of Time* contains the director's choice and arrangement of independently supplied arguments. The declarative is rendered suggestive. Morris's film employs a rather humorous example of broken symmetry applied to visual rhetoric. The first thing you see after the opening credits in front of a field of receding stars is a chicken; finally replaced by Hawking's famous cybernetic wheelchair, complete with vanity plate, just before the closing credits. Hawking's mother provides interior bookends of a sort, since she is the first and last natural human voice you hear. The closing sentence of her first appearance is made in a sustained shot of her in a chair: 'Some people disappear and are never seen again'. This observation sets the tone for the rest of the film. Every time our hypothetical astronaut hurtles towards oblivion he stands in not just for her son but humans in general. Near the end she portrays her son as a 'searcher' who may as often as not be talking 'nonsense, well don't we all'. Her final line—spoken over a shot taken from an astronomical atlas—is, 'You don't know what your taking off point is'. Her comment pinpoints a difficulty with interweaving intuition, logic and scientific methodology at a time of technological advancement when observations must be predicted and then instigated in order to be made at all. Once again her statement applies to humans in general, since she is the most immediate candidate for one of these 'just ordinary people' Hawking invites to universal discussion, both at the close of the film and his book of the same name. Images of her son bookend her appearances. Finally the furthermost matching shots are of a backdrop of stars (illustration B). The standouts are two different images framed by that backdrop—the chicken and the wheelchair—unified by the stars and Hawking's mechanical voice.

Stars framing image ——▶ Montage of Stephen ——▶ Isobel with inserts

Isobel with inserts ——▶ Montage of Stephen ——▶ Stars framing image

*Illustration B*

Morris thereby places Hawking as the intermediary between individuals with their respective philosophical worldviews and society's transforming relationship with the physical world, rather than between heaven and earth or life and afterlife. We define our humanity the way we define the God of Genesis—passively, in a manner that invites paradox. God fills the void between the ever-expanding boundaries set by the difference between our knowledge and inexperience. We, after that fashion, fill the void between the mute animals we dominate and the talking machines we invent (illustration C). This failure is not the Greco-Roman tragic irony of a fall from grace, but the Yahwist irony of unresolved conflict or inadequacy.

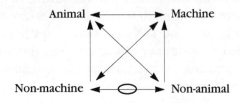

*Illustration C*

Hawking's decade-old invocation of the God of Genesis continues to irritate regardless. Margaret Wertheim accuses Hawking of taking the phrase 'mind of God' from the end of his book *A Brief History of Time* to open Morris's film adaptation (Wertheim 1995: 218) but she is wrong. Such an opening would employ hubris by misrepresenting the scientific investigations that follow as substitutes for religion. Morris's film really opens with the clicking noises Hawking makes when composing his communications, followed by the metaphorically unanswerable riddle, 'Which came first, the chicken or the egg?' announced in Fredspeak. The film ends as the book does, with a cryptic story of redemption. The man who could spare no more time to argue theology after being diagnosed with a fatal disease imagines a future when we will all be free to do so at our leisure. The projected end of physics will take place when we have answered the what and how of the universe, in a way that even non-specialists can appreciate. The next to last sentence in both versions of *A Brief History of Time* sets the stage for us then to ask that question philosophers now have no time, interest or intellectual wherewithal to ask: 'Then we shall all, philosophers, scientists, and just ordinary people, be able to take part in the discussion of why it is that we and the universe exist'. This penultimate sentence is neither anti-God nor anti-religion, nor does it subsume theology into science. It rather provides some means by which theology outlives science to mark our final intellectual destiny. Hawking quailed at the idea of leaving in the last sentence when the book went to press, but later joked that cutting it would have halved his sales (Hawking 1994: 37) the way the equation of $E = mc^2$ purportedly halved his sales. He was quite probably right to worry on both counts, since it is such an audacious yet faithful thing to say. This famous closing line speculates on an even more distant future in which there truly are no more questions left to ask and no more stories to tell; as if the 'whirling and flashing' sword has been halted and our view of Eden is no longer obscured. Humans for whom the answer to the ultimate 'Why?' is known instead of unknown will by definition 'know the mind of God'.

## Shared Stories, Divergent Emphases

The second and last example of a semiotic square here compares the same character in two stories, told by opposing factions, drawn from a shared source in laboratory physics. Our mysterious electron from the two-slit experiment mentioned earlier stars in a scientific *Gedanken* turned pop culture *Märchen* at once. Semioticians will recognize the little trickster as a liminal figure, one which might balance the 'intolerable oppositions' (Bible and Culture Collective 1995: 78) of a culture beset by violently shifting modes of expression. The graph (illustration D) adapts the Aristotelian semiotic square template as a representation of the two-slit experiment and its range of all possible experimental statements, including inconclusive ones.

The square in turn symbolizes the tensions between two different approaches to storytelling rather than a gulf between two cultures. To place our electron on the top horizontal arrow between A and B would be equivalent to the statement that it is 'A and B'—liminal in the sense of a supernatural hybrid or hermaphrodite. To place it on the bottom horizontal arrow between Not A and Not B would be equivalent to the probability statement in quantum or classical physics that it is 'not A nor B'—liminal in the sense of being describable only in negative terms. The dramatic myth of a hybrid 'A and B' electron and the dynamic myth of an indeterminate 'not A nor B' electron are of equal importance and plausibility. We are free to identify with that monstrous 'A and B' electron as well as the unspeakable 'not A nor B' electron, as long as we do not privilege one as more real or more knowable than the other. Such stories may be cold comfort for us in a postmodern/postedenic world, but they will have to do for now.

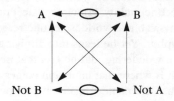

*Illustration D*

While scientific stories are available to be told by and commented on by us all, they could be more valuable if treated as opportunities for mutual enrichment. The work of science does not require its practitioners, though they will eventually resist mystical or artistic tendencies in practice, to surrender religious convictions or even eschew literary flights of fancy. Scientific storytelling however, based in mathematical mapping (Clapham 1990: 111), presents its own difficulties. It does not allow for the allusion, metaphor or insinuation inherent in common spoken language. One must look in geometric modeling or laboratory observations for a new ending to an old story; then only if it promises to explain the previously unexplainable. Elaborations based on accepted theoretical norms are commonly rejected as trivial in science because of this requirement alone, one that rules the discipline above anything describable as a god. That does not restrict careful use of elaborations in other arenas, if they contribute to developing some common understanding of non-literary enterprise. The bigger challenge remains to develop the 'discovery communication' skills used within theoretical science across a wider range of disciplines.

## APPENDIX

The following is an interview with Dudley Herschbach, Nobel Prize winning chemist, Harvard professor and *The Nobel Legacy* TV series co-host, conducted by Jennifer Kramer on October 28th, 1995, after that summer's Flight From Science And Reason conference at the New York Academy of Sciences:

Q1
K:    There is a point [in *The Ascent of Man*] where [Bronowski] makes a point of renaming The Uncertainty Principle 'The Principle of Tolerance'. There seems to be a physical, real-world, scientific reason for naming it that, that it's not just a metaphor. Yet he leaps into applying it as a metaphor for moral responsibility. I'm wondering, did he feel that he had to leave out the math, and the math of it is where that limitation comes in?
H:    It's unfortunate that the name 'Uncertainty Principle' got attached to it. There's a great irony, as there often is. It goes this way: the uncertainty aspect really only makes what little sense it does if you're thinking of things in a classical mechanics point of view. In classical mechanics, of course, you could to arbitrary accuracy—in principle—find both the position and the momentum of a particle at the same moment. What quantum mechanics tells you is that because things really have this intrinsic wave/particle duality, you cannot specify both the momentum and position—with arbitrary accuracy—at the same moment. Now actually, in practice, it's almost the other way around. In classical mechanics, you discover that you can't specify that in practice, in practical terms, the position and momentum accurately enough to follow them indefinitely in the time development. You will lose track of where the particle is eventually, later, because you didn't know where it was well enough to start with. The philosophical thing was that in classical mechanics, in principle, it was possible to imagine that if you knew the position and momentum or velocity of a particle, you could predict exactly what happens in the future. The laws allow you to have that information on what happens in the future. But in practice you cannot specify accurately enough the position, to know after awhile, where it is: it

becomes more and more uncertain. The longer the time goes by, it takes more precise [measurements]; the more accurately you have to know things *originally*, in order to integrate the equations, and make note in that time interval what happened.

Q2

K:    And what does that tell me?

H:    What it tells you is that, in the first place, there's no possibility of specifying those things. Furthermore, you don't need it! In quantum mechanics, the whole description of states and motion is different than in classical mechanics. It asks for less information. Here's an example: I speak a little in my paper [for The Flight From Science and Reason] about this notion of 'nuclear spin' that comes into magnetic resonance [MRI] and so forth. In classical mechanics, you'd say, 'OK, this particle—be it a nucleus or an atom, whatever— has a little magnet in it. That magnet can have any orientation, any angle with respect to, let's say, up'. Any angle! So in classical mechanics to take exactly the configuration or state of that particle, you'd have to give that angle to *whatever accuracy you need*. In quantum mechanics it says, that angle has no meaning. That spin can only be 'up' or 'down'. It has only two possibilities. And we can know exactly by an experiment which way it is! You see, so quantum mechanics is much more definite than classical mechanics! So most people haven't studied it, The Uncertainty Principle, and assume what it might mean, and of course it doesn't mean anything like that.

Q3

K:    You probably aren't familiar with this article. I just stumbled across it not too long ago. It's by two men named Goldberg and McDermott. It was called 'An Investigation of Student Understanding of the Real Image Formed by a Converging Lens or Concave Mirror' in *American Journal of Physics* in 1987. They had a whole series of kids that they brought in. And they showed [the students] a mirror reflecting onto a screen in a particular setup. Then they took the screen away and asked, 'Is the image still there?' Only the very, very brightest of the kids got it immediately, that of course it's still there. For everyone else who needed hints, it didn't matter how much math or preparatory work they had...

H:    I'm familiar with a lot of studies—not this particular one—but studies for science education that show that even when people have had physics courses and so on, if they encounter a situation that's outside their realm of experience in the courses, where they worked on certain kinds of problems and came to understood how to look at them, that they fall back on primitive ideas that really don't make sense in terms of the understanding they later acquired in the course, but nonetheless they fall back on it! So it's a pedagogic phenomenon you need to be aware of. But there's nothing wrong with that!

Q4

K:     I know you teach undergraduates... Do you actually get up and say, 'When I was in high school, and I had to deal with chemistry, I had this problem?'

H:     Maybe an example would be this: There's a class of chemical reactions called 'unimolecular' meaning that the molecule itself falls apart and rearranges. Well, for about thirty years this totally mystified chemists. They couldn't understand. By that time they knew, in the early years of this century, you needed a certain amount of energy for the molecule to be able to break a bond or rearrange to another configuration of bonds. But the only way they knew for a molecule to acquire energy was by bumping into another one! So that meant that you had to have two things interacting to transfer enough energy. But the rate of reaction seemed to depend just on the one thing. How could that be? Well, people eventually came to realize that if you had a collision and it deposited enough energy so the molecule could break a bond, it still usually wasn't in the right place. That energy might have been in the wrong bond and had to migrate around until by chance enough of it accumulated in the bond that would break, to let it break. In the meantime, while that was happening, the molecule might suffer another collision and get deactivated, so it no longer had enough energy to break the bond. When you put in that step and work out how these compete, then you discover a certain range in which the activating and deactivating happen very fast, then the bottleneck step is the slow thing, the time lag. That therefore makes the overall thing look as if it just depends on the one molecule. I use many examples like that along the way so they see that scientists don't understand what's going on right off the bat. Usually if you're working in some new area it's completely mystifying; just the way chemistry's mystifying to most people when they start studying it. And you have to be patient; you have to really work at it. Then you reach the point of view where you say, 'Yeah, yeah, really, that's obvious'. [Laughs]

## Works Cited

Bartusiak, M.
    1993        *Through a Universe Darkly: A Cosmic Tale of Ancient Ethers, Dark Matter, and the Fate of the Universe* (New York: Avon Books).
The Bible and Culture Collective
    1995        *The Postmodern Bible* (New Haven: Yale University Press).
Bronowski, J.
    1973        *The Ascent of Man* (Boston: Little, Brown and Company).
Clapham, C.
    1990        *A Concise Oxford Dictionary of Mathematics* (Oxford: Oxford University Press).

Coulthard, E.
1992        *The Making of A Brief History of Time* (Anglia Television Limited).
Courant, R., and H. Robbins
1941        *What Is Mathematics? An Elementary Approach to Ideas and Methods* (Oxford: Oxford University Press).
Davies, P.
1994        *The Last Three Minutes: Conjectures about the Ultimate Fate of the Universe* (Science Masters, 3; New York: BasicBooks/ HarperCollins Publishers).
Gabel, J.B., C.B. Wheeler and A.D. York (eds.)
1996        *The Bible as Literature: An Introduction* (New York: Oxford University Press, 3rd edn).
Frye, N.
1983        *The Great Code: The Bible and Literature* (San Diego/New York: Harvest/HBJ).
Hahn, Liang-shin
1994        *Complex Numbers & Geometry* (Spectrum Series, 1; Washington, DC: Mathematical Association of America).
Hawking, S.W.
1988        *A Brief History of Time: From The Big Bang to Black Holes* (New York: Bantam Books).
1994        *Black Holes and Baby Universes* (New York: Bantam Books).
Horgan, J.
1996        *The End of Science: Facing the Limits of Knowledge in the Twilight of the Scientific Age* (Reading, MA: Helix Books/Addison-Wesley Publishing Company).
Johnson, G.
1996        *Fire in the Mind: Science, Faith, and the Search for Order* (New York: Alfred A. Knopf).
Kaplan, R.A.
1981        *The Living Torah: The Five Books of Moses and the Haftarot* (new trans.; Brooklyn, NY: Maznaim Publishing Corporation).
Lindley, D.
1993        *The End of Physics: The Myth of a Unified Theory* (New York: BasicBooks/HarperCollins Publishers).
Luthi, M.
1984        *The Fairytale as Art Form and Portrait of Man* (trans. J. Erickson; Bloomington: Indiana University Press).
Metz, C.
1991        *Film Language: A Semiotics of the Cinema* (repr.; trans. M. Taylor; Chicago: University of Chicago Press [1964]).
Morris, E. (dir.)
1992        *A Brief History of Time* (Triton Pictures).
Ochs, E., S. Jacoby and P. Gonzales
1994        'Interpretive Journeys: How Physicists Talk and Travel through Graphic Space', *Configurations* 2: 151-71.

Overbye, D.
1992        *Lonely Hearts of the Cosmos: The Story of the Scientific Quest for the Secret of the Universe* (New York: HarperPerennial/ HarperCollins Publishers).

Schenda, R.
1986        'Telling Tales—Spreading Tales: Change in the Communicative Forms of a Popular Genre', *Fairy Tales and Society: Illusion, Allusion, and Paradigm* (ed. and trans. R.B. Bottigheimer; Philadelphia: University of Pennsylvania Press).

Schwartzman, S.
1994        *The Words of Mathematics: An Etymological Dictionary of Mathematical Terms Used in English* (Spectrum Series, 20; Washington, DC: Mathematical Association of America).

Stewart, I., and M. Golubitsky
1992        *Fearful Symmetry: Is God a Geometer?* (Cambridge, MA: Blackwell).

Suggs, M.J., K.D. Sakenfeld and J.R. Mueller (eds.)
1992        *The Oxford Study Bible: Revised English Bible with the Apocrypha* (New York: Oxford University Press).

Tavis, A.
1986        'Fairy Tales from a Semiotic Perspective', *Fairy Tales and Society: Illusion, Allusion, and Paradigm* (ed. R.B. Bottigheimer; Philadelphia: University of Pennsylvania Press).

Wertheim, M.
1995        *Pythagoras' Trousers: God, Physics, and the Gender Wars* (New York: Times Books/Random House).

White, M., and J. Gribbin
1993        *Stephen Hawking: A Life in Science* (New York: Plume/Penguin Books).

Young, R.M.
1992        *Excursions in Calculus: An Interplay of the Continuous and the Discrete* (Dolciani Mathematical Expositions, 13; Washington, DC: Mathematical Association of America).

# RICHARD WALSH

## Ancient Biblical Worlds and Recent Magical Realism: Affirming and Denying Reality

### Reality, Realities and Narrative Worlds

Once upon a more hierarchical, traditional age, 'reality' was a well-known, stable commodity. Reality was what the authorities said or what common sense dictated. In short, reality was taken for granted. Modern pluralism has rendered 'reality' more suspect. The constantly competing realities of various tribes, interest groups, institutions, and cultures reveal 'reality' to be an ideological, social construct. Following Roland Barthes, one might say that 'reality' is myth, a particular society's common-sense assumptions about life (1972: 129-30).

Pluralist competition has not, however, decreased the fervor and certainty with which various 'realities' are defended. Ideologues and propagandists are no less frequent now than then. Reality remains a deadly serious business. In this fractured, dangerous world, fantasy intrigues because it challenges 'reality': 'The practice of imagination is a subversive activity not because it yields concrete acts of defiance (which it may) but because it keeps the present provisional and refuses to absolutize it' (Brueggemann 1978: 119). Fantasy plays beyond and across tribal myths. As it plays, fantasy gives readers pause (Todorov 1973: 25). Like the religious mysterium tremendum, fantasy leaves one awefully wondering (Otto 1958: 12-30).

Fantasy, however, seldom survives. Typically, it gives way to the human desire for certainty and order. Thus, humans create myth. They construct various exclusionary realities. With the certainties of myth, fantasy degenerates into the incredible or the marvelous (Todorov 1973: 41). Awe gives way to reason or magic. Wonder dies in certainty. Only prophets and poets can live hesitantly.

Thus, while every narrative, even those of documentary realism, creates an alternative world, narratives tend to have either a mythic or fantastic relationship to readerly realities. Narrative either supports or subverts 'reality' (cf. Crossan 1975: 47-62; Torgovnick 1981):

| *Myth* | *Theodicy* | *Satire* | *Fantasy* |
|---|---|---|---|
| 'Realism' | History | Humor | Irony |
| Support readerly reality | Defend/Elucidate readerly reality | Critique/Deconstruct readerly reality playfully | Subvert readerly reality constructively |

Myth 'founds world' (Crossan 1975: 62; cf. Eliade 1958). Even when it incorporates supernatural and magical elements, myth is 'realistic' narrative. Literary realism—history and documentary—build upon and explicate myth's world. Theodicy defends that tenuous social construct against anomie and critique. Myth celebrates, explains, transmits and/or defends reality.

On the other hand, fantasy 'subverts world' (Crossan 1975: 62). It denies reality's 'taken-for-grantedness'. Such challenges can, of course, be either deconstructive or constructive. Satire and humor represent the former option. Leaving 'reality' in place, they parasitically play with and against it. Such fantasies are aesthetic subcreations of alternative literary worlds which do not intend to create new orders. They are poetry or the play which 'suspends our living unto death'.

By contrast, irony is surreptitiously constructive. It critiques 'reality' from some transcendant perspective and entices the reader to accept that perspective as reality. Such fantasies intend, then, to replace readerly reality altogether. They are prophetic, not aesthetic, fantasies. Obviously, if successful, such fantasies become myth in their own right. If unsuccessful, they become merely incredible.

## Modern Rationalism and Fantasy

For the modern, post-Enlightenment world, reality is rational. Reason and its associates—philosophy, science, technology, individualism, and bureaucratic institutions—define life. Philosophy and science, reason's advance guard, typify the methodological doubt characteristic of Enlightenment reason (so Krentz

1975). That skepticism rejects authorities as the standards of truth in favor of a scrutiny of assumptions and/or an empirical testing of various hypotheses. Technology applies the fruits of this critique to produce the 'good life' for the atomistic, free individuals who reason. Finally, bureaucracy is merely the rational ordering of political and social power/life. For the Enlightenment, then, reality is bureaucratically-connected, technologically-supported critical individuals.

If the rational defines the possible, fantasy subverts science with magic, the individual with family/folk, and bureaucracy with critique. Such fantasies appear in two disparate locations: (1) in ancient narratives like the Bible; and (2) in modern fantasy (or postmodern disenchantment) like the magical realism of Gabriel García Márquez. The formal similarity here, of course, is the a-rationality of these narrative worlds.

## Biblical Fantasies and Imperial Reality

Of course, the Bible and García Márquez's narrative worlds have a different relationship to modernity. The Bible antedates modernity while García Márquez lives in or looks back upon it. The Bible, then, does not stand deliberately athwart modernity. If it once was fantastic, it was so as it subverted other, older realities. The Bible's ancient 'central impossibility' (Irwin 1976) was its commitment to the divine sovereignty as a fantastic alternative to various imperial sovereignties.

In Exodus 1–15, for example, an unknown deity reveals himself to a fugitive to order him to return to Egypt to free certain Hebrew slaves. Miraculously, this slave-God defeats Pharoah with plagues and by throwing his armies into the sea. The lowly slaves leave bedecked in Egyptian spoil and march through the wilderness to a mountainous encounter with their leader's deity.

Similarly, Daniel subverts the reigning bestial empires with a vision of their overthrow by a kingdom of one 'like a son of man' (Dan. 7). In Revelation's related visions, the bestial kingdoms fall to a slain lamb. For that fantastic millenial dream, the lamb triumphs through and because of its death (Rev. 4–5; cf. 18–20).

While various religious communities enacted these visions in worship, no readers ever lived in such fantastic kingdoms. In each case, these narrative worlds (and many others) subvert the powers-that-be with alternative images of power epitomized in the following words:

> If any want to become my followers, let them deny themselves and take up their cross and follow me. For those who want to save their life will lose it and those who lose their life for my sake, and for the sake of the gospel will save it (Mk 8.34-35).
>
> You know that among the Gentiles those whom they recognize as their rulers lord it over them, and their great ones are tyrants over them. But it is not so among you; but whoever wishes to become great among you must be your servant, and whoever wishes to be first among you must be slave of all (Mk 10.42-44).

While the miraculous politics of these narrative worlds is arational and corporate, it fantastically subverts ancient imperial worlds, not modern rationalism. The fantasy 'simply' envisions God's exaltation of the meek:

> The bows of the mighty are broken,
> but the feeble gird on strength...
> The Lord kills and brings to life;
> he brings down to Sheol and raises up.
> The Lord makes poor and makes rich;
> he brings low, he also exalts (1 Sam. 2.4, 6-7).

## Biblical Myth, the Enlightenment, and New Biblical Fantasies

With Constantine the fantasy ended. The revolutionary kingdom became simply a spiritual addendum to the present. The subversive stories became the establishment's property and were made the mythic basis of institutional religion. As a result, the biblical narratives ceased to challenge 'reality' and became its basis. Premoderns lived in the biblical narrative between creation and consummation (so Frei 1974).

The Enlightenment, of course, destroyed the Bible's mythic status. Reason, methodological doubt, became the arbiter of reality. The Bible's dethronement by reason, however, created new fantastic possibilities (Thompson 1978). Read in and after the Enlightenment, the ancient biblical narrative became an alternative to reason's hegemony. Now, the fantastic crux, the 'central impossibility', was miracle, rather than alternative politics.

As readers dislike instability, modern Bible readers often hurry beyond hesitancy to incredulity or faith. Put differently, readers reconstruct their world in order to accommodate sensibly the biblical narrative. The common choices are either rationalism or supernaturalism (cf. Schweitzer 1968: 78-95).

Rationalism reduces the biblical narrative to the uncanny. Incredulous before the biblical story, the rationalist explicates the miracles as tales beyond the ken of pre-scientific observers. For example, God did not turn the Nile to blood to deliver the Hebrew slaves. Instead, red bacteria made the Nile undrinkable, forced the frogs to flee, which died en masse causing the insect population to increase and disease to reach epidemic proportions, and so forth. Nor did the Lord part the sea to allow his people to pass safely. Instead, the slaves went through a swampy region while the Egyptian chariots bogged down (cf. Exod. 6–15). This rationalization of biblical 'reality' reduces the Bible to antiquarian or ethical interest.

On the other hand, supernaturalism believes the Bible with a vehemence that leaves no rationalist stone upon another. Here, the biblical fantasy becomes the marvelous revelation of a supernatural reality. Such a reading, of course, requires one to believe more than seven incredible things before breakfast.

This marvelous reading returns divine intervention. While the supernaturalist may romanticize such a world as one of salvific miracle and answered petition, it would also be, if it resembled the biblical stories, a world of the inexplicably suffering righteous (e.g. Job) and the forsaken prophet (e.g. the Jesus of Mark's gospel). In short, from a post-Enlightenment perspective, it would be a world of divine caprice:

> Does disaster befall a city,
> unless the Lord has done it? (Amos 3.6b)
> I form light and create darkness,
> I make weal and create woe;
> I the Lord do all these things (Isa. 45.7).
> Is not Esau Jacob's brother? says the Lord.
> Yet I have loved Jacob but I have hated Esau... (Mal. 1.2b-3).

Enlightenment reason and its benefits would, of course, be gone.

The free, atomistic individual who reasons would also vanish. As feminists and others have rightly noted, the Bible depicts God as a sovereign, liege, king, and patriarchal father. This centralized, hierarchical power dehumanizes:

> Then the Lord God said, 'See, the man has become like one of us, knowing good and evil; and now, he might reach out his hand and take also from the tree of life, and eat, and live forever'—therefore the Lord God sent him forth from the garden of Eden... (Gen. 3.22-23; cf. 11.6-8).
>
> And the Lord said to Moses, 'When you go back to Egypt, see that you perform before Pharoah all the wonders that I have put in your power; but I will harden his heart, so that he will not let the people go' (Exod. 4.21; cf. 7.3; 9.12; 10.1, 20, 27; 11.10; 14.4, 9).

Submission to such a sovereign is, from a modern perspective, masochistic (cf. Berger 1969: 73-80).

In the light of this dilemma between rationalistic disenchantment and masochistic morals, hesitation becomes more attractive. Is fantasy recoverable? Are there poets and prophets 'among us'?

## Magical Realism and The Critique of Modernity

One might find such fantasies in the move in aesthetics from modern realism to perspectivism and pluralism typified by the Latin American 'Boom' novelists. The most famous member of the group, which includes Cortázar, Fuentes, and Donoso, is Gabriel García Márquez. Following Joyce, Kafka, Faulkner, and Borges, these novelists explore aesthetic techniques and internal, subjective 'realities'. Further, they insist on the author's absolute rights of invention.

All these trends are apparent in the Boom's most famous novel, *One Hundred Years of Solitude*. The work is the episodic, epic tale of the Buendía family and the village of Macondo. The family story begins with married cousins who fear that their incest will result in a pig-tailed child. The threat is soon by-passed, however, and the Buendía line produces various vigorous José Arcadios and reflective Aurelianos. Five generations later another two Buendía cousins marry. This time, a Buendía, the last, is born with a pig's tail. The family's solitude, its incest, is its undoing.

The family founds the village of Macondo. For a time, the village lives paradisically. Outside influences—technology, the church, political revolution, and American capitalism—ultimately puncture this peaceful solitude. Macondo deteriorates. Ultimately, the banana plague, torrential rains, and a hurricane bring an apocalyptic end. The pig-tailed child dies, and his father reads the gypsy's tale of the end.

The work's charm does not lie in this plot, based both on the Bible and *Oedipus Rex*, but in its almost constant ability to surprise. The surprises begin with the novel's delightful opening sentence: 'Many years later, as he faced the firing squad, Colonel Aureliano Buendía was to remember that distant afternoon when his father took him to discover ice' (García Márquez 1971: 1). The reader is caught immediately in a mysterious narrative between 'once upon a time', the discovery of ice, and a later 'historical event', the firing squad. Continuing the unexpected, Colonel Buendía does not die before the firing squad although another Buendía does.

The work's self-referential conclusion is also amazing. The tale ends when the remaining Buendía deciphers a gypsy's narrative, which is the story of Macondo and the Buendías:

> Before reaching the final line, however, he had already understood that he would never leave that room, for it was forseen that the city of mirrors (or mirages) would be wiped out by the wind and exiled from the memory of men at the precise moment when Aureliano Babilonia would finish deciphering the parchments, and that everything written on them was unrepeatable since time immemorial and forever more, because races condemned to one hundred years of solitude did not have a second opportunity on earth (1971: 383).

This narrative apocalypse reminds the reader that one 'only reads'. By so doing, it remains hesitantly outside readerly reality.

Within this wondrous narrative, the line between fantasy and reality is not clear. Anything is possible in Macondo. People fly on magic carpets. Murdered ghosts come back to live happily

with their murderers. The blood of a murdered son finds its way
through town to his mother. An insomina plague strikes the village. The resulting memory loss requires a Buendía to put labels
on items so people will remember what they are. A gypsy dies
and returns because he cannot bear the solitude. A room
remains untouched by time. A virgin ascends to heaven. It rains
butterflies and dead birds. Finally, it simply rains and rains.

García Márquez renders these 'impossibles' through a
detached, matter-of-fact narration which scarcely notes that
they strain credulity and reality. According to García Márquez,
this narrative voice is simply one like his grandmother's, who
could tell the most absurd stories credibly. In fact, García
Márquez's style is two-fold: he renders the ordinary as marvelous and the marvelous as ordinary.

Thus, it is the gypsies, not scientists or teachers, who first
bring technology to Macondo. The justly famous scene when
José Arcadio first sees ice typifies the ordinary rendered marvelous. José Arcadio

> ...put his hand on the ice and held it there for several minutes as
> his heart filled with fear and jubilation at the contact with mys-
> tery. Without knowing what to say, he paid ten reales more so
> that his sons could have that prodigious experience... He paid
> another five reales and with his hand on the cake, as if giving tes-
> timony on the holy scriptures, he exclaimed: 'This is the great
> invention of our time' (1971: 26).

The Bible can also transfigure the ordinary:

> The kingdom of heaven is like yeast that a woman took and mixed
> in with three measures of flour until all of it was leavened (Mt.
> 13.33).

In religion such transfigurations are the very heart of symbol
and of hierophany in which one

> ...becomes aware of the sacred because it manifests itself, shows
> itself, as something wholly different from the profane. To desig-
> nate the act of manifestation of the sacred, we have proposed the
> term hierophany... It could be said that the history of religions—
> from the most primitive to the most highly developed—is consti-
> tuted by a great number of hierophanies... In each case we are
> confronted by the same mysterious act—the manifestation of
> something of a wholly different order, a reality that does not

belong to our world, in objects that are an integral part of our natural 'profane' world (Eliade 1958: 11).

Some critics refer to this hierophanic style, which defamiliarizes reality, as 'magical realism'. Originally used in art criticism, the term referred to the move from expressionism and exoticism to the 'magical' treatment of ordinary reality (Williams 1984: 77-78; Janes 1991: 100). The result is a new perspective:

> It is the discovery of a whole new world. One paints pots and piles of rubbish and sees these things in a completely different way as if one had never before seen a pot. One paints a landscape, trees, houses, vehicles, and one sees the world anew. One discovers like a child a land of adventure. [Jurgens, cited in Janes 1991: 97).

García Márquez also renders the marvelous as ordinary. In the midst of a 'realistic' narrative, he includes flying carpets, levitating priests, and ascending virgins. The Bible does the same. For example, in Joshua 10, after a detailed recounting of the names and places of a military campaign, the narrative offers matter-of-factly:

> So Joshua came upon them all suddenly, having marched up all night from Gilgal. And the Lord threw them into a panic before Israel, who inflicted a great slaughter... As they fled before Israel...the Lord threw down huge stones from heaven...and they died... (Josh. 10.9-11).
> On the day when the Lord gave the Amorites over to the Israelites... The sun stopped in midheaven, and did not hurry to set for about a whole day (Josh. 10.12-13).

After the supernatural astronomical events, 'realistic' documentation continues (Josh. 10.15-43). Such magical realism expands 'reality' by including the marvelous.

Critics interpret this magical realism differently. Latin American critics call it a realistic depiction of the 'marvelous reality of Latin America' (Carpentier's term in his preface to *The Kingdom of this World*). Anglo-American critics see it as a mix of fantasy and realism (cf. Janes 1991: 97-106). The former treats *One Hundred Years* as myth. The latter treats it as fantasy.

## Magical Realism and Myth

García Márquez himself has insisted that his fiction is a realistic portrayal of Latin America. Thus, in his Nobel speech, after providing a litany of Latin American marvels and tragedies, he opines,

> I dare to think that it is this outsized reality, and not just its literary expression that has deserved the attention of the Swedish Academy of Letters... Poets and beggars, musicians and prophets, warriors and scoundrels, all creatures of that unbridled reality, we have had to ask but little of our imagination, for our crucial problem has been a lack of conventional means to render our lives believable. This, my friends, is the crux of our solitude (1988: 89).

The incredible is real. The fantasy is a marvelous report.

Not surprisingly, then, some readers have transformed *One Hundred Years* into an allegory of Colombian or Latin American history. More abstractly, others have compared the novel to the American myth of discovery, development, and decay. In either case, García Márquez becomes a priest, not a prophet.

On other occasions, García Márquez has also claimed that the novel simply gives 'poetic permanence to the world of my childhood', that is, to the village and house of his grandparents (cited in Janes 1991: 39). If so, García Márquez is not a prophet, but a scribe of folk traditions. That realistic, mythic urge, however, creates a myth which threatens official 'realities':

> But I realized that reality is also the myths of the common people, it is the beliefs, their legends; they are their everyday life and they affect their triumphs and failures. I realized that reality isn't just the police that kill people, but also everything that forms part of the life of the common people (cited in Williams 1984: 79).

This alternative mythic memory borders on the fantastic (cf. the banana plague, García Márquez 1971: 272-90; McNerney 1989: 26-27).

## Magical Realism and Fantasy

Despite realistic protestations, García Márquez has also insisted on his artistic right of invention. In fact, he has playfully asserted more than once that he would rather be a magician, like the gypsy-narrator Meliquíades, than an author (McMurray 1977: 86). García Márquez likes illusion. *One Hundred Years'* self-referential ending, then, will not let one forget that one reads. The book's sheer facticity stands as an alternative to or an expansion of, at least, Anglo-reader reality. Refusing assimilation, the book keeps alive the hesitation between the marvelous (myth) and the uncanny (disbelief).

That hesitation relativizes modern reality. Flying carpets, levitating priests, the undead, and ascending virgins subvert science. Imagination rules, rather than logic. The fact that Macondo's paradise decays after the introduction of technology questions technology's value. The association of technology with gypsies renders technology itself magical.

The repetition of names subverts individualism. One needs a genealogical chart to keep up with the Arcadios and Aurelianos. Even a character senses that they are merely repeated mythic types:

> Throughout the long history of the family the insistent repetition of names had made her draw some conclusions that seemed to be certain. While the Aurelianos were withdrawn, but with lucid minds, the José Arcadios were impulsive and enterprising, but they were marked with a tragic sign (1971: 174).

Further, the absence of a protagonist in favor of a family and a village questions individualism. So, too, does the motif of solitude. With that theme, García Márquez muses upon the despairing, alienated, modern individual.

Finally, the novel critiques powerful political and economic institutions. Political revolt seems futile when Colonel Aureliano Buendía, despite a gift of prescience, fights and loses 32 wars only to learn that war is for power and not principle or honor (García Márquez 1971: 160-63). The unofficial account of the banana plague similarly lampoons foreign capitalism. Only a flood of biblical proportions ends that debacle. Thereafter, despite a brief resurgence, Macondo is doomed.

Thus, one can read *One Hundred Years* as a fantastic subversion of every major lineament in modern reality. The book's last three self-referrential pages, as well as the devastating critiques of García Márquez's failure to take a political stand with the work, suggest that the book is a poetic, rather than prophetic, fantasy. García Márquez deconstructs reality; he does not offer a new liveable myth. The magician does, however, open a way through the looking glass.

## Conclusion: Magical Realism, the Bible and Transcendence

That magic portal 'signals' transcendence (Berger 1990) or mediates mystery. Ritual, of course, has always served as such a doorway. Through ritual, worshipers escape the everyday for another realm. There they can experience, for example, the reign of God and Christ in vision, text, and ritual while living in the larger realm of the Roman empire (cf. Rev. 21). Biblical narrative can also serve this function, if it can be recovered from the rationalist-fundamentalist dilemma.

Transcendence's importance is well-known to the religious, but their pleas for it are no more forceful than García Márquez's Nobel speech conclusion:

> On a day like today, my master William Faulkner said, 'I decline to accept the end of man'. I would feel unworthy of standing in this place that was his, if I were not fully aware that the colossal tragedy he refused to recognize thirty-two years ago is now, for the first time since the beginning of humanity, nothing more than a scientific possibility. Faced with this awesome reality that must have seemed a mere utopia through all of human time, we, the inventors of tales, who will believe anything, feel entitled to believe that it is not yet too late to engage in the creation of the opposite utopia. A new and sweeping utopia of life, where no one will be able to decide for others how they die, where love will prove true and happiness be possible, and where the races condemned to one hundred years of solitude will have, at last and forever, a second opportunity on earth (1988: 90-91).

In short, life is in transcendence, not in myth.

## Works Cited

Barthes, R.
    1972          *Mythologies* (New York: Hill and Wang).

Berger, P.L.
   1969       *The Sacred Canopy* (Garden City, NY: Anchor Books).
   1990       *A Rumor of Angels* (Garden City, NY: Doubleday).
Brueggemann, W.
   1978       *The Prophetic Imagination* (Philadelphia: Fortress Press).
Crossan, J.D.
   1975       *The Dark Interval* (Niles, IL: Argus).
Eliade, M.
   1958       *The Sacred and the Profane* (New York: Harcourt Brace).
Frei, H.W.
   1974       *The Eclipse of Biblical Narrative* (New Haven: Yale University Press).
García Márquez, G.
   1971       *One Hundred Years of Solitude* (trans. G. Rabassa; New York: Avon).
   1988       'The Solitude of Latin America', Nobel Lecture, 1982, in J. Ortega (ed.), *Gabriel García Márquez and the Powers of Fiction* (trans. M. Castaneda; Austin: University of Texas Press).
Irwin, W.R.
   1976       *The Game of the Impossible* (Urbana: University of Illinois Press).
Janes, R.
   1991       *One Hundred Years of Solitude: Modes of Reading* (Boston: Twayne Publishers).
Krentz, E.J.
   1975       *The Historical-Critical Method* (Philadelphia: Fortress Press).
McMurray, G.R.
   1977       *Gabriel García Márquez* (Literature and Life Series; New York: Frederick Ungar).
McNerney, K.
   1989       *Understanding Gabriel García Márquez* (Columbia: University of South Carolina Press).
Otto, R.
   1958       *The Idea of the Holy* (New York: Oxford University Press).
Schweitzer, A.
   1968       *The Quest of the Historical Jesus* (New York: Macmillan).
Thompson, L.
   1978       *Introducing Biblical Literature* (Englewood Cliffs: Prentice-Hall).
Todorov, T.
   1973       *The Fantastic: A Structural Approach to a Literary Genre* (Cleveland: Case Western Reserve University Press).
Torgovnick, M.
   1981       *Closure in the Novel* (Princeton: Princeton University Press).
Williams, R.L.
   1984       *Gabriel García Márquez* (Boston: Twayne Publishers).

CONARD CARROLL

# Hermes, the Fantastic and the Burning Heart

> They said to each other, 'Did not our hearts burn within us while
> he talked to us on the road, while he opened to us the Scriptures?'
> (Luke 24.32).[1]

Fantastic: Middle English *fantastik*, from Old French *fantastique*, from Medieval Latin *fantasticus*, from Late Latin *phantasticus*, imaginary, from Greek *phantastikos*, able to produce the appearance of, perception, faculty of imagination, from *phantazein*, to make visible, from *phainein*, to show, to bring to light (*bha-1*, to shine; *bha-2*, to speak).[2]

Some appellations of Hermes:[3]

| | | |
|---|---|---|
| shining like gold | in the heart | invisible |
| beautiful, famous | heart-delighting | guide |
| loud-shouting | light-bringer | messenger |

1. Revised Standard Version of the Bible. Translation—obviously an aspect of Hermes—is problematic. Translations make the original 'heart' of Lk. 24.32 'hearts'. Most assert that this small alteration is necessary because it makes the meaning more logical, more easily understood. This tendency to ignore the 'heart' for the sake of 'explanation under the guise of translation' (Alter 1996: xiv). Since I cannot offer my own translation of the original language, I take heart in the fact that the three on the road to Emmaus probably did not speak Luke's Greek. Still, translation, at best, is a creative tension. Later, when attention is turned to Acts 14 and Luke 24 various translations will be considered. Since Hermes 'is remembered as the symbol of the acquisitive way of life' (Brown 1990: 98), it seems appropriate to offer one's own sense of translation. That such translation would be considered indignant and suspicious corresponds with Hermes, as will be seen later.

2. *The American Heritage Dictionary* and *The Oxford English Dictionary*.

3. Though this is from Doty's list, Farnell offers the sources of the appellations (1909: 62-66). Kerenyi 1976 and Brown 1990 correlate. An appellation is a name, an entreaty, a calling out from one to the other, emotive and of the ritual, the prayer.

| brilliant, shining | man-loving | wayfarer |
|---|---|---|
| greedling | luck-bringer | of the cave |
| bravest, best | one who descends | spellbinder |
| fond of jeering | mover of spirits | guide of dreams |
| presider over games | joy-giver | at the boundary |
| belonging to night | psychopomp | of the gateway |
| inventor/discoverer | artificer | hinge of the city |
| evil-averter | savior | shameless one |
| minister | servant | thief |
| trickster | deceiver/cheat | interpreter |
| skilled in words | many-turning | herald |
| bringer of good news | shifty | overflowing with babble |
| persuader of the mind | inventor | ram-bearer |

> ...etymological fantasies, those forces which have always run wild at certain moments and which, as soon as the science of language has imposed practically certain gains, no longer appear as anything but follies: a language revery, the play of desire destined to free itself from knowledge even while exhibiting the lexical mirage, or to mime, simply for fun, the usage of the unconscious (Blanchot 1986: 97).

I toss this[4] toward the stones heaped beside the road. The usually invisible, silent companion may or may not guide this crossing of boundaries.[5] On the way, the unfamiliar and strange are

4.   Most note this act, with Farnell (1909: 17-18) being most complete: '...heaping up stones at certain intervals along the way, and consecrating them to Hermes may well be of immemorial antiquity' (1909: 18). 'The stone-heaps were a primitive sort of boundary-stone, marking a point of communication between strangers' (Brown 1990: 32). Along with this 'secular purpose' the herms 'can be put under a religious *tapu* by consecration to the way-god, and could be regarded as a thank-offering to him on part of the traveller; also the latter could establish communion between himself and the god by throwing his stone on the pile. The heaps thus became charged with the power of the god, just as in the aniconic age the pillar was full of the divinity, and therefore could be regarded as acts of worship' (Farnell 1909: 18). 'Intercourse with strangers was surrounded with magical safeguards: meetings occasioned magico-religious ceremonies; points of habitual contact were regarded as hallowed ground' (Brown 1990: 33). This magico-religious act also protected the traveller from ghosts (Farnell 1909: 17), an aspect Hermes shares with Hekate. Hermes can also go the whole way with the wayfarer.
5.   The 'boundaries' of scholarship and critical activity. See Brown's

common, the uncanny, near and far, a constant. So the cross-road is clear: this heap, these stones, each with a prayer, a story, departure and destination. Each with a way.[6] And now, even if there were no ghosts to reckon with, no thieves to cajole, even if there were time to consider every stone, what could be gathered, how read such desire? Maybe the sense of loss that comes with remembering how only gods are given such interpretation proves to be good fortune. Few can long endure burning hearts.

Among other things, the Bible appears to be what Kerenyi, sounding the Greek sense of 'beginnings or first principles', names 'the Boundless'—'No mere "causes", therefore, but primary substances or primary states...inexhaustible, invincible in timeless primordiality, in a past that proves imperishable because of its eternally repeated rebirths' (Jung and Kerenyi 1963: 7). Approaching the Bible usually brings about a reasonable measure of supplement within equally reasonable discursive positionings. Never bound or de-fined by discourse, the Boundless compels a correspondence that repulses such rational limits, rendering critical distance an illusion. Merleau-Ponty describes the 'expressive moment...where the book takes

'Boundary' (141-64) in *Love's Body*: 'To give up boundaries is to give up the reality-principle...a false boundary drawn between inside and outside; subject and object; real and imaginary' (1966: 149). Brown reminds us that such boundaries create a 'kind of Argus-eyed tenseness' (148), but doesn't remind us that Hermes lulls to sleep every eye with his music and then slays the 'tenseness', making possible phantasy and fantasy-making. With Blake and Whitehead, Brown asserts that 'Reality is energy' (1966: 155). Whereas reality is static, fantasy moves, the flux that is Hermes. Burke offers a succinct and substantive discussion of hermeneutics, reminding us that, 'although the distinctions once made are no longer always so clearly drawn', it was and may be now concerned with 'the rules and methodologies applied in the movement from exegesis to interpretation. The distinction between and among these three interrelated disciplines neither was nor is always easily made' (1982: 863). Exegesis determines the meaning the text had for the writer and first audience; interpretation seeks the meaning for the present. It is easy to see Hermes being a part of this movement, this translation and transcription.

6.   The first line of Clarke's poem, 'Herm'—'In anybody's way there must be a way' (1979: 21).

possession of the reader' who builds within 'a strange expressive organism which can not only interpret the conventional meaning of the book's works and techniques but can even allow itself to be transformed and endowed with new organs by the book' (1973: 12-14). It is expected that this rapt merging and metamorphosis will produce reasonable address.[7] Might this 'strange expressive organism' find the discursive limiting? Might definition dissolve, discourse crack? Might these 'new organs' become another way of approaching the Boundless, the Bible? Might this strange organism, while tracing the fantastic in the Bible, invite the fantastic within interpretation and the expression of the interpretation?[8]

The Bible appears and fragments happen. What is the Bible but fragments gathered? The fact that this gathering covered millennia emphasizes the correlative utility of fragments. After these fragments became one, the interpreters then fragmented the text into chapters and verses. Now, supplement stitches the text, rendering an image of a binding of the text, a curious cemented fragmentation that could suggest a tenuous unity of the book. Hence these correspondent fragments: as the book so the response, as the text so the interpretation, as the message so the messenger: 'like curing like',[9] the burning heart.[10]

7.   This strange expressive organism correlates with Plato's poet who is the interpreter of the gods, the creative act and creation—the poem—interpretation. This writing, obviously, does not intend poetry.

8.   The fantastic brings to light and even the traditional critical event brings-to-light-that-which-is-present-yet-not-seen, yet in traditional discourse the fantastic element, which could be the origin of the whole event, is never made manifest.

9.   'In fact, sublimation requires going with the fire, like curing like, raising the temperature to a white heat so as to destroy all coagulations in the intensity of desire, so that what one desires no longer matters, even as it matters most, mattering now sublimed, translucent, all flame' (Hillman 1982: 70). This burning clears the way for fantasy: 'Imagination begins in a heart aware that there is both true and false imagining and that these are not contradictions, but rather correlatives, even co-terminous' (Hillman 1982: 73). As will be seen later, Hermes juxtaposes, even connects contradictions, and is the urge toward correlation.

10. See Jabes's *The Book of Shares* for the correlation of fragments and the burning that is writing—the burning heart of interpretation. 'Make

Though Blanchot's book appears to be the near philosophical figurings of literary theory, the emotive, which manifests in the italicized fragments, compels this elaboration. Reflecting upon writing and desire, fear, loss, dread and death, the writer, *'Listening, not to the words, but to the suffering that endlessly, from one word to the next, runs through the words'* (1992: 86), comes to and becomes 'The fragmentary: writing belongs to the fragmentary when all has been said' (1992: 42). Though all has not been said or written about the Bible, its closure warns that the one who adds to or takes away from the book will be erased from the Book of Life. This turn to the fragment is a way away from 'the infinitely continuous discourse whose content is "its own continuity", continuity that is assured if itself only in giving itself as circular' (1992: 43). This circular continuity, intentionally or not, binds, splits Hermes. Though this deprivation seems to limit the god who is closest and friendliest to humans, the god of the alphabet and writing (Graves 1955: 182-84), will not be written down. The 'running back and forth' of dis-course only occludes the Hermes the Greeks sensed: 'a splendor out of the depths (that) must once have struck the eye that perceived a world in the god and the god in the whole world' (Otto 1954: 124). To recover this *world in the god*, that which was hidden or removed is now uncovered, returned, the fragmentary becoming 'a play of limits in which no limitations play' (Blanchot 1992: 44); a play that 'invisibly destroys surface and depth, real and possible, above and below, manifest and hidden' (Blanchot 1992: 50). The fragmentary 'refers to nothing and has no proper reference' (Blanchot 1992: 49), thereby clearing a way for the recovery of wholeness. Where 'there is constant change...Hermes begins to manifest as ongoing disruption and disorder' (Paris 1990: 111). The writing that traces the fantastic in the Bible first 'sees through'[11] the Hermes hermeneutics involves. 'For if we are to

---

allowance for fire where writing spreads': 'Ah, write to keep alive the fire of creation' (1989: 99). Jer. 36, surely deserving a close reading, offers another perspective upon the configuration of writing, fragments, interpretation (and the absence of it) and burning.

11. Ever devoted to imagining and fantasy, Hillman describes how seeing through, 'an activity that opens' (1975: 163), correlates 'idea' and 'fantasy'

have success in reviving the God's image in its fullness, we must be prepared not only for what is immediately intelligible, but also for what is strangely uncanny' (Kerenyi 1976: 5). Amidst this confusion, the tracing of the fantastic in the Bible first sees through the Hermes hermeneutics involves to *Hamlet*, wherein the unexpected, the strange and uncanny become common.[12]

Huge and elusive, tremendous yet subtle, the Bible, as Ghost in *Hamlet*, appears, demanding recognition, appropriation and action. *Hamlet* and Hamlet embody a fantasy of interpretation. In the opening, the three who have gathered in the dark share an anxiety intensified by the previous night's events and the prearrangement of the encounter which appears to promise understanding. The guards and Horatio believe reasonable speech will verify the existence of Ghost and deliver the reason for its appearance. Their certitude is not the least bit phased by their inability to name what they have seen and anticipate—'it' / 'figure' / 'image' / 'he' / 'apparition' / 'dreaded sight' / 'form' / 'illusion' / 'fantasy' / 'something more than fantasy'. Dialogical engagement is their only course of action with the fantastic they have discerned has obvious implications for their shared reality. Five lines into their story, as if the words of their narrative conjured it, the fantasy manifests. The disbelieving confidence of the logical 'scholar' (I.i.42) instantly splits into 'fear

(1975: 141). Is it Hermetic luck that Kerenyi attributes seeing through' (1976: 26) to Hermes, using the god's coming upon the tortoise and *seeing* the lyre? For Hillman, seeing through is a 'subjectivizing' which asserts that 'what lies behind or within is truer and more real, powerful or valuable than what is evident... This ultimate hidden value justifying the entire operation can also be the hidden God (*deus absconditus*) who appears only in concealment' (1975: 140). As the herm mutely contains the charge of power, the Hermes that lies behind hermeneutics, I believe, is more real and potent than the evident. Hermes, who still appears in the concealment hermeneutics continues, is hidden and revealed. The ultimate hidden value of Hermes may be that he brings to light the original darkness: the ultimate fantasy?

12. Thiselton, referring to Torrance's remark about how 'a transforming understanding of the scriptures may be more likely to occur when we feel disturbed by the unexpected than when Biblical texts have already been tamed of all that is strange and unfamiliar' (1992: 257).

and wonder' (I.i.44) that stun speech, so that he forgets his purpose until reminded by the guards. Then reason's rhetoric of quick questions and imperatives demands the disclosure of identity. As with the weapons they pull when Ghost returns, Horatio's words attack with logical severity. With both appearances, Horatio expects the fantasy to speak before he speaks to it. Logic's need to know through speech cancels engagement. Though language is supposed to distinguish fantasy from reality, the apparition's refusal to enter dialogue neither diminishes its existence or appropriation. The silence of the fantastic proves real enough to affect the future when the guards' deduction leads them from Elsinore's edge to Hamlet: 'This spirit, dumb to us, will speak to him' (I.i.171). After they report the appearance of Ghost, rational interpretation gives way to Hamlet's fantasy of interpretation that involves risk, creation and the pathological. Though Hamlet also feels the 'fear and wonder', his language neither attacks Ghost nor implores disclosure. He encounters the fantastic, names it, and engages conversation: 'Thou comest in such a questionable shape / That I will speak to thee. I'll call thee Hamlet' (I.iv.43-44). The fantastic moves Hamlet, unlike Horatio's distancing demands, to question, to interpretation: 'Say, why is this? Wherefore? What should we do?' (I.iv.57) Horatio reasons that Hamlet 'waxes desperate with imagination' (I.iv.87) and surmises that following the fantastic 'might deprive your soverignty of reason / And draw you into madness' (I.iv.73-74). Hamlet welcomes the fantastic and whatever imagination and madness interpretation requires. Ghost becomes the guide, 'the uncanny guidance' (Otto 1954: 112), who will seemingly abandon him later on his journey. Alone, after Ghost delivers the fantasy that sets the play in motion, Hamlet's first words are inward: 'Hold, hold, my heart' (I.v.93). Heart steadied, Hamlet's erasure commences interpretation:

> I'll wipe away all trivial find records,
> All saws of books, all pressures past
> That youth and observation copied there,
> And thy commandment all alone shall live
> Within the book and volume of my brain,
> Unmixed with baser matter (I.v.99-104).

Interpretation's erasure of the palimpsest of consciousness and
the book of his brain leads to a writing the reader/audience
does not see: '[Writes]'—a direction not marked as a line in the
text—a writing that never becomes 'the written' because it is
never read.[13] Hamlet's 'wild and whirling words' (I.v.133)
confuse the reasonable guards and scholar. These words become
the first display of the 'antic dispositions' (I.v.172) and
'ambiguous giving out' (I.v.178) of the interpretation that first
experiences the fantastic and appropriates its narrative, seeking
to know through its own imagining and making, deception and
play; through reasonable and pathological means: 'By indirec-
tions find direction out' (II.i.66). Later, this merging of the
pathological and interpretation, of secrecy and tricks, apparently leads Hamlet away from interpretation when he is sent to
England. On this journey, though, he secures the gain 'wholly
unexpected'[14] that seals interpretation. When all appears lost
suddenly, paradoxically, all becomes right. Returning from the
sea—as with '[Writes]' above, the journey and its fantasy is not
manifest—a transformed Hamlet, after much interpretation and
reading and writing, enters the final act through the graveyard.
Though, as Otto describes Hermes the psychopomp, there 'is
something of a ghostly quality about his arrival and appearance'
(Otto 1954: 115), the pathological flux has become an awareness both calm and open: 'The readiness is all. Since no man of
aught he leaves knows, what is't to leave betimes? Let be'
(V.ii.224-26). This readiness will lead, as Hamlet himself says
about Fortinbras's army on his way to England, to 'immenent
death...for a fantasy and trick of fame' (IV.iv.61-62). This interpretation is invention, for Hamlet, like Hermes 'the inventor',
devises and creates. At the close of the play, Horatio, who

13. This is the burning heart of interpretation, the burning that is writing,
the unseen burning that makes way for the fantastic, the possibility that
Hermes, the god of writing, always brings. This unseen writing that never
becomes "the written" because it is never read is the 'the lexical mirage' of
the etymological fantasy. Consider Jn 7.53–8.11, an ephemeral pericope
questioned for its belatedness, wherein Jesus writes on the ground in the
midst of interpretation. This writing is never read yet his interpretation
turns all present inward, toward their hearts.
14. The scholar calls this Hermes' 'true characterization' (Otto 1954:
108).

'deliver(s)' (V.ii.376) the message given him by Hamlet, tells Fortinbras that he will 'hear / Of carnal, bloody, and unnatural acts, / Of accidental judgements, casual slaughters, / Of deaths put on by cunning…purposes mistook / Fall'n on th' inventors' heads' (V.ii.372-75).

Whereas Hamlet had 'a father killed, a mother stained' (IV.iv. 57) and a charge to kill the king, his step-father, Metis indirectly assists Zeus in the destruction of Kronos. Metis—'Wise Counsel'—the daughter of Okeanos and Tethys, of Air and Mother Earth (Graves 1955: 33-34). Metis, 'the mother of Athene, the encompasser of all righteous things, she who knew more than all other gods or men' (Kerenyi 1951: 118), who enabled Zeus' ascent to Olympus. She directed Zeus to Rhea who arranged it for Zeus to be the 'cup-bearer' of the 'emetic potion' (Graves 1955: 40). Some say Metis informed him how to mix the potion and others that she gave him the 'potion that put the dreadful father to sleep' (Kerenyi 1951: 118) so the swallowed would return. She then became Zeus' first wife, 'But when she was about to bear gray-eyed Athena', Hesiod sang, 'he deceived the mind of Metis with guile / and coaxing words, and lodged her in his belly' (889-91). Fearing the oracle's words about Metis's 'keen-minded children' (894), 'something stronger than lightning' (Kerenyi 1951: 119), doing to him what he did to Kronos, Zeus turned his 'honeyed' (Graves 1955: 46) and 'flattering words' (Kerenyi 1951: 118) upon Metis and 'tricked her' 'secretly' (Graves 1955: 119).[15]

Later, on Lake Triton's shore Zeus' skull ached and the god howled. 'Up ran Hermes, who at once divined the cause of Zeus' discomforts' and asked either Hephaistos or Prometheus to bring the 'wedge and beetle and make a breach in Zeus' skull, from which Athene sprang, fully armed, with a mighty shout' (Graves 1955: 46). Unless Hermes the 'contriver' (Doty

15. All quotes here trace aspects of Hermes—servant, sleep, wisdom, the flash in darkness, flattering words, deceiver, trickster, secrecy and death. The 'wedge and beetle' correlate with Hermes splitting the tortoise with such a tool when he makes the lyre. That some say the Kyklop Brontes, 'the Thunderer', may be Athene's father is significant for he depicts the dark from which the lightning drops.

1980: 123) knew about Zeus swallowing Metis (and Athene, which is possible), this divination is more intuitive than reasonable. Or does it make sense that 'Hermes, the primal lover' (Kerenyi 1976: 64), would assist this birth since he is 'the first evocation of the purely masculine through the feminine' (Kerenyi 1976: 62)? Though Hermes and Metis never meet in the textual remains of myth, their correspondence (as is Hamlet's with Hermes) is unmistakable. Metis, as do Hamlet and Hermes, 'appears more or less intaglio, immersed in a practice that has not the slightest interest, at any moment, in explicating its nature or justifying its procedures'.[16] 'The word *metis* always signifies practical understanding and thinking through, which is more valuable than physical strength even in the life of one who desires battle and victory' (Otto 1954: 52). This practical thinking is non-linear and seemingly erratic. Metic-thought, which Plato dismissed as 'deception and lie' (Klein 1986: 3), is a 'fluid mental attitude which operates between dichotomies' (4) and 'through association, analogy, and intuition' (Paris 1990: 92) with 'the duplicity of disguise' (Klein 1986: 2). Chased by Zeus, Metis transforms herself, depicting 'the one who is coming into existence' (Klein 1986: 19). This Becoming is also the world of Hermes, 'where the act of becoming takes place' (Kerenyi 1976: 51) and the guide leads one to the 'place of fulfillment' (Otto 1954: 112). As the one 'at the boundary' (Doty 1980: 126), Hermes surely parallels this Becoming that 'lose boundaries' (Klein 1986: 6) within a 'continuous swinging movement' so that seeking metic-thought becomes 'the impossible, improbable synthesis'.[17]

Correspondingly, Blanchot encourages one to 'write in the thrall of the impossible real' (1986: 38). Metis and metic-thought, 'whose existence must always be presupposed but can never be demonstrably produced' (Klein 1986: 3), correlates

16. Klein (1986: 3) translates the French of Marcel Detienne and Jean-Pierre Vernant's *Les ruses de l'intelligence des grecs*. Klein's translations of their words will be marked as 'translation'.

17. Klein (1986: 4-6), translation: Klein emphasizes Detienne and Vernant's method of seeking to articulate metic-thought through mirroring its own 'dissembling' and 'trick of circling back [*retournement*] and the duplicity of disguise' (1986: 2).

with how Hermes is 'suddenly and magically present, with no announcement' (Otto 1954: 115). Hermes, the 'beaming' (Doty 1980: 121), paradoxically embodies an 'experiential wisdom (that) is nocturnal and feminine, the intuition of Metis' (Paris 1990: 113). As does Metis and Hamlet and metic-thought, a fulfilled Hermes, ever 'resembling the elusive other', will ultimately 'transform' (Klein 1986: 5) the seeker and follower, when 'the hermeneutical task is thought to be the restoration of meaning instead of the reduction of illusion'.[18]

Hermeneutics evades definition.[19] Huge and elusive, it has the capacity to disrupt dialogue, to stun conversation.[20] Often regarded as theoretical jargon, hermeneutics incites sarcasm, provokes dismay. It means so much that most are not sure what it means. Many feel that it can mean anything, or nothing. Hermeneutics is nebulous substance. The possibilities of translation inciting separation, of interpretation closing instead of opening, prove to an irony that comes with the territory of the way. To ignore this irony is to avoid the thing itself; to explain away this irony is to malign the event; to attempt to understand it through scholarship and critical enterprise would become a task titanic. And to engage this irony may lead to extermination. A mere glance towards hermeneutics gleans complexity.[21] Luke, though, on the road to Emmaus (to be considered more fully later), presents the event simply: 'Then starting with Moses and

18. Winquist states: 'Interpretation is always an imaginative expansion into the realm of possible forms...' (1978: 33).

19. Mueller-Vollmer relates: 'The problem is that hermeneutics is both a historical concept and the name for an ongoing concern in the human and social sciences; and for the historical aspect of hermeneutics a simple definition will not do. As Nietzsche succinctly put it: "all concepts in which an entire process is semiotically concentrated elude definitions; only that which has no history is definable"' (1985: x). Or does hermeneutics avoiding definition give evidence that Hermes still sojourns within the word?

20. When silence happened in a conversation it was said that Hermes had entered the room. Otto 1954 cites Plutarch as a source (115).

21. Torrance's first chapter is 'The Complex Background of Biblical Interpretation' (1995: 15-39). Mueller-Vollmer offers a 'clear warning as to the complexities underlying the term hermeneutics and the hermeneutics enterprise itself' (1985: 1). This complexity, though, should be a given.

all the prophets, he interpreted (*hermeneo*) for them every passage of scripture that referred to himself' (24.27).[22] But does the effort to discern simplicity within interpretation confuse or enhance the multiple meanings the etymon of hermeneutics— Hermes/herm—presents? Is ascribing the complexity of hermeneutics to Hermes a lack of reason or imagination? Or both?[23] Hermes, in his complete configuration, is complexity, a complexity other than logical. The reasonable and theoritical 'Words, words, words' (*Hamlet*, II.ii.193) of hermeneutics turn from the shadows only one aspect of Hermes. Kerenyi, at length, illuminates further:

> It belongs to the Hermetic wisdom of the Greek language itself, to one of its most ingenious chance hits, that the word for the simplest mute stone monument, *herma*, from which the name of the God stems, corresponds phonetically to the Latin *sermo*, or 'speech' or any verbal 'exposition'. The word *herma*, which in Greek does not have this meaning, does however form the basic verbal root for hermeneia, 'explanation'. Hermes is *hermeneus* ('interpreter'), a linguistic mediator, and this not merely on verbal grounds. By nature he is the begetter and bringer of something light-like, a clarifier, a God of ex-position and inter-pretation (of the kind also that we are engaged in) which seeks and in his spirit—the spirit of the shameless exposition of his parents' love affair—is led forward to the deepest mystery. For the great mystery, which remains a mystery even after all our discussing and explaining, is this: the appearance of a speaking figure, the very embodiment as it were in a human-divine form of clear, articulated, play-related and therefore enchanting, language—its

22. Note that Luke presents none of this interpretation; the *hermeneia* never actually manifests. One wonders if Jesus, in traditional fashion, gathered the various fragments 'of scripture that referred to himself' (24.27) and delivered them.

23. Mueller-Vollmer ascribes the complexity of hermeneutics to the task of Hermes: 'In order to deliver the message of the gods, Hermes had to be conversant in their idiom as well as that of mortals for whom the message was destined. He had to understand and interpret for himself what the gods wanted to convey before he could proceed to translate, articulate, and explicate their intention to mortals' (1985: 1). Though I do not deny that Hermes did engage in such a process, does Mueller-Vollmer forget? Hermes is a god. Why ascribe complexity to Hermes when there is surely huge heaps of human complexity that could be (if there were time, energy and space) regarded?

appearance in that deep primordial darkness where one expects
only animal muteness, wordless silence, or cries of pleasure or
pain (Kerenyi 1976: 88).[24]

This 'something light-like' does not always expose and explain.
Blanchot's words correlate: 'Light breaks forth: the burst of
light, the dispersion that resonates or vibrates dazzlingly—and
in clarity clamors but does not clarify' (1986: 39). Aware that
the interpreter can and does clarify and explain, the etymological fantasy, ever aware of the innocent becoming of the
mystery,[25] seeks with 'play-related' course the Hermes hermeneutics appears to overlook or ignore: that sudden gleam.

Hermes, as all attest, is no stranger to transformation: from
herm to angelos, from phallos to musician, from dog-throttler to
law-giver, from thief to businessman, from shepherd to the glo-
rious, from loud-shouter to herald, from the cave to Olympus,
from attendant to savior.[26] Though understanding the transition
from Hermes to hermeneutics may prove impossible, imagining
the translation from Olympian to the word denoting the theory
of biblical interpretation, perhaps equally titanic, offers
a perspective from which to consider how hermeneutics
depicts[27] Hermes. This imagining is fantasy and so within the
range of the many-turning, dream-sender, guide of dreams,
spellbinder, magician, spirit of Night, psychopomp.[28]

Etymological fantasy sees through the Hermes hermeneutics
depicts a partial interpreter, void of the aberrant, of much of
'his irreducible, highly personal totality' (Kerenyi 1976: 2)—
'this diverse whole, which is inexhaustible and yet nowhere
denies the unity of its being' (Otto 1981: 8)—the 'heart delight-
ing' and 'gracious' 'companion' (Doty 1980: 121-22) who offers
'kindly protection or dangerous leading astray' (Otto 1954:

24. I wonder if Zeus' howling on lake Triton's shores were animal-like
cries of muted pain?

25. As hermeneutics mediates between exegesis and interpretation,
Hermes' territory of the way is between reading and writing, hence the
*mystos*, the silence.

26. See Doty 1980 and Farnell 1909.

27. I wonder if it is possible for systemization to depict at all.

28. See Doty (1980: 19), Otto (1954: 118-20) and Kerenyi (1976: 44-52)
describe Hermes' relationship with Night.

116). Hermeneutics appears to deprive the interpreter of pathological aspects—theft, trickery, deceit, jeering, contriving,
magic, shamelessness, intrigue, 'using evil practices' (Doty
1980: 127)—fragmenting the world of the god and god of the
world. Does hermeneutics disfigure or disguise Hermes? Can one
imagine Hermes being caught? He is kinesis, becoming, the fluid
force that goes down and ascends. Or has Hermes accepted,
Mephistopheles-like, the guise of the academic-exegete? If so,
might this acceptance that appears to cover be a matter of dissembling duplicity, a resembling of the elusive other? The
response to this robing, this fragmentation, is re-turn and reclaiming the pathological, for the aberrant, *infirmitas* is 'is
essential to complete configuration' (Hillman 1980: 4): negation
becomes movement toward fulfillment.

This metic-movement 'of inversion, of turning the tables'
(Klein 1986: 4) returns, recovers the pathological aspects and
completes the configuration. Otto discusses how Hermes is
'questionable from a moral point of view, nevertheless it is a
configuration which belongs to the fundamental aspects of
living reality, and hence, according to Greek feeling, demands
reverence, if not for all its individual expressions, at least for
the totality of its meaning and being' (Otto 1954: 122). An
*apokalupsis*, this un-covering brings to light the aberrations
through which Hermes, the fluid one who turns loss into gain,
expresses an essence nobody discusses: inclusion. Doty apparently intuits—'My hermeneutics leads me to emphasize *what a
mytheme sets in motion*' (1980: 117). Hermes sets in motion
inclusion. His theft of Apollo's cattle gains for him a place on
Olympus. His shameless song about his parents moves Apollo to
trade cattle for the thief's lyre. Hermes splits Zeus' skull and
Athene is brought to light. He helps bring Odysseus home and
steals the corpse of Agamemnon for Priam. The psychopomp
guides Eurydike to Orpheus. His whispers and tricks bring
lovers together. As shepherd he juxtaposes animal and human.
Hermes provides opposites with boundaries, borders: the living
and the dead, consciousness and sleep, child and adult, the feminine and masculine—the hermaphrodite. 'The mythology of the
trickster is derived from the rituals of the boundary' (Brown
1990: 46) that made possible relationships between families,

tribes and strangers. The 'trickster may evolve into any one of such contrasting figures as benevolent culture hero nearly indistinguishable from the Supreme God, a demiurge in strong opposition to the heavenly powers' (Brown 1990: 46). The trickster can evolve into the herald, 'the ceremonial expert in the rituals that center around...the public assembly place' (Brown 1990: 26). At these rituals, the herald's 'function' was 'to calm things down and maintain an atmosphere that allowed each person to express...so that a decision might be reached' (Paris 1990: 78). This decision often meant inclusion. Though the trickster, unlike the sacred herald, can seem 'trivial' or 'destructive and pathological', Hermes' 'presence reminds us that the crossing of every threshold is a sacred event'.

> Hermes is associated with all boundaries—and with their transgression. He teaches that the violation of taboos may be a creative act, that to accept the importance of boundaries is not necessarily to be bound by them. Hermes moves back and forth between worlds (Downing 1993: 65-66).

Pathological transgression of boundaries may become 'a sacred event'. Otto regards Hermes' transgressions as 'undignified' (Otto 1954: 123) and 'questionable from a moral point of view, nevertheless it is a configuration which belongs to the fundamental aspects of living reality, and hence...demands reverence' (Otto 1954: 122).

Tracing Hermes in the Bible, a questionable violation that may be an undignified creative act, brings to light the correspondence of the fantastic, the pathological and interpretation. All along the way, this writing has followed Hermes' 'mobility, ingenuity, briskness...and the goal is the treasure that suddenly bursts into light' (Otto 1954: 120)—Acts 14 and Luke 24—two fragments, woven, both explicitly and implicitly, with Hermetic traces that figure the burning hearts of interpretation.[29]

Luke 24 and Acts 14 evince aspects and motions of Hermes:

29. The following paragraphs figure upon Winquist's assertions: 'it appears that imaginative generalization is a device for the expansion of consciousness. There are no uninterpreted facts. Description is interpretation' (1978: 33). All in all, Hermes' intent is the expansion and the inclusion of consciousness with something, someone else.

journey, the road, new territory, boundary-crossing, messenger/
message, signs and wonders, interpretation (oral and textual),
sudden gain and loss, ritual, burning, wounds, and Jerusalem.
As would be expected with Hermes, these traces bear a dissembling similitude that brings to light a relationship of the fantastic and interpretation. These Hermetic traces bring to light
burning hearts.

Acts 14 relates an appearance of the fantastic that brings to
light the burning heart of sacrifice that disrupts interpretation.
After speaking in the Antioch synagogue about how Jesus fulfills
Scripture, Paul and Barnabas take the light and message to the
Gentiles. In the synagogue interpretation happens and in the
street the message and 'signs and wonders' (14.3). The
hermeneut-evangelos controls the situation until the appearance
of the fantastic when Paul suddenly heals the lame man crip-
pled since birth and the crowd is moved to believe that
Barnabas is Zeus and Paul Hermes because he is the speaker.
The Lycaonians take the messengers for gods and desire to
expiate the pathological treatment rendered them by Lycaon in
Ovid's tale. These hearts begin to burn with partial interpretation and desire sacrifice. Paul's speech about a benevolent
Creator and merciful God appears to intensify the ritualistic
sacrifice that leads to aberration, the stoning of Paul by the
travellers from Iconium and Antioch who unexpectedly arrive
just after Paul's speech ironically fuels their hearts that burning
with the desire of expiation. Paul's own knowledge of the
pathological, the act of stoning, no doubt keeps death at bay.
Not dead, but with wounds that will become stigmata that signify the way to the kingdom of God is through the pathology of
persecution, Paul returns to Lystra. The two resume their way
the next day and return to Antioch where 'they called the congregation together and related all that God had helped them
accomplish' (14.27) before they go to Jerusalem for the interpretation of the Council.

Whereas Acts 14 depicts mis-interpretation and pathological
destruction, Luke 24 brings to light instances of the fantastic
leading to interpretation and knowledge. More intense than
Paul and Barnabas' movement, Luke 24 is constant coming and
going, departing and returning, appearance and disappearance.

The playful cunning of a trickster manifests in the chapter
instead of pathological Hermetic traces. The fantastic commences the chapter when the women go to the empty tomb and
encounter the two shining figures who ask them why they
search for the living among the dead. Their story is interpreted
to be fantasy by those who stayed, until Peter followed their
route and 'returned home, marveling at what had happened'
(24.12). His return and verification of the supposed fantasy
marks the two's departure to Emmaus. On the road, 'engaged in
conversation about all that had taken place' (24.14), the two
are unexpectedly joined by Jesus whom they cannot recognize.
The stranger, with simple questions, is immediately part of the
conversation. Either playing with or tricking the two, he evokes
his own story from the travellers. Suddenly, the companion,
remarking their sluggish hearts, 'interpreted (*hermeneo*) for
them every passage of scripture that referred to himself'
(24.27). Jesus pretends to be 'going on' further but accepts their
invitation to stay the night. At the meal he becomes the server,
blesses, breaks and passes the bread. In this gesture 'their eyes
were opened and they recognized him; and he vanished from
their sight' (24.31).

With this appearance of the fantastic, when interpretation is
consummated with instant recognition and disappearance of
the messenger/ message, the burning heart of interpretation surfaces. 'They said to each other, "Weren't our hearts burning
within us while he was talking to us on the road"' (24.32)?
Though their hearts burned as he interpreted 'the written', they
remained silent, but with the interpreter's departure comes
expression. The appearance of the fantastic is at the same
instant the disappearance of message/messenger. Not yet understanding, the burning heart the fantastic set in motion is interpretation. When the two retrace their steps and return to
Jerusalem they are instantly greeted with news of the risen
Lord. Before they can tell their story the fantastic occurs again
when Jesus is standing in the room and they 'figured they were
seeing a ghost' (24.37). When Jesus speaks, 'they still didn't
know what to believe and were bewildered' (24.41). The
appearance of the fantastic again accompanies interpretation as
he tells them he has fulfilled 'the written'. Then 'he prepared

their minds to understand the scriptures' (24.45). In a curious echo of Acts 14, Jesus instructs them that 'all peoples will be called to undergo a change of heart for the forgiveness of sins' (24.47). They are told to stay in Jerusalem, the place where the travellers prepare to go at the close of Acts 14.

The appearance of the fantastic in both chapters ignites burning hearts. The burning heart of mis-interpreted sacrifice, while trying to expiate the past, leads astray to the pathological disruption of the journey. The burning heart of interpretation guides the two to another appearance of the fantastic that completes their journey with preparatory opening toward the future. Actually, both burning hearts create openings. Enduring the pathological burning heart of mis-interpreted sacrifice, their journey opened 'a door' (Acts 14.27) and brought the light to the Gentiles. Hermes is the light-bringer and the one 'watching at the door' (Doty 1980: 126). Though the burning heart is not a matter of understanding, 'he opened their minds to the understanding of the Scriptures' (Lk. 24.45), a hermeneutics of the heart (Acts 28.27). The fantastic brings to light the *hermeneus*, 'interpreter', (Doty 1980: 128) who is *enkardios*, 'in the heart, close to one' (Doty 1980: 121): the 'savior' (Doty 1980: 126), whose 'superior smile...illuminates' (Otto 1954: 123) even the darkest way. Maybe it is not what is brought to light but the bringing to light itself that is the core which the fantastic and Hermes share.

## Works Cited

Alter, R.
    1996        *Genesis: Translation and Commentary* (New York: Norton).
Blanchot, M.
    1986        *The Writing of the Disaster* (trans. A. Smock; Lincoln: The University of Nebraska Press).
    1992        *The Step Not Beyond* (trans. L. Nelson; Albany: State University of New York Press).
Brown, N.O.
    1966        *Love's Body* (Berkeley, CA: University of California Press).
    1990        *Hermes the Thief: The Evolution of a Myth* (Great Barrington, MA: Lindisfarne Press).

Burke, D.G.
1982        'Interpret; Interpretation', in G.W. Bromiley (ed.), *The Inter-
            national Standard Bible Encyclopedia* (2 vols.; Grand Rapids:
            Eerdmans): 861-63.
Clarke, J.
1979        *The End of This Side* (Bowling Green: Black Book).
Doty, W.G.
1980        'Hermes' Heteronymous Appellation', in Hillman, *Facing the Gods*:
            115-33.
Downing, C.
1993        *Gods in Our Midst: Mythological Images of the Masculine: A
            Woman's View* (New York: Crossroad).
Farnell, R.L.
1909        *The Cults of the Greek States* (5 vols.; Oxford: Clarendon Press).
Graves, R.
1955        *The Greek Myths* (New York: Penguin).
Hillman, J.
1975        *Revisioning Psychology* (New York: Harper & Row).
1980        'On the Necessity of Abnormal Psychology: Ananke and Athene', in
            J. Hillman (ed.), *Facing the Gods* (Dallas: Spring).
1982        *The Thought of the Heart and the Soul of the World* (Dallas:
            Spring).
Jabes, E.
1989        *The Book of Shares* (trans. R. Waldrop; Chicago: University of
            Chicago Press).
Jung, C.G., and C. Kerenyi
1963        *Essays on a Science of Mythology: The Myth of the Divine and the
            Mysteries of Eleusis* (trans. R.F.C. Hull; Princeton: Princeton
            University Press).
Kerenyi, K.
1951        *The Gods of the Greeks* (trans. N. Cameron; London: Thames and
            Hudson).
1976        *Hermes: Guide of Souls* (trans. M. Stein; Dallas: Spring).
Klein, R.
1986        'The Metis of Centaurs', *Diacritics* 16: 2-13.
Merleau-Ponty, M.
1973        *The Prose of the World* (trans. J. O'Neill; ed. C. Lefort; Evanston, IL:
            Northwestern University Press).
Mueller-Volmer, K. (ed.)
1985        *The Hermeneutics Reader: Texts of the German Tradition From
            the Enlightment to the Present* (New York: Continuum).
Otto, W.F.
1954        *The Homeric Gods: The Spiritual Significance of Greek Religion*
            (trans. M. Hadas; New York: Pantheon).
1981        *Dionysius: Myth and Cult* (trans. R.R. Palmer; Dallas: Spring).
Paris, G.
1990        *Pagan Grace* (Dallas: Spring).

Shakespeare, W.
1969        *William Shakespeare: The Complete Works* (ed. A. Harbage; New
            York: Viking Press).
Thiselton, A.C.
1992        *New Horizons in Hermeneutics* (Grand Rapids: Zondervan).
Torrance, T.F.
1995        *Divine Naming: Studies in Patristic Hermeneutics* (Edinburgh: T.
            & T. Clark).
Winquist, C.E.
1978        *Homecoming: Interpretation, Transformation and Individuation*
            (Ann Arbor, MI: Scholars Press).

LLOYD WORLEY

# Impaling, Dracula, and the Bible

## The Tradition of Impaling

When Boston College professors and historians McNally and Florescu first published their best-seller *In Search of Dracula* (1972; repr. 1994), the Renaissance Romanian Prince Vlad Dracula was first introduced to the general public. In addition to being fascinated with the fact that there really was someone named 'Dracula' who had a connection with the famous fictional vampire, the public's interest in Vlad has focused on his use of the unspeakable torture/execution method known as impaling—the thrusting of a long stake or shaft through the anus, through the intestines to the diaphragm muscle. The naked victim was then hoisted up and the pole fixed in the ground. Subsequent writhing eventually forced the stake upward to pierce the heart, causing death (if the victim had not already died of shock or blood loss). Even after death, the impaling process continued, with gravity often finally causing the stake to exit through the mouth.

Impaling was a slow and horrible death designed to strike fear and loathing into the observer. That it did so (and does so) is evident, and when the life and times of Vlad are unveiled to audiences in presentations—scholarly or not—the inevitable, astonished questions are posed: What kind of man would do this? Is impaling Vlad's creation? Who else did this? The questions about and reactions to impaling show that Vlad knew what he was doing, for even today merely the idea of the act itself scrapes a raw nerve. Indeed, impaling has been scraping that nerve for some two millennia before Vlad 'the Impaler' ruled Romania.

According to Stegemann (1993: 135), impaling was known to the people of Israel at least as early as 701 BCE when Assyrian King Sennacherib conquered the Israelite town of Lachish. The

Assyrian reliefs of this victory show depictions of three nude
Israelites impaled on stakes, which is probably the first depiction of the gruesome torture/execution method. The term for
impaling is *tālâ 'al ha-'ēṣ* (Stegemann 1993: 135), meaning
'hanging on a pole', but the Assyrian reliefs show that the word
'hanging' does not precisely describe the method of fixation.
Stegemann (1993: 135) indicates that in the Temple Scroll (one
of the Dead Sea Scrolls discovered at the Qumran Community),
the 'evil-doer' will be executed by live *tālâ 'al ha-'ēṣ*, not by the
method at Deut. 21.22-23:

> And if a man have committed a sin worthy of death, and he be to
> be put to death, and thou hang him on a tree: His body shall not
> remain all night upon the tree, but thou shalt in any wise bury him
> that day; (for he that is hanged is accursed of God) (AV).

That is, the criminal is executed first, then impaled.

The Temple Scroll probably dates from 150–125 BCE (Yadin
1993: 94), so the death by impaling (*tālâ 'al ha-'ēṣ*) could be a
memory of the execution method introduced Sennacherib in
701 BCE. Yet, the same phrase, *tālâ 'al ha-'ēṣ*, occurs in Deut.
21.22-23, and the date of Deuteronomy is at least 621 BCE
(Dummelow 1964: 123), some 80 years prior to Sennacherib.
Thus, it is possible to conclude that Sennacherib of Assyria did
not introduce impaling to the Israelites, but that these ancient
Hebrew peoples knew of it prior to the Assyrian invasions,
having first seen impaling or suffered from it or a version of it
under the Pharaohs (at Gen. 40.19). The difference is that in
Deut. 21.22-23 the victim is a criminal who is first executed,
then displayed for a while via impalement, whereas Sennacherib's economy combined three steps, making impalement at
once a torture, an execution, and a public intimidation. The
Israelites saw impalement as a temporary public warning to be
followed by burial; the Assyrians saw impalement as a personal
torture and long-term humiliation which precluded burial or further postmortem care by the family of the accused.

However, at Deut. 21.22-23, we do not find a reference to
impaling as such. In the 1611 AV, the phrase is 'hang him on a
tree' and 'his body shall not remain all night upon the tree'.
Even in a modern translation such as the Oxford and Cambridge
REB, we find 'hang him on a gibbet' and later, the word 'there'

to refer to 'gibbet'. The impression given by these translations is
as to one who has been lynched or who is held by ropes to a
tree. To understand the original words being used, the dictionary apparatus of *Strong's Exhaustive Concordance* is helpful.
The word at Deut. 21.22-23 which is translated as 'tree' is *'ēṣ*,
meaning 'stick', 'staff', 'stock', or 'timber'. The noun appears to
be derived from the infinitive *'aṣâ*, meaning 'to fasten' or 'make
firm'. The *'ēṣ* ('stick', 'staff', 'stock', or 'timber') of Deut. 21.22-
23 is quite different from terms which definitely mean 'tree',
such as *'îlān* (a tree) or *'ēlôn* (an oak tree). Thus, it is not a 'tree'
that the criminal is hanged on, but the *'ēṣ*, the stake upon which
the criminal is impaled.

Even the verb for 'hang' in Deut. 21.22-23 is different from
the verb for 'hang' found only a few verses later in Deuteronomy. At 21.22-23 is *tālâ*, meaning 'to suspend', 'to hang up',
and 'to gibbet' (hence the NEB use of 'gibbet'), and at Deut.
28.66, 'hang' is *tālā'*, meaning 'to suspend' as the term is
usually understood (*tālā* can also mean 'to be uncertain'). The
words are similar, but they are not identical in meaning, where
*tālâ* is understood to mean 'impaled' as on a spit. The meaning
of *tālâ* is clearly explained in Dummelow (1964: 132): 'The tree
was a stake on which the dead body of the criminal was
impaled, in token of infamy'.

Once the true meaning of *tālâ 'al ha-'ēṣ* is understood to mean
'impaled', the phrase can be followed through the Old
Testament (using Strong's *Concordance*). The first mention of
impalement is at Gen. 40.19 where Joseph interprets a dream
for one of Pharaoh's prisoners who, not having the ability to
interpret its meaning, learns to his sorrow: 'Yet within three
days shall Pharaoh lift up thy head from off thee, and shall hang
thee on a tree; and the birds shall eat thy flesh from off thee'
(Gen. 40.19). This verse suggests that the Israelites first learned
of impalement not from the Assyrians but from the Egyptians.

Other impalement references follow, and in each case, the
phrase is *tālâ 'al ha-'ēṣ*:

> And if a man have committed a sin worthy of death, and he be to
> be put to death, and thou hang him on a tree: His body shall not
> remain all night upon the tree, but thou shalt in any wise bury him
> that day; (for he that is hanged is accursed of God) (Deut. 21.22-
> 23).

> And the king of Ai he hanged on a tree until eventide: and as soon as the sun was down, Joshua commanded that they should take his carcase down from the tree, and cast it at the entering of the gate of the city, and raise thereon a great heap of stones, that remaineth unto this day (Josh. 8.29). And afterward Joshua smote them, and slew them, and hanged them on five trees: and they were hanging upon the trees until the evening (Josh. 10.26).
>
> And when inquisition was made of the matter, it was found out; therefore they were both hanged on a tree: and it was written in the book of the chronicles before the king (Est. 2.23).
>
> It is sharpened to make a sore slaughter; it is furbished that it may glitter: should we then make mirth? it contemneth the rod of my son, as every tree (Ezek. 21.10).

Other 'trees' (*'îlan* = 'tree') are not associated with the verb 'hang' (*tālâ*) and are not the 'stake' (*'ēṣ*). It can be seen that the method precedes Sennacherib in Israel, and the composition dates of the succession of Old Testament books where impaling is found show an unchanged progression of the phrase *tālâ 'al ha-'ēṣ* which means the act of impaling. Mention of impaling does not stop at Ezekiel, but crosses the bridge into New Testament times when Paul writes at Gal. 3.13. 'Christ hath redeemed us from the curse of the law, being made a curse for us: for it is written, cursed is every one that hangeth on a tree'. Paul's reference is to Deut. 21.22-23. The words are Greek. Paul's *kremannumi* means 'hang', but his 'tree' is *xulon*, meaning 'stick', 'club', 'staff', 'stock', or, finally, 'tree'. If we understand that Paul could read the Hebrew Scriptures, he quotes the meaning and intent, in Greek, to mean 'impaled'. Paul does not mean that Christ was impaled, but, rather, he refers to the shame and horror associated with impaling, his theological meaning being to reinterpret the shame and horror in terms of Christ's saving grace. The important point is that the Galatians would know about impaling and its history not only in Assyria but in their own Jewish tradition. One of the tenets of Deut. 21.22-23 is that impaling is so terrible, so horrible, so shameful, that the sufferer is 'cursed of God', an accusation leveled against Jesus by certain anti-Christian Jews to show that he could not have been the messiah because of his manner of death. That such an accusation could have been made and that the accusation needed a rebuttal show both the psychic and social scars impaling left on its victims and the society to which they belonged. References to impaling are made in four other places in the New Testament:

1.   'The God of our fathers raised up Jesus, whom ye slew and hanged on a tree' (Acts 5.30).
2.   'And we are witnesses of all things which he did both in the land of the Jews, and in Jerusalem; whom they slew and hanged on a tree' (Acts 10.39).
3.   'And when they had fulfilled all that was written of him, they took him down from the tree, and laid him in a sepulchre (Acts 13.29).
4.   'Who in his own self bare our sins in his own body on the tree, that we, being dead to sins, should live unto righteousness: by whose stripes ye were healed' (1 Pet. 2.24).

In each instance of mention in the New Testament, the reference is made to signify the shame associated with impaling, not to imply that Christ was impaled as is seen in the reliefs of Sennacherib's victory. It does not appear that the Romans impaled, but instead crucified their criminals. Indeed, considering the lack of reference to impaling, it seems that impaling was not used—or was rarely used—in the Middle East. However, it does appear that it was talked about, as any catastrophe would be, and that the impact on society by impaling was strong enough to be used against and rebutted by early Christians who were defending their belief in Jesus as messiah.

Impaling executed criminals seems to have been an Egyptian as well as an Israelite practice (Gen. 40.19 and Deut. 21.22-23). Likewise, the Assyrians also impaled, but they impaled the living for the purposes of torture and execution, as well as to terrorize the conquered populace. The memories of that shame and terror continued over the centuries well into New Testament times, and while it seems impossible to think that impaling as a matter of public policy would have stopped, it appears that no records of the practice surface until the Crusades. Runciman (1994: 116) relates an incident in June/July of 1096 in which a renegade band of Franks, on their way to join Godfrey de Bouillon's army in Jerusalem, entered Hungary to pillage the countryside. The peasants resisted, so the Franks impaled a Hungarian boy. Where had the Franks learned such a thing? Runciman does not say, but McNally and Florescu (1994: 91) refer to a single instance of impaling carried out by John Tiptoft, Earl of Worcester, during the War of the Roses, saying that 'he had learned it from the Turks'. Perhaps the Franks invading Hungary heard tales of impaling from the surrounding Ottomans. It is likely that impalement probably occurred in the Middle East sporadically as a terrorist method. The return to Hungary and the world of mass impalings as a public policy awaited the rise to power of the Turkish-educated Vlad Dracula some 400 years later.

The definitive work on Transylvanian Prince Vlad II is *Dracula: Prince of Many Faces* (Florescu and McNally 1989), with most other works drawing upon either this work or upon *In Search of Dracula* (McNally and Florescu 1994). A synopsis of the life of Vlad II can be found in Melton (1994: 665-70), but two major events in Vlad's life concern the topic of impalement. First, in 1438, Vlad's father, Vlad Dracul (whose surname is derived from the Coat of Arms of the Order of the Dragon, an exclusive Imperial Order of Chivalry) gave his sons Vlad and Radu as hostages to the Turks as part of a loyalty 'non-aggression' pact. While the younger Radu became thoroughly 'Easternized', Vlad learned the Turkish culture without adopting it as his own—except, apparently, impaling. Whether impaling was then regularly practiced by the Turks is not known, but considering the fact that the practice was familar enough to enter the Old Testament records in the eighth century BCE (or sooner) and that the memory of impaling still was strong enough in New Testament times to be used as anti-messiah propaganda, it could be concluded that Vlad II at least heard stories about impaling, even if he never witnessed the act. As Melton says (1994: 666), Vlad 'learned Turkish language and customs'.

Upon the murder of Vlad Dracul and the execution of Mircea, Vlad II ascended the throne in 1447 as 'Vlad Dracula', meaning 'Vlad the son of Dracul' (McNally and Florescu 1994: 63). However, Vlad Dracula not only had to ascend the throne, he had to take it and secure it, so it was some nine years before Dracula

was in a position to finally establish his power. In 1456 Vlad
Dracula, in the courtyard of his palace, reintroduced *tālâ 'al ha-
'ēṣ* as public policy by impaling en masse the elder boyars
(noblemen) of Wallachia whom he had invited to a meeting
(McNally and Florescu 1994: 91). This was not a random act,
but was carried out by Dracula in order to destroy the noble
families whose power had broken his father and to serve as a
warning to his own countrymen who might move to take the
newly-acquired throne from him. During his short reign (1447–
76), Vlad Dracula imposed *tālâ 'al ha-'ēṣ* so often, so spectacu-
larly that he was popularly known, not as Vlad Dracula, but as
Vlad Tepes (pronounced teh-pesh), meaning 'Vlad the Impaler'.
Henceforth, the Middle-Eastern Egyptian/Israelite/Assyrian practice of *tālâ 'al ha-'ēṣ* became associated solely with one man,
the Prince of Wallachia, Vlad the Impaler.

While Dracula was complex enough a man to have many reasons for impaling his enemies (he did seem to enjoy it), it is logical to think that one reason would have been the emotional
impact the practice would have had on both enemies and
friends. That is, Dracula knew that mere rumor of impaling
would have nearly the same result as impaling itself. And talk
there was. As McNally and Florescu indicate (1994: 86),
Romanian Dracula stories have been orally transmitted even
into the twentieth century, and the accuracy of the stories is
supported by contemporary letters and documents. Woodcuts
from two editions of the 1499 sensational pamphlet published
by Ambrosius Huber (McNally and Florescu 1994: frontispiece
and 79) show Dracula presiding at an impaling. The two woodcuts differ slightly, showing impalements (a) with the body
upright, the pole thrust through the anus; (b) with the body face
up, the pole thrust through the back into the heart; (c) with the
body face down, the pole thrust through the navel. If public
policy was a major factor in Dracula's impaling (as it seems to
have been), then his use of the method would be aligned with
the Assyrians' practice rather than with the considerably more
modest Israelites' use. This alignment would make sense, given
Dracula's education by the Turks during his formative years.

Yet, for all its gruesome fascination, impaling would have
remained a passing mention for Bible scholars, and Prince

Dracula would have remained an interest for Slavic scholars had it not been for a decision by an Irish novelist and theater manager to connect the Wallachian prince with a Transylvanian vampire.

## Dracula and Christ

Bram Stoker's *Dracula* is one of the world's literary achievements. A great success in its own day, it has never gone out of print, and, as Aldiss writes (1986: 143), 'wretched must be the language which contains no translation of it'. How Stoker came to select Vlad Dracula as a prototype for Count Dracula was first told in McNally and Florescu (1994: 133-55) and then given in close detail in Belford's (1996) biography of Stoker. A major source for Stoker was Emily de Laszkowska Gerard's 1888 travel book, *Land Beyond the Forest* (McNally and Florescu 1994: 150), which contained valuable information about vampire folklore in Transylvania, as well as information about Vlad Dracula. Stoker became fascinated with the name 'Dracula' (he would not be the last to have the fascination), and so it was that the name (and even a bit of Vlad's history) was imported into Stoker's novel, *Dracula*, first published in May of 1897.

Examination of vampire folklore in Dracula and elsewhere shows striking points of similarity with the impaling practice of the Old Testament, the New Testament, and the use of it by Vlad Dracula: staking, nailing, dismemberment, and blood-drinking. Summers (1991: 217-27) discusses the vampire in Assyria and the Middle East and in a long banishing liturgical prayer (1991: 220-22) used by Assyrian clergy are found many characteristics that we recognize in the later vampire legends (walking about at night, preying on the living, stealing of life), but for the Assyrian, banishments drove away the 'Ekimmu'. That was not the case for the vampire of the Slavs, the Russians, and other Baltics. For them, the stake was the answer, and even certain types of wood were recommended, especially whitethorn, since it was believed that Christ's crown of thorns came from this plant (Summers 1991: 203). Other woods fit to kill the vampire included ash and oak (Barber 1988: 72).

The vampire-killing stake one sees in dramatic movie scenes is encountered again and again in the folklore, where the stake is driven through the heart (Barber 1988: 7) or a nail is driven into its forehead (Barber 1988: 45). Barber (1988: 53) even mentions a Romanian practice of driving a stake, not into the vampire, but into the grave so that if the person is a vampire, then the revenant, in rising, actually impales itself. Summers (1996: 309) describes the Romanian practice of driving a needle or stake through the heart or navel. Barber (1988: 52-53; 73) also mentions the occasional practice of driving sharp implements into the mouth of the supposed vampire. The staking ritual appears again and again and is reported in Summers, Copper, Florescu and McNally, Auerbach, Guiley, and many others. Auerbach (1995: 134) discusses variations in impaling by Vlad, but the illustrations from Huber show impalements that closely correspond to these folkloric anti-vampire staking methods: through the heart, through the navel, and (by psychological displacement, i.e. anus = mouth) through the mouth.

Of course, vampire folklore and legend not only precede Vlad Dracula, but even precede the New Testament and the Old Testament (Varma 1989: 14-29), yet the similarities between revenant-killing folklore and impalements are impressive. For the Assyrian and other Middle-Eastern peoples of BCE, prayers of banishment such as found in Summers (1991: 220-22) are sufficient to rid society of vampires, but for the later Orthodox Slavs and Baltics, exorcisms and imprecatory prayers are insufficient—there must also be impalings, beheadings, dismemberments, and heart removals (Barber 1988: 73). These are all methods of torture and execution used by Vlad.

Why was there a shift in the practice from the use of religious power to the use of rather more 'secular' methods? A major theme of Auerbach's insightful *Our Vampires, Ourselves* (1995) is that vampire lore not only permeates modern society, but that modern society permeates and changes vampire lore. It appears quite likely that such interpenetration can occur in all cultures in all periods and that as the tales of Vlad Dracula's impalements spread (mostly through the flight of his enemies who took their tales with them), these true reports would mix in with vampire lore to produce the similarities so noted. As Barber points out (1988: 72), the methods that kill a vampire would kill a living person as well, thus introducing an interesting question into the lore: if a vampire is a supernatural creature, then why are not supernatural death methods such as prayer, imprecations, and exorcisms sufficient to eliminate the vampire offender? Every indication is that supernatural methods were once used. Why did not these continue for vampires as they did, for example, for the devil himself? The answer to these questions may well be that as the horror of impaling gripped the popular terrorized mind of the mid-1400s, there was a mix of folklore mythology with Vlad's reality. Richardson (1992: 420) discusses the 'oral-anal-genital sado-masochistic' elements of the vampire lore in Dracula, and Barber reveals (1988: 86) the frantic vampire-hunting that developed in Europe over a period of several hundred years. The mix of lore, fact, frenzy, and fear congealed into the 'practical' legends of the vampire that dominated not only the fifteenth century, but that dominates the twentieth century as well. The vampiric 'practicality' works well in modern American society where Dresser reports (1989: 79-119) that the vampire in the media is selling throat lozenges, batteries, and even refrigerator storage bags. That is, both in ancient and modern times, the vampire has a 'solidarity' that allows him to move in the world, not as an insubstantiality, but with a power to move and change the physical world. The driving force of this 'substantiality' is the lingering attraction/repulsion of impaling.

The Church itself was not immune to the mix of lore and fact of the vampire legend, nor, considering the similarities between impaling and crucifixion, would we expect the Church to be immune. Where Christ was hanged 'on a tree' (the euphemism for *tālâ 'al ha-'ēṣ*, 'impaled'), the vampire—and Vlad's enemies—was also impaled. Where Christ was nailed to the cross, the vampire was nailed in the head (which image also recalls the crown of thorns). Where Christ was speared through the heart, the vampire is staked through the heart. Where Christ shed his blood to give life, the vampire takes blood and gives death or a 'living-in-death'. However, the Church did not institutionalize any of the vampiric lore and allowed these elements to remain on the fringe of religious practice—except, perhaps, for one element, the image of the heart.

In almost all references, the reader finds the requirement that to destroy the vampire, the stake must penetrate the heart. Indeed, the heart of the vampire began to receive such attention that its removal from the vampiric body became, for a while, important (Barber 1988: 73). In the Middle Ages, we find that a popular devotion to the pierced heart of Jesus developed—the devotion to the Sacred Heart. While the devotion had a biblical basis (Jn 7.37-39; 19.33-37), iconography developed showing, not the divine corpus, but the pierced heart of Jesus on the cross. The theology of the devotion was that spiritual life was fostered in the veneration of Jesus's physical heart, 'united to his divinity', as a symbol of his redemptive love (Connelly 1995: 1150). Depictions of the devotion show Jesus, not on a cross, but standing, with a radiant, somewhat stylized, heart exposed at the center of his chest. Horizontally around the heart at its midpoint is a wreath of thorns, and surmounting the heart is a crown and cross.

Even today, Sacred Heart statues, holy cards, and pictures can be easily found in abundance in church supply businesses which cater to the Roman Catholic public. Beneath the veneer of this imagery lurks the vampire/Vlad/impaling images seared into public consciousness in the seventh and eighth centuries BCE and the fifteenth and sixteenth centuries CE. Barber (1988: 51-52) and many others establish that the pricking (the 'mini-impalement') power of the hawthorne repels and immobilizes the vampire. The hawthorne wreath surrounds the Sacred Heart. The surmounting cross is driven into the Sacred Heart, just as any vampire's heart is impaled on a stake, and only the addition of the crown shows that this impalement is divine, not demonic. This imagery does not equate Christ with the vampire; rather, the imagery shows the popular consciousness transferring what it fears—impalement—over to faith and religion which protect from fear. The result is that two separate but similar popular beliefs flourished side by side: in the divine world, the Sacred Heart offered the terrible image of impaling as a path to holiness; in the secular world, vampire lore offered the terrible image of impaling as an uncertain method of dealing with evil uncleanness. They are the same, but they are not the same. In that uncertainty can be discovered the power of impaling, Dracula, and the Bible.

## Works Cited

Aldiss, B.W., and D. Wingrove
    1986      *Trillion Year Spree: The History of Science Fiction* (New York: Atheneum).
Auerbach, N.
    1995      *Our Vampires, Ourselves* (Chicago: University of Chicago Press).
Barber, P.
    1988      *Vampires, Burial, and Death: Folklore and Reality* (New Haven: Yale University Press).
Belford, B.
    1996      *Bram Stoker: A Biography of the Author of Dracula* (New York: Knopf).
Connelly, J.T.
    1995      'Sacred Heart, devotion to the', in R.P. MacBrien (ed.), *The HarperCollins Encyclopedia of Catholicism* (San Francisco: HarperCollins): 1150.
Copper, B.
    1973      *The Vampire in Legend and Fact* (New York: Citadel Press).
Dresser, N.
    1989      *American Vampires: Fans, Victims and Practitioners* (New York: Norton).
Dummelow, J.R. (ed.)
    1964      *A Commentary on the Whole Bible by Various Writers* (repr.; New York: Macmillan [1908, 1909]).
Florescu, R.R., and R.T. McNally
    1989      *Dracula, Prince of Many Faces: His Life and Times* (Boston: Little, Brown).
Guiley, R.E., and J.B. Macabre
    1994      *The Complete Vampire Companion* (New York: Macmillan).
McNally, R., and R.R. Florescu
    1994      *In Search of Dracula: The History of Dracula and Vampires* (repr.; Boston: Houghton Mifflin [1972]).
Melton, J.G.
    1994      *The Vampire Book: The Encyclopedia of the Undead* (Detroit: Gale Research).
Richardson, M.
    1992      'The Psychoanalysis of Count Dracula', in C. Frayling (ed.), *Vampyres: Lord Byron to Count Dracula* (London: Faber & Faber): 418-22.
Runciman, S.
    1994      *A History of the Crusades.* I. *The First Crusade and the Foundation of the Kingdom of Jerusalem* (London: The Folio Society).

Stegemann, H.
1993        'Is the Temple Scroll a Sixth Book of the Torah-Lost for 2,500
            Years?', in H. Shanks (ed.), *Understanding the Dead Sea Scrolls*
            (New York: Vintage): 126-36.

Strong, J. *et al.*
1975        *The Exhaustive Concordance of the Bible* (repr.; Nashville:
            Abingdon Press [1890]).

Summers, M.
1991        *The Vampire: His Kith and Kin* (repr.; New York: Dorset Press
            [1928]).

1996        *The Vampire in Europe* (repr.; New Jersey: Random House
            [1929]).

Varma, D.P.
1989        'The Vampire in Legend, Lore, and Literature', in M. Carter (ed.),
            *The Vampire in Literature: A Critical Bibliography* (Ann Arbor,
            MI: UMI Research Press): 13-29.

Yadin, Y.
1993        'The Temple Scroll—the Longest Dead Sea Scroll', in H. Shanks
            (ed.), *Understanding the Dead Sea Scrolls* (New York: Vintage):
            87-112.

LARRY J. KREITZER

## The Scandal of the Cross:
## *Crucifixion Imagery and Bram Stoker's* Dracula

A couple of years ago some friends came to visit me from the United States, a distinguished couple who teach in the English Faculty of a liberal arts college in the bluegrass heartlands of Kentucky. One evening we were discussing the way in which the basic facts of the Christian story seemed to be unknown to many people within the modern world. They told me of an experience that they had had in King's Road in London when they entered a jewelry store and were browsing for something to purchase. They overheard an exchange between another customer and a young sales clerk in which the customer expressed an interest in purchasing a necklace with a cross on it. 'Do you want a plain one or one with a little man on it?' was the clerk's reply. Apparently the significance of the 'little man on the cross' was something which escaped her.

The purpose of this study is to explore the ways in which imagery of the cross of Christ and its most potent symbol, the crucifix, have become part of our literary and cultural inheritance, and to note one particular way in which this imagery has evolved within popular culture in recent years. I propose to do this by using Bram Stoker's classic horror story *Dracula* (1897), together with some of the numerous cinematic adaptations of the story which have appeared in recent years. Thus, we shall have occasion to discuss not only Francis Ford Coppola's ambitious *Bram Stoker's Dracula* (1992), but one or two of the more significant vampire films in recent years, including Werner Herzog's *Nosferatu: The Vampyre* (1979) and Neil Jordan's *Interview With the Vampire* (1994). Several other films from the 1970s and 1980s have also captured the imagination of a youthful public and are worth considering in exploring this theme, notably Tobe Hooper's *'Salem's Lot* (1979) and Tony Scott's *The Hunger* (1983). Each in its own way contributes to a

discussion of the role that crucifixion imagery plays in perpetu-
ating the ever-adaptable mythology arising from Stoker's original
novel *Dracula*.

We shall pursue the study in three parts: (1) the place of the
cross in Paul's thought; (2) crucifixion imagery in Bram Stoker's
*Dracula* (1897); (3) crucifixion imagery in some film adaptations of *Dracula*.

## The Place of the Cross in Paul's Thought

Nowhere in the New Testament is Christ's sacrificial death on
the cross of Calvary more theologically important than it is in
Paul's letters. It is clear that the death of Jesus of Nazareth on a
Roman gibbet holds a central place in the theological thought of
Paul, with 'the preaching of the cross' becoming a summary
statement for all that the apostle to the Gentiles held to be dear
to his calling and ministry.[1]

The easiest places to see the centrality of the cross are those
where Paul appears to add references to the death of Jesus of
Nazareth by crucifixion to the christological hymns of the early
church. For example, we note the theologically significant inclusion of the phrases 'even death on a cross' in Phil. 2.8c and
'through the blood of his cross' in Col. 1.20 to illustrate the
point.[2] In both of these instances it appears that Paul goes out
of his way to focus attention on the cross of Calvary, and the
death of Jesus the Messiah of God that took place there, as the
central point in the Christian drama of redemption. It is a
common assumption by many New Testament scholars that
Paul's insertion of these explicit references to the cross into earlier creedal hymns suggests that the cross did not have a very
prominent place within the earliest layers of Christian thought.

1.    The so-called Pauline 'theology of the cross' has been the subject of
much recent discussion, particularly as it has provided a rich basis for dialogue between biblical specialists and systematic theologians. See Käsemann
1971: 32-59; Stuhlmacher 1986: 155-168; Cousar 1990; McGrath 1993:
192-97.

2.    The christological hymns contained in Phil. 2.6-11 and Col. 1.15-20
have been subjected to intense scholarly scrutiny. See Martin 1993: 419-23
for an introduction to this matter.

However, this is a conclusion which is methodologically suspect and one which is open to severe criticism. Quite simply, it is extremely difficult to determine what in the midst of Paul's letters is pre-Pauline traditional material and what are Paul's own rhetorical flourishes written in the heat of his correspondence. Even if we were to agree that the earliest christological hymns did not contain *explicit* reference to the cross itself, there is little doubt that a declaration of the death of Jesus Christ was an integral feature of these hymns (Phil. 2.8b is a case in point). If this is so, then perhaps the best way to describe Paul's contribution to the matter is to say that he is merely making explicit what was implicit from the very beginning of Christian belief and proclamation.

In any event, what is certain is that Paul uses 'the cross' and crucifixion imagery at several key points in his letters, most frequently in polemical contexts where he is engaging with opponents over the true nature of the Christian faith.[3] In fact the noun 'cross' (σταυρός) appears only ten times in the Pauline corpus (1 Cor. 1.17, 18; Gal. 5.11; 6.12, 14; Phil. 2.8; 3.18; Col. 1.20; 2.14; Eph. 2.16) and the verb 'to crucify' (σταυρόω) appears only eight times (1 Cor. 1.13, 23; 2.2, 8; 2 Cor. 13.4; Gal. 3.1; 5.24; 6.4). In the main these passages all refer to the *literal* crucifixion of Jesus on Calvary, although crucifixion is occasionally used in a *metaphorical* sense, as in Col. 2.14 ('having nailed the certificate of debt to the cross') where it appears as a symbol of the place where the legal demands of the guilty are met and forgiveness is thereby effected, or in Gal. 6.14 ('the world has been crucified to me and I to the world') where it appears as a symbol of Christian discipleship.[4] Similarly the use of the verb 'co-crucified' (συνσταυρόω) in Rom. 6.6 and Gal. 2.19 also points to the adaptability of the imagery as a symbol of discipleship and the union of believers with Christ.

Perhaps the two most interesting texts for our concerns are 1 Cor. 1.23 and Gal. 5.11 where Paul speaks of Jewish reaction to 'the scandal' (σκάνδαλον) of the cross and describes the assessment of it by Greeks as 'foolishness' (μωρίαν). These curious phrases suggest that there was originally something

3. See Ellis 1974: 69-75 on this point.
4. Minear 1979: 395-407 offers an interesting discussion of this.

offensive about the message of the cross, that Jesus's death was the focus of humiliation, shame and embarrassment.[5] Far from the cross being the object of religious reverence and pride so familiar to us today, it was instead a stumbling-block to the followers who committed themselves to the Messiah who had been crucified upon it.[6] Why was it such an object of ridicule and contempt? It is generally agreed that the execution of the Jewish Messiah as a common criminal lies at the heart of the matter, and that the offense that this kind of death represented in terms of the Torah was too much for many devout people to bear. Paul states as much, and attempts to turn the tables on the matter when he cites Deut. 21.23 in Gal. 3.13: 'Christ redeemed us from the curse of the Law, having become a curse for us—for it is written, "Cursed is everyone who hangs on a tree"'. The cryptic passage from Deuteronomy was the subject of considerable midrashic interest among pre-Christian Jewish writers and it is hardly surprising that it becomes associated with the crucifixion by Paul in the way that it does here.[7] What is important for us to see in this regard is the way in which the cross quickly evolves from being an object of ridicule to being a symbol of power. Originally the cross was a source of dishonor; quite quickly it became a source of power and wonder and developed into a focal point for Christian worship and religious reverence.

How does this help in terms of a fresh consideration of Bram Stoker's *Dracula*? I would like to suggest that there is something of a reversal of fortunes concerning the place that the cross has in the developing Dracula mythology when it is compared to that seen in early Christianity. In other words, Stoker's *Dracula* starts with an understanding of the cross which builds

5.   Heb. 12.2 similarly speaks of the shame that Jesus Christ suffered on the cross.

6.   Hengel (1977) contains a fine discussion of the way in which crucifixion was viewed within the ancient world, including many Jewish, Greek and Latin writers of antiquity.

7.   See Wilcox 1977: 85-99; Fitzmyer 1978: 493-513. There is some evidence that the wicked figure of Haman in the Book of Esther may have served as a precursor for the crucified Jesus. See Thornton 1986: 419-26 on this point.

upon the position that is arrived at within the Pauline letters. Throughout the novel the cross is surrounded by a sense of reverence; it is held in respect and it is recognized as possessing great protective power. Indeed, it is perhaps *the* primary means of defense against the evil Count Dracula, with garlic flowers and communion wafers and hawthorn bushes serving as supplementary weapons in the vampire killer's armory. And yet, this is only the first stage in how crucifixion imagery is portrayed within the Dracula mythology, for as we shall see below, subsequent cinematic adaptations of the story have differing assessments of the significance of the cross within them. The power of the cross as a symbolic weapon against Dracula is no longer quite what it was in Stoker's day, and it is our task to draw attention to some of the shifts in emphasis.

## Crucifixion Imagery in Bram Stoker's *Dracula* (1897)

Before we turn to examine the place that the crucifixion imagery has within *Dracula* itself, it is worth reviewing how it was that Stoker came to write the novel and what sorts of critical discussion it has engendered, not least in the realm of theological matters. A brief consideration of some of these issues will also serve to set the religious imagery we are concentrating on here in this essay within its proper context.

### *Bram Stoker and the Writing of* Dracula

The year 1997 marks the centenary of the publication of *Dracula*. The novel has been phenomenally successful; it has been translated into approximately 20 languages worldwide and it has never been out of print in English since it first appeared in June of 1897, sporting a mustard-yellow cover and blood-red lettering.[8] Paradoxically, the author of the celebrated novel, which is often described as the quintessential Gothic horror story, remains something of an obscure figure. Many modern people today know of his creation largely because of the numerous film adaptations of the novel, but remain totally unaware

---

8. Originally published by Archibald Constable and Company, Westminster.

of the author's identity. Indeed, the recent biography of Bram Stoker by Barbara Belford goes so far as to describe him as 'the soulless invisible man' and suggests that the paper trail left by him is very faint indeed, so much so that it was difficult to write a detailed biography about him (1995: x).[9] Stoker wrote a total of 18 novels, but it is only *Dracula* which has stood the test of time, and it is generally only by this single work that he is known to the public.[10]

What influenced Stoker to write the story, and under what circumstances he produced the work, are matters of considerable dispute.[11] Much scholarly attention has been directed to establishing the historical basis for the story of Count Dracula. It is now generally agreed that the figure of Vlad the Impaler, a fifteenth-century prince of Wallachia in what is now southern Romania, is the figure most likely to be behind it all.[12] It will come as no surprise to know that the association of Prince Vlad with the Dracula legend is something which the post-communist Romania is eager to exploit; sites associated with the Prince have now become tourist attractions and there are many travel companies which offer a Dracula tour to the relevant areas.[13] Yet, whatever the historical anchors for them

9.   This is now the standard biography of Stoker and replaces the other two inferior biographies by Harry Ludlam *A Biography of Dracula: The Life Story of Bram Stoker* (London: Foulsham, 1962) and Daniel Farson *The Man Who Wrote Dracula: A Biography of Bram Stoker* (London: Michael Joseph, 1975).

10. Although an increasing number of people are aware of his last novel, *The Lair of the White Worm* (1911), largely through British director Ken Russell's film from 1989 which is based on the story.

11. The discovery in 1970 in the Rosenbach Library and Museum in Philadelphia of Stoker's working notes for *Dracula* puts paid to the suggestion that the novel was a rush-job. It now seems clear that *Dracula* was meticulously planned and researched as a novel, in contrast to what was commonly assumed among earlier critics. Stoker spent at least six years researching and preparing the book. For further discussion along these lines, see Bierman 1977: 39-41; Haining and Tremayne 1997.

12. See McNally and Florescu 1975, 1995; Leatherdale 1993: 13-44; Nandris 1966: 367-96; Porter 1992.

13. Elizabeth Miller, a Professor in the Department of English at the Memorial University in Newfoundland, Canada, manages an Internet site on the subject which is entitled 'Dracula's Home Page' (<http://www.ucs.

might be, vampire legends and myths have been around since the Middle Ages and stories of them became a standard feature of Gothic horror.[14] There is good evidence that Stoker was familiar with many of these stories, notably Joseph Sheridan Le Fanu's *Carmilla* (1872).[15]

The relationship between Bram Stoker and the celebrated actor Sir Henry Irving, with whom Stoker had a long and intimate friendship both as business manager of *The Lyceum* and as a personal friend, is sometimes said to be the inspiration behind *Dracula*.[16] In this sense, it is Irving who, as Count Dracula, sucks the life out of the devoted Stoker, who serves as the Jonathan Harker figure. In such a scenario Stoker's own wife Florence is reflected in the character Lucy Westenra, who is socially frivolous and seemingly unable to keep herself from seeking after and accepting the attentions of a myriad suitors. Nowhere is the power of Irving over Stoker more evident than in the fact that Stoker hurriedly wedded Florence and postponed his honeymoon with her in order to comply with Irving's demands that Stoker join him in Birmingham and begin the theater season; in *Dracula* we find an echo of this in the fact that Jonathan Harker's wedding to Mina is postponed when Count Dracula demands that Harker come to Transylvania in order to finalize the arrangements for his move to England.

Both the narrative style and the structural design of *Dracula* have been focal points of investigation within recent years.[17]

mun.ca/~emiller/>). She includes color photographs of most of the tourist spots in Romania.

14. One of the best treatments of the subject is Twitchell 1981. Also worth considering is Punter 1980. Several good anthologies of vampire stories are available which show the range and diversity of the subject. For example, see Ryan 1987, Haining 1995.

15. See A.N. Wilson, 'Introduction' to Stoker 1983: ix-xii. Le Fanu was, like Stoker, an Irishman from Dublin. He was joint owner of the Dublin *Evening Mail* and thus was at one time Stoker's employer (when Stoker was writing theater reviews for the paper).

16. A suggestion which is no doubt responsible for the decision to have a cover photograph of Henry Irving (as Mephistopheles) in the Penguin Classics edition of Stoker's *Dracula* (1993).

17. See Senf 1979: 160-70; Seed 1985: 61-75; Johnson 1984a: 17-24; Miller 1994: 27-30.

The novel is divided into 27 chapters but they are not as straightforward as one might expect.[18] The fact that the narrative throughout is conducted by means of a series of journals and letters, of diary entries and newspaper clippings, means that the way in which the story is communicated to the reader is somewhat unusual; there is always a sense of distancing involved, and there is no omniscient narrator to be found. The reader is never quite able to identify with the narrator of the story directly but is forced to engage with the narrative through a multiplicity of characters. The result is somewhat unexpected, yet spectacular: the reader encounters Dracula in a secondary sense. Count Dracula himself never assumes the role of the narrator in the novel; he is met only through the eyes and ears of the other characters in the story. Yet, paradoxically this mediated encounter with the central figure of evil is all the more suspenseful as a result and the dramatic effect of the novel is enhanced by it.

The sexual imagery underlying the vampire story is generally recognized, and there have been many studies specifically given over to exploring this theme, perhaps the most discussed aspect of *Dracula* within the critical literature.[19] The illicit pursuit and capture of an unsuspecting victim, culminating in an intimate embrace and a bite to the throat, lies at the heart of the horror of the vampire story. Little wonder then that the marks left on the necks and throats of passionate lovers in Great Britain are commonly described as 'love bites' (the American equivalent of 'hickey' is rather lame in comparison). Given the thinly disguised submerged sexual nature of the novel it comes as no surprise that *Dracula* has been the happy hunting-ground for those pursuing a Freudian reading of the story. Many argue, for example, that it is the incest taboo which is foundational to the

18. We shall cite passages from the novel by noting their chapter and page number (thus 1:5 denotes page five of chapter one). The edition used here is that within the Penguin Classics series (London: Penguin Books, 1993). The edition contains an Introduction by Maurice Hindle (vii-xl).

19. See Fry 1972: 20-22; Weissman 1977: 392-405; Griffin 1980: 454-65; Wood 1983: 175-87; Craft 1984: 107-133; Stevenson 1988: 139-49; Howes 1988: 104-19; Hogan 1988: 138-63; Case 1991: 1-20; Leatherdale 1993: 155-71; Krumm 1995: 5-11; Belford 1995: 5-9; Auerbach 1995: 140-48.

story and that the novel is best interpreted as a Victorian version of the Oedipus myth.[20]

The novel has been the focus of a number of other interpretative readings. For example, it has been analyzed by some feminist critics for what it contributes to the late-Victorian view of the sexual roles of men and women, with Stoker being both hailed by some as an early feminist and at the same time condemned by others as a chauvinistic traditionalist.[21] The novel has also been subjected to various political interpretations, with the rich blend of metaphor and symbol inherent in the story readily lending itself to application. Thus, it has been read as a text primarily concerned with political and economic matters arising out of the English imperial system and the role of England as an enlightened Western democracy in the face of the political chaos which threatened from the East.[22] Some have detected in the novel echoes of the debate over Irish Home Rule which so dominated the domestic political agenda in Stoker's own day.[23] There has also been a school of thought which views *Dracula* as an illustration of the Marxist class-struggle in which Count Dracula, as the personification of bourgeois capitalism constantly in search of new victims (or 'markets'?), preys upon the working-class and sucks them dry.[24] The interpretation of *Dracula* as an anti-Semitic work, in which Stoker employs the stereotypical nineteenth-century images of the Jew and sets these over against the virtues of Christianity, has also been put forward.[25] This leads us to consider the theological dimensions of the novel, an area which has not received the attention that

20. Bentley 1972: 27-34.

21. Demetrakopoulos 1977: 104-13; Roth 1977: 113-21; Senf 1982: 33-49; Johnson 1984b: 20-39; Williams 1991: 445-63; McDonald 1993: 80-104.

22. For discussion of the social and geo-political dimensions of the novel, see Wasson 1966: 24-27; Hennelly 1977: 13-26; Arata 1990: 621-45; Wicke 1992: 467-93; Sutherland 1996: 233-38.

23. Glover 1996.

24. Moretti 1983: 83-108; Hatlen 1980: 80-97; Jancovich 1992: 48-52.

25. Halberstam 1993: 333-52 offers some interesting ideas along these lines, calling attention to the possible influence of Henry Irving's portrayal of the Jew Shylock in Shakespeare's *The Merchant of Venice* upon Stoker's imagination.

it is due, but one that promises much in terms of understanding the evolving nature of the religious mythology surrounding *Dracula*.

### Theological Imagery and Biblical Allusions in the Novel

Leonard Wolf describes *Dracula* as displaying 'the perpetual tension between the dark and the light; the wrestling match between Christ and Satan' (1993: vii). Certainly it is true that *Dracula* is a profoundly theological novel which contains a host of interlocking ideas commonly associated with historic Christianity. At the same time the novel contains a dozen or so clear allusions to biblical stories or texts which help to set the tone for the theological exploration which lies at its core. These come from a wide range of biblical strata, embracing both Old Testament and New Testament writings.

For example, in 5:80, in one of Lucy Westenra's letters to Mina Murray, there is an allusion to the Parable of the Ten Virgins (Mt. 25.1-10). This comes in the form of Lucy's recounting to her friend the proposal made to her by the Bowie-brandishing Texan Quincey P. Morris. Technically speaking, Morris is made to misquote the central image of the parable (he mentions the '*seven* young women with the lamps'), perhaps under the weight of seven as an image of perfection and the fact that in his eyes Lucy is the perfect woman. Similarly, in 10.156-157 there is an allusion to the parable of the sower (Mt. 13.1-9/Mk 4.1-9/Lk. 8.4-8) as Van Helsing explains to Dr Seward that they need to be patient in order to let the true nature of Lucy Westenra's vampiric condition be revealed in due course.

Meanwhile, in 6:99 Mina Murray's journal contains an allusion to the story of the healing of the blind man of Bethsaida (Mk 8.24) when she offers a description of seeing people half-shrouded in the seaside mists of Whitby, and notes that they 'seem "like trees walking"'. In 8:133 there is an allusion to the saying of Jesus recorded in Mt. 10.29-31/Lk. 12.6-7 in which God's concern for the life of a sparrow (as compared to that for the life of an eagle) is asserted. The same section of Dr Seward's Diary describes the religious mania of the lunatic patient Renfield in language which is reminiscent of Jn 3.29 where John the Baptist declares the imminent arrival of 'the Master' (the description here makes use of bridegroom imagery, perhaps building upon Isa. 62.5). In effect, this is to make Renfield something of an anti-type to John the Baptist and carries with it the implication that Count Dracula is the anti-type to Jesus Christ himself.

The idea is even carried on further in the chapter when Seward remarks that Renfield 'thinks of the loaves and fishes even when he believes he is in a Real Presence' (8:135). The Feeding of the Five Thousand is clearly alluded to in this comment, as is the eucharistic sub-text of the gospel story (Mt. 14.13-21/Mk 6.32-44/Lk. 9.10-17/Jn 6.1-15). In 20:346 Dr Seward reports on a further conversation that he has had with his patient in which Renfield cites Gen. 5.24 ('Enoch walked with God') as part of how the lunatic perceives his relationship with Count Dracula. He is to be rewarded with unending terrestrial life (as opposed to Enoch's unending spiritual life) from his Master and Lord, Count Dracula. In the next chapter this allegiance is tested in a passage which is a parody of the temptation of Christ in the wilderness. Here, in 21:360, the zoophagous Renfield, mortally wounded by Dracula for having attempted to protect Mina from him, relates to Dr Seward how Dracula had offered him thousands of rats to eat, as well as dogs and cats. Dracula promised him, 'All these lives I will give you, ay, and many more and greater, through countless ages, if you will fall down and worship me!' The parallel with Mt. 4.9/Lk. 4.7 is obvious. In 25:441 Van Helsing explains that Dracula's hypnotic power over Mina will be his undoing, alluding to Ps. 69.22 when he says, 'The hunter is taken in his own snare'. The agelessness of Dracula is alluded to in 14:247 by comparing him with the biblical patriarch Methuselah who, according to Gen. 5.27, lived to be 969 years old.

Meanwhile, the story of Noah's ark in Gen. 8.8-12 is alluded to in 4:64 where Jonathan Harker describes Dracula's castle in Transylvania as perched on a spot so high that it 'seemed to me as if the dove from the ark had lighted there'. In 19:333 there is an allusion to Exod. 40.34-38 with its mention of 'a pillar of cloud by day and fire by night' as part of 'Mina Harker's Journal'. Mina uses the image to describe her dream-like pseudo-sexual encounter with the Count and the fact that he enters her bedroom as a thick and mysterious mist.

Even Dracula himself occasionally alludes to Scripture, as in 2:31 where he uses a phrase from Exod. 2.22, 'a stranger in a strange land', to describe how he fears he may feel when he makes the anticipated move to London. In the Old Testament story these are the words on the lips of Moses which denote his period of life in Egypt.

Perhaps the most significant, and best known, quotation of a biblical text within the novel appears in 11:184 where again in Dr Seward's Diary the words of the maniac Renfield are cited. Following the knife attack by Renfield upon Seward, the attendants come to restrain Renfield and return him to his cell. As they do so Renfield repeats over and over again, 'The blood is the life! the blood is the life!', a line from Deut. 12.23 which could be described as one of the interpretative keys to the novel as a whole. The same line is repeated one other time by Renfield in 18:301.

Our particular focus within this article is the crucifixion imagery within *Dracula*, the way in which it uses and adapts Christian iconography. But just how prevalent is this within the novel? The word 'crucifix' occurs twenty times during the course of the narrative (1:12 (three times); 2:38; 3:41 (twice); 3:48; 7:106; 7:117; 13:213; 13:215; 15:261; 16:272 (twice); 18:306; 18:309; 19:321; 21:363; 21:365; 23:394). One of the most interesting examples of this concerns the captain of the sailing ship *Demeter* which unwittingly transports Dracula and his earth-laden coffins to Whitby. The captain is found dead, tied to the wheel of the ship with a 'crucifix and beads' (i.e. a rosary) sandwiched between his hands and a spoke of the wheel. In addition to these references to a crucifix, there are two references to 'the cross' (1:15 and 22:382), and one reference to an 'impaled obstacle' (1:23). The idea of people making a 'sign of the cross' to protect themselves against Dracula and his power occurs fourteen times, most prominently in the introductory chapter of the novel, as if to alert the reader to the need for such protection (1:11; 1:13; 1:14; 1:15 (twice); 1:17; 1:18; 1:19 (twice); 7:110; 9:137; 9:153; 19:321; 27:464). Generally this 'crossing' is done by superstitious Transylvanian peasants, either when they encounter Dracula himself or when the evil Count is mentioned in conversation. A good example is found in 1:13-14, as the young solicitor Harker leaves the inn where he has been staying and, boarding the coach, begins his fateful journey to Count Dracula's castle:

> When we started, the crowd round the inn door which had by this time swelled to a considerable size, all made the sign of the cross and pointed two fingers towards me. With some difficulty I got a fellow-passenger to tell me what they meant; he would not answer at first, but on learning that I was English he explained that it was a charm or guard against the evil eye. This was not very pleasant for me, just starting for an unknown place to meet an unknown man; but every one seemed so kind-hearted, and so sorrowful, and so sympathetic that I could not but be touched. I shall never forget the last glimpse which I had of the inn-yard and its crowd of picturesque figures, *all crossing themselves*.

One could legitimately extend the crucifixion imagery to include the idea of the 'stake' which is used to dispatch Dracula and other vampires in the novel. The term 'stake' is used thirteen times in a literal sense (15:259; 15:262; 16:275 (twice); 16:277 (four times); 16:279; 18:309; 25:425; 25:430; 27:477), as well as some seven times in a metaphorical sense (16:269; 19:326; 21:357; 23:390; 25:424 (twice); 27:469). It seems clear that Stoker was playing with the word when he says, for example, that 'there is a soul at *stake*!' (21:357), or 'The *stake* we play for is life and death' (27:469). Perhaps the most theologically significant use of 'stake' occurs in 16:277 where the phrase 'mercy-bearing stake' is used. This occurs in connection with the (in)famous scene in which Arthur Holmwood drives a stake through the heart of his beloved Lucy as she lies in her coffin, thus ending her vampiric existence:

> Arthur placed the point over the heart, and as I looked I could see its dint in the white flesh. Then he struck with all his might.
> The Thing in the coffin writhed; and a hideous, blood-curdling screech came from the opened red lips. The body shook and quivered and twisted in wild contortions; the sharp white teeth champed together till the lips were cut, and the mouth was smeared with a crimson foam. But Arthur never faltered. He looked like a figure of Thor as his untrembling arm rose and fell, driving deeper and deeper *the mercy-bearing stake*, whilst the blood from the pierced heart welled and spurted up around it.

It is difficult to read this without finding one's mind recall that the cross of Christ might well be described as a 'mercy-bearing stake'. In this sense, *Dracula* might be described as a novel which expresses an interesting theology of atonement, albeit covertly. There are several other allusions to the passion and crucifixion of Christ which help to establish this as *the* key theological idea for the sub-text of the *Dracula* story-line. Three of these are worth noting briefly.

First, in 21:367 Mina pronounces 'God's will be done!' when she is informed of Renfield's death; clearly this is an allusion to Jesus's words in the Garden of Gethsemane recorded in Mt. 26.39/Mk 14.36/Lk. 22.42. In all three Gospel accounts this prayer of Jesus that the Father's will might be done is linked to mention of the 'cup' of suffering which he must shortly endure on the cross. Secondly, in 18:305 there is an allusion to Christ's being pierced by the soldier's spear while hanging on the cross at Golgotha. This occurs in 'Mina Harker's Journal' when she mentions 'an arrow in the side of Him who died for man'. What is significant about this allusion is that it is recorded only in John's Gospel (in 19.34), and it is immediately followed by a mention of the '*blood* and water' which flowed from Christ's side—a fitting allusion considering the emphasis that blood has within the story line of *Dracula* itself. Thirdly, in 19:321, as part of Jonathan Harker's Journal, there is a recollection of how Professor Van Helsing bravely enters the lair of Count Dracula in Carfax in Purfleet, London. As he enters the house in which Dracula has hidden his earth-filled coffins, Van Helsing crosses himself and utters the Latin words '*In manus tuas, Domine!*', an adaptation of the final words of Jesus on the cross according to Lk. 23.46 ('Father, into your hands I commit my spirit').

There seems little doubt that Stoker's *Dracula* is a novel which is shot through with frequent allusions to biblical imagery, most notably to the cross and the crucifixion of Jesus Christ. In particular, the use of a crucifix as a means of fending off the vampire occurs frequently in the course of the story, although other Christian rituals like baptism and Holy Communion also appear at key points.[26] Let us now move to

---

26. I plan to explore the sacramental theme more fully in my forthcoming *Pauline Images in Fiction and Film* (Sheffield: Sheffield Academic Press).

consider some of the ways in which this crucifixion imagery is developed in some recent cinematic adaptations of the *Dracula* story.

## Crucifixion Imagery in Some Film Adaptations of Dracula

Without doubt the popularity of the figure of Dracula is due in no small measure to the various cinematic portrayals of him—a mythologically rich character as vibrant as this readily lends itself to such artistic expression. This was recognized very early on; even during Stoker's lifetime the novel *Dracula* was adapted for the London stage.[27] However, it was not until F.W. Murnau's film classic *Nosferatu: Eine Symphonie des Grauens* (1922) that the rich potential of Stoker's creation began to be explored cinematically, and even here it was not without controversy. The film, now regarded as a seminal work of German expressionism,[28] was an unauthorized adaptation of Bram Stoker's novel, and Stoker's widow Florence vigorously pursued her legal rights through the courts. She eventually won her case in 1925 and all copies of the film were ordered destroyed, a legal injunction which fortunately (from the stand-point of cinematic history) was not successfully carried out since a few copies survived.[29] Given this inauspicious beginning, it is indeed remarkable that over 200 Dracula and vampire movies have been made by film directors from all around the world.[30] Perhaps most prominent among these, at least as far as shaping the popular understanding of the Dracula myth, are the various films produced by the British Hammer House of Horror films in the 1950s, 1960s and 1970s, which made the actors

27. See Skal 1990.
28. This silent classic has been restored and is available through Redemption Films Ltd, London. The restoration contains English-text announcement panels and remains a must for anyone interested in the popular development of Dracula mythology. For more on this, see Wood 1979: 43-49 and 1983: 175-87.
29. Skal 1990: 40-63 discusses this.
30. A number of books catalogue this rich explosion of films. See Jones 1993, Silver and Ursini 1993; Gelder 1994: 86-107.

Christopher Lee and Peter Cushing household names.[31] However, the vampire film remains a perennial favourite and it has experienced something of a revival in the past fifteen years or so (particularly for the teenage audience). It is on these more recent films that I will concentrate. I shall arrange the discussion under three headings according to how the crucifix imagery is handled within them.

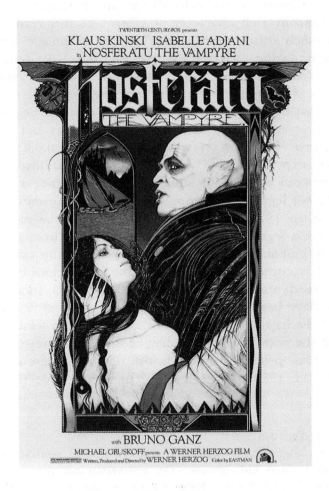

Figure 1

31.  See Eyles, Adkinson and Fry 1973, Hutchings 1993: 115-27. Each of the fifteen Hammer films which develop the Dracula myth depicts, to a greater or lesser extent, the crucifix as a weapon against vampirism.

## The Cross: Revered as a Symbol of Faith

I first consider Werner Herzog's *Nosferatu: The Vampyre* (1979)
which stars the accomplished German actor Klaus Kinski as
Count Dracula in striking makeup and costuming (see Fig. 1).
The film is a remake of F.W. Murnau's classic *Nosferatu:
Eine Symphonie des Grauens* (1922) and is largely dependent
upon it, as indeed are most of the cinematic adaptations of
*Dracula*.[32] Cross and crucifixion imagery appears a couple of
times in the film (in contrast to Murnau's original where it is
hardly used at all). For example, in the opening dream sequence
of Lucy Harker, we see the young woman (played by Isabelle
Adjani) wake up screaming, a gold crucifix-necklace clearly visible. There is also an interesting scene in which Jonathan Harker
(played by Bruno Ganz) is staying overnight in an inn while he is
on his way to Count Dracula's castle. As he prepares for bed at
night he is visited by a peasant maid who brings him a rosary
with a crucifix on it and places it around his neck. She also
gives him a book about vampires before she leaves the room,
crossing herself as she exits. In a scene from the middle of the
film Count Dracula is shown moving his earth-laden coffins into
the Carfax property he has purchased. The coffins are placed in
a room which obviously has been a chapel, for there is a cross
on one wall. As Dracula sees the cross he raises his arms and
cowers in fear, quickly moving away from it. Later he similarly
turns away from Lucy Harker, groaning in the process, when he
realizes that she is wearing her cross necklace. A cross-necklace
also figures at the end of the film when Jonathan Harker, who
has been turned into Dracula's successor after having suffered
the vampire's bite, yanks his own cross from his neck and
throws it to the floor. Finally, we note a scene in which Lucy

32. For an adaptation of the screenplay into a novel see Monette 1979.
Herzog's *Nosferatu: The Vampyre* (1979) was followed by a sequel, entitled *Vampire in Venice* (1988), in which Klaus Kinski reprised his haunt-
ingly memorable portrayal of Count Dracula. Unfortunately the sequel is
not really a worthy follow-up to the earlier effort and need not detain us
here beyond noting that Kinski refused to continue the make-up and characterization of the earlier film. Apparently even the homage paid to F.W.
Murnau in this regard has its limits.

reads from Jonathan's book about vampires and discovers how to defeat Dracula whose presence in the city is linked to the arrival of the plague. We hear the voice-over: 'The sign of the cross bans him. The consecrated host can bar his retreat. And should a woman pure of heart make him forget the cry of the cock, the first light of day will destroy him'. It is her own love for Jonathan which drives her to sacrifice herself in an attempt to save him. In short, the cross is consistently presented as a positive symbol of faith. Dracula is repelled by it, and those who wear a cross are thus protected by it. Little wonder that it could be described as an object of reverence.

I next consider two further films from 1979, both of which deal with crucifixion imagery in similar fashion. The first of these is Tobe Hooper's film entitled *'Salem's Lot*. This above-average made-for-TV movie is an adaptation of the 1975 novel by Stephen King and represents the best-selling novelist's venture into the genre of the vampire story. Stephen King has done more than perhaps any other modern writer to create a neo-Gothic style of horror fiction in which the best elements of classic Gothic writing are given contemporary settings. *'Salem's Lot* relates a tale of the spread of vampirism through a small, sleepy town in New England and the attempts by one concerned writer to discover the sinister goings-on and put a stop to them, assisted by a young teenager named Mark Petrie who is interested in matters of the occult and understands what is happening. The actor David Soul (of *Starsky and Hutch* fame) plays the writer Ben Mears who returns to his hometown of Salem's Lot in Maine and finds himself embroiled in these supernatural events, in which the Master Vampire, known as Mr Barlow (played by Reggie Nalder) preys upon an unsuspecting public, assisted by his aide-de-camp Mr Straker (played by the veteran actor James Mason). The blend of dramatic suspense and special effects is impressive and helps to make this film one which is both entertaining and thought-provoking. It is clear from the novel that King knows and uses Stoker's *Dracula* extensively in his own creative adaptation; there are several scenes in which this is quite evident.[33] As a case in point, there is a scene in

33. 1981: 40-42. Also see Twitchell 1989: 90-128, on this point. The influence of F.W. Murnau's *Nosferatu* upon Tobe Hooper's film is also

which Mears and his friend and colleague Bill Norton, the local town doctor, are examining one of the female victims of the vampiric attack upon the town. The woman, who is lying in the morgue on an autopsy table, suddenly comes to life and advances menacingly towards Mears. He fends her off by raising a hastily-constructed cross made from two medical tongue-depressors. The vampiress is driven back, obviously frightened by the cross, and Mears moves forward to press the cross against her forehead. She screams in pain, with the cross branded upon her forehead, and dissolves into oblivion. This is an extremely interesting scene, one which has often been depicted in vampire movies over the years. It demonstrates not only the power that the cross/crucifix has within the story-line, but also the abiding influence of Stoker's *Dracula* upon the film. In Stoker's story (in 23.381) we recall that it is Professor Van Helsing who similarly brands Mina on the forehead with a communion wafer.

*'Salem's Lot* contains a number of other scenes in which a cross or crucifix is presented as the key means of defence against the Master vampire and his subordinates. Indeed, there is only one point in which the efficacy of the cross is ever brought into question. This occurs in a scene in which the Master Vampire invades the house of Mark Petrie just when the youngster's concerned parents have invited the town's Roman Catholic priest, Father Callahan, to discuss their son's fate. This leads to a dramatic scene in which the significance of the cross as an expression of faith is emphasized. The mysterious Mr Straker challenges the priest to put his faith to the test, thereby freeing the young Mark whom the Master Vampire holds in a death grip. The priest holds up a crucifix before him in defence:

> *Straker:* You can do nothing against the Master. Stop, holy man! Or he will cut the boy's throat! Back, back holy man! Back shaman, back priest! What would you give for this miserable boy?
> *Father Callahan:* What do you ask?
> *Straker:* What would you give to reprieve him this night to save him for another night?
> *Father Callahan:* What do you want?

clear, most notably in the physical appearance of the Master Vampire (complete with elongated Spock-like ears and rat-tooth fangs!).

> *Straker:* The Master wants you! Throw away your cross, face the
> Master. Your faith against his faith! Could you do that? Is your
> faith enough?
> *(The boy is released and departs from the room, vowing revenge
> against the Master Vampire.)*
> *Straker:* Now for your part of the bargain.
> *Father Callahan (in desperation as he holds the crucifix before
> him):* I am a priest!
> *Straker (mockingly):* A priest! Throw away the cross! Face the
> Master! Faith against faith!
> *(The Master Vampire advances and, grabbing the crucifix from
> the priest's hand, throws it ignominiously to the floor. The cross
> is bent, its symbolic power broken).*

What is significant here is that the cross (or crucifix) in and of
itself is not deemed powerful enough to repel the Master
Vampire, although elsewhere in the film it is sufficient to challenge his minions. The power of the cross is linked to the faith
of the bearer of it; without belief in the Christian faith that it
represents, the cross appears worthless.[34]

John Badham's *Dracula* (1979) is a revival of the 1924 play
by John Balderston and Hamilton Dean and is scripted by W.D.
Richter. It stars Frank Langella as Count Dracula (recreating his
role from the Broadway production), Laurence Olivier as
Abraham Van Helsing, Donald Pleasance as Dr Seward, Kate
Nelligan as Lucy, Trevor Eve as Jonathan Harker, and Jan Francis
as Mina Van Helsing. This production plays fast and loose with
the plot and characters of Stoker's novel, making Mina the
daughter of the vampire hunter Professor Van Helsing, for
instance, and transforming Dracula's castle in Transylvania into
Carfax Abbey in Whitby. Nevertheless, there are several memorable scenes from the film which use crucifixes within them and
help to demonstrate how the cross is retained as an essential
feature of Dracula-mythology. Perhaps the most unforgettable
scene of the film is when Van Helsing encounters his daughter
Mina, who has been vampirized, in an underground cavern. She
attempts to bite him in the neck, and he has to fight her off

---

34. Precisely the same point is made in Tom Holland's *Fright Night*
(1985), in which the main vampire figure dismisses those who try to fend
him off with a crucifix by saying, 'You have to *believe* for this to have
power over me!'

with the help of Dr Seward, who comes to the rescue brandishing a crucifix. Eventually Professor Van Helsing brands Mina's forehead with the cross in a manner similar to that noted above in *'Salem's Lot*. There are a number of other scenes in which crucifixes, cross-necklaces and rosaries figure within the story (including one of the few film depictions of the *Demeter's* captain being found dead with a rosary in his hand). In virtually every instance these are used in such a way as to present the cross as a potent symbol with which to fend off Dracula and those whom he has vampirized. The one exception occurs when Van Helsing and Jonathan Harker go to Carfax Abbey in an attempt to destroy Count Dracula. In the dark and dank bowels of his coffin-room they confront Dracula, and Harker raises a cross in a gesture of defiance against the evil he represents. Dracula grabs the cross derisorily and it bursts into flame (apparently on his home turf and under cover of darkness the cross is not the threat it is in the daylight!). He casts the cross aside and then proclaims: 'You fools! Do you think with your crosses and your wafers you can destroy me?' All in all, the film is rich in crucifixion imagery, blending it effectively with several scenes in which consecrated hosts also serve to repel Dracula and the women he has seduced.

To summarize, many of the cinematic adaptations of *Dracula* contain a fairly faithful presentation of the importance of the crucifix imagery as it appears in the original novel. Indeed, we could go so far as to say that the majority of Dracula and vampire films offer a positive portrayal of the cross and present it as *an object of worship and reverence*. That is not to say that Dracula himself worships the cross; but he certainly does fear it as having power over him, and in this sense his revulsion at being confronted by a crucifix is the mirror-image of the reverence in which it is held by others. Thus, somewhat paradoxically, the reviling of the cross by Dracula and his followers could legitimately be viewed as a form of reverence for it. This should not overly surprise us since religious awe is often very closely linked to fear, at least at a very primal level. [35]

35. Perhaps this helps explain why William Friedkin's film of William Peter Blatty's *The Exorcist* (1971) remains one of the few Oscar-winning films on general cinematic release which has never got past British censors

I move now to consider a second way in which crucifixion imagery is expressed in the most ambitious *Dracula* film of the past decade, that directed by Francis Ford Coppola.

## *The Cross: Renounced in the Name of Love*

Francis Ford Coppola's *Bram Stoker's Dracula* (1992) has been the focus of considerable debate, not least because of the vision that it presents of Victorian England and the way in which it handles, or mishandles, the Gothic themes so central to the original novel.[36] Thus, despite the brash claim of the film's title, in many ways this is barely recognizable as Bram Stoker's story of Count Dracula. To be fair, the major characters are all in place and the costuming is certainly reflective of the late-Victorian age in which Stoker lived, but the guts of the story, its pulse, as it were, is missing. The film boasts an all-star cast, including Gary Oldman as Count Dracula, Anthony Hopkins as Abraham Van Helsing, Winona Ryder as Mina Murray/Elizabeta, Keanu Reaves as Jonathan Harker, Richard E. Grant as Arthur Holmwood, and newcomer Sadie Frost as Lucy Westenra.[37]

Most damaging to the original plot of the novel is the way in which the relationship between Dracula and Mina Harker is transformed into a tale of lost love, as she becomes the reincarnation of Dracula's wife Elizabeta who committed suicide over

and has never enjoyed a UK video release. The infamous scene in which the demon-possessed eleven year-old Regan MacNiel masturbates with a crucifix is controversial to say the least and was deemed to have crossed the line of moral acceptance. Apparently Friedkin committed the unpardonable sin of reviling that which the Censorship Board revered.

36. The screenplay for the film was written by James V. Hart, who together with Coppola has produced *Bram Stoker's Dracula: The Film and the Legend* (London: Pan Books, 1993) which contains a number of stills from the film together with the shooting script and some interesting interviews with people connected with the film. Saberhagen 1992 is a popular novel based on the screenplay as a movie tie-in. The book contains an *Afterword* by Francis Ford Coppola and eight pages of color photos from the movie.

37. The film is readily available on video distributed by Columbia Tristar Home Video (1992). A 30-minute supplemental video entitled *The Making of Bram Stoker's Dracula* is also available from Columbia Tristar Home Video (1993).

four centuries before. Thus promotional posters for the film proclaim it as a story whose major message is 'Love Never Dies' (see Fig. 2). In effect this makes the film into an overly senti-mental love-story with *Aliens*-like special effects and bodily transformations galore gratuitously thrown in along the way. This substitution of romantic sentimentality for Gothic horror is all rather unfortunate. Nowhere in Stoker's novel is Dracula said to *love* Mina in this way; on the contrary, he is animalistic and predatory in his approach to the women he pursues. Coppola's film paints him as rather a noble figure, whose love for Mina eventually culminates in his own destruction as he sacrifices himself rather than contaminate the woman he loves with his vampirism. Indeed, even the erotic power of Stoker's work, his indirect association of vampiric activity with sexuality, is seri-ously undermined, for the film leaves nothing to the imagination and makes Mina and Dracula lovers. One wonders how much of the motivation behind this (mis)interpretation of Stoker's vision is due to the sexual climate of the 1990s and the ever-real threat of AIDS as a sexually-transmitted disease; in effect vampirism becomes a thinly disguised cipher for HIV infection.[38] Unfortunately, the attempt to update the message of the film and make it relevant for the contemporary viewing audience has lost something essential, something mysterious, in the process.

Nowhere is the film more open to criticism than in the way in which it alters Stoker's conclusion to the novel. Never in the film is there any mention of Mina giving birth to a son, symboli-cally named after the men who risked their lives to save her from Dracula's curse (see 27:485). Instead, within the film we have the love between Dracula and Mina serving as the focus in the final confrontation at Dracula's castle in Transylvania. Indeed, it is Mina herself who rises to the awful demands of her love for Dracula as she challenges Van Helsing and the band of vampire hunters, and withdraws to the chapel with the wounded Dracula. There she dispatches him by driving Quincey Morris's Bowie knife through the Count's heart before retrieving

38. Thus Stewart 1995: 184-85, says, '(Dracula's) readiness to sacrifice comes across as a biomedical parable of tragic self-control in an age when the exchange of bodily fluids, blood or otherwise, is ruled by thanatos rather than eros'. See also Auerbach 1995: 175-81.

the blade and decapitating him. All of this is said to be an expression of her love for him. As she says, holding the Count in her arms as he lies dying on the chapel floor, 'There in the presence of God, I understood at last how my love could release us all from the powers of darkness. Our love is stronger than death'. This may be highly romantic, tear-jerking stuff, but it is certainly *not* Bram Stoker's *Dracula*.

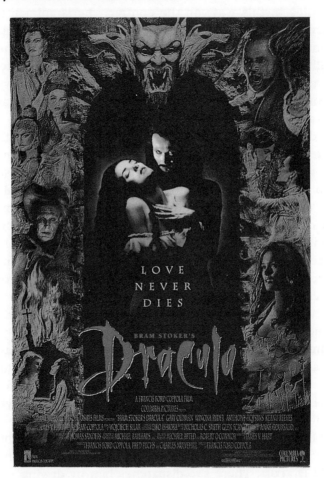

Figure 2

Nevertheless, there are one or two interesting features of the film adaptation which contribute to my examination of the place that crucifixion imagery has in the retelling of *Dracula*. The most important of these concerns the way in which the medieval legends about Prince Vlad the Impaler are combined with the Stoker story line. The film opens with an all-important five-minute sequence which presents the Prince as a Crusader doing his Christian duty in fighting the Turks in 1462. In fact the very first image we see is of a church in Constantinople which has the Maltese cross atop its cupola toppled and replaced by a star-and-crescent as the Islamic forces conquer the city. Vlad, a Romanian knight of the Sacred Order of the Dragon (hence the name *Dracula*—dragon), helps to defend his homeland against the invaders, kissing a crucifix which he wears around his neck and giving thanks to God for his victory over the enemy.

Meanwhile, Vlad has left his beloved wife Elizabeta back at home in his castle. She receives a false message that he has been killed in battle and, unable to contemplate going on without him, commits suicide. The Prince returns just as she is about to be interred without the Church's blessing. She lies on the floor of the castle chapel, surrounded by a number of monks bearing crucifixes on standards. The chief priest among them is named Chesare (played by Anthony Hopkins in a cameo role), and he informs Vlad that since Elizabeta was a suicide she is outside of grace, her soul damned. The dead body of Elizabeta lies on the floor of the chapel, the shadow of a cross falling across her face as Chesare pronounces her damnation (the same image is repeated in a flashback episode in the middle of the film wherein Mina Murray asks Dracula about his Princess Elizabeta). The injustice of this so incenses the Prince that he curses the Christian faith for which he had so bravely fought and renounces God. He moves menacingly towards Chesare, who crosses himself in a futile gesture of defence. Vlad brutally brushes aside the crucifix which the priest holds up to protect himself and, drawing his sword, rushes across the chapel to stab the sword into the centre of a large cross which stands behind the chapel altar. Blood begins to flow from the cross and soon the chapel is engulfed in a torrent of free-flowing blood. Vlad grabs a chalice and, filling it with some of the blood which comes down from the cross, drinks it, declaring, 'The blood is the life...and it shall be mine!' The scene is now set for a story of revenge and blood-lust. This opening sequence sets the tone for much that follows and offers a clever means of explaining why it is that Dracula has come to despise the cross and all it represents. This, of course, builds upon one of the most important features of *Dracula* mythology, the Count's antipathy to the cross of Christ. Indeed, the film offers us an historical reason for this antipathy and intertwines it with a vision of romantic love.

Several subsequent scenes recall this opening renunciation of both God and the cross of Christ. For example, as Dracula entertains Jonathan Harker for his first meal in the Count's castle, Harker calls attention to a painting which hangs in the dining hall, a fascinating version of Albrecht Dürer's *Self-Portrait* (1498). This introduces the subject of the Order of the Dragon, and the Count explains that this was 'an ancient society pledging my forefathers to defend the Church against all enemies of Christ. That relationship was not entirely successful'. Later on in the film, as Van Helsing attempts to discover the true story of what is taking place among them now that Dracula has arrived in London, he visits the British Museum and reads some forbidden records housed there relating to Dracula's background. As he reads, the arch vampire-hunter comes to an important realization. 'Ja, Draculea! The blood is the life!' he intones, recalling the earlier declaration by the Count himself as he drank blood from the chalice in his castle chapel.

As one might expect given this renunciation of the Christian faith by Vlad/Dracula, there are a number of instances in the film where images of a cross or a crucifix appear. At times these come directly from passages contained in Stoker's novel and at times they are added by the film's screenwriter. As examples of the former we could note, for example, the scene early in the film in which Jonathan Harker is riding on his way to Dracula's castle in a coach. One of the women who is with him in the coach gives him a small crucifix to serve as a talisman against evil. Also worth noting is the scene in which Count Dracula sneaks up behind Harker as he is shaving the morning after his arrival in the castle. Dracula is invisible in the shaving-mirror and his sudden appearance in the room causes Jonathan to nick himself. This leads to a delightfully inventive scene (not contained within the novel) in which the Count surreptitiously licks

Harker's blood from the razor in near-orgasmic delight. This sequence concludes with Dracula shaving Harker and, as he catches sight of the crucifix which Harker wears around his neck through its reflection in the blade of the straight-razor, admonishing the young solicitor not to place his faith in such 'trinkets of deceit'. This is an important scene, one which *does* have its basis within the original novel and which demonstrates the importance of the crucifix as a central motif within the story.

The crucifix-bearing Abraham Van Helsing is certainly integral to the novel, and there are several scenes in the film in which either his pectoral cross is visible, or he is portrayed brandishing a crucifix before himself. For example, in the scene set in Lucy Westenra's mausoleum in which she is 'staked' by Van Helsing and his band of vampire-hunters it is noticeable that throughout Van Helsing wears a prominent pectoral crucifix. Indeed, Van Helsing drives the vampiress Lucy back to her coffin by flashing a large crucifix before him and proclaiming no less than five times, 'Be strong in the Lord and in the power of His might!' Likewise, the defilement of Dracula's earth-laden coffins in Carfax Abbey is accomplished, in part, by the placing of a crucifix within the coffins while Van Helsing reads from an ancient exorcism manual. Here Van Helsing pronounces his final declaration over the assembled coffins of Dracula while waving a crucifix over them as they are set alight and destroyed. Toward the end of the film, Van Helsing holds up a cross against Dracula as the intrepid band of vampire-hunters burst in upon the Count and Mina in the infamous scene in which she drinks blood from his breast. Professor Van Helsing's pectoral cross is also clearly visible in the scene in which he decapitates the three vampiresses in Dracula's castle toward the end of the film.

As mentioned above, there are also some interesting scenes in which the image of a crucifix is added in the film screenplay to the story line of the novel. A good example occurs when Jonathan Harker is being seduced by the three vampiresses in Dracula's castle. As one of the women positions herself above him, preparing to bite him in the throat, she catches sight of a crucifix around his neck. She recoils from it, and then snarls at the object which instantly melts away like quicksilver, and she continues her sexual assault upon him. Another good example occurs when Mina Murray goes to the room of her friend Lucy Westenra just prior to Dracula's vampirization of her during a sleepwalking episode. She discovers Lucy's bed empty, her crucifix-necklace left lying among the bed clothes.

Finally, we note that in the final sequence of the film where Mina and Dracula lie together in the chapel of the castle in Transylvania there is an interesting combination of two of Jesus's sayings from the cross. Dracula lies prostrate on the chapel floor, mortally wounded, and laments to Mina, 'Where is my God? He has forsaken me! It is finished!' These words allude to the words of Jesus from the cross recorded in Mt. 27.46/Mk 15.34 from Ps. 22.1 ('My God, my God! Why have you forsaken me?') and Jn 19.30 ('It is finished!'). The overall effect of this is to transform Dracula into something of a Christ-figure, one who has to undergo the abuse and misunderstanding of his fellow creatures as well as rejection by God. This he willingly accepts out of love, *for Mina*.

Whatever else we might say about the way in which Francis Ford Coppola's film interprets the novel by Bram Stoker, whether we would choose to describe it as a creative adaptation of the book or as a seriously misguided reading of the work, it is clear that crucifixion imagery has an important role to play in the film. And yet, the haunting thing about James V. Hart's screenplay is that it manages to build a consistent portrayal of Dracula as a man who has been forced to renounce one thing that he held dear (the church and the cross of Christ) because of the all-consuming love that he has for another thing he holds dear (his wife Elizabeta and her reincarnation in the form of Mina).

To summarize: Coppola's film *Bram Stoker's Dracula* is about the *renunciation* of the cross of Christ by a man who is driven to such action by his love for a woman and the hypocrisy of the Christian church over her death. Dracula is here presented as the noble warrior, a victim of ecclesiastical prejudice whose own qualities of love and self-sacrifice take him beyond the church and transform him into a Christ-figure motivated by love and ageless devotion for his wife. The traditional presentation of the cross as something antithetical to the very existence of Dracula is altered under the weight of the neo-Romantic retelling of the story.

I turn now to consider one final way in which the cross is presented in vampire films which build upon Stoker's novel *Dracula*.

## The Cross: Ridiculed, Replaced and Rejected as Irrelevant

In a growing number of films the cross is either ridiculed as a worthless religious trinket of a by-gone era, or replaced by another symbol, or simply rejected altogether as redundant to the concerns of the modern world. In each instance the cross of Christ has become something of an irrelevancy, at least as far as the lives of the vampires portrayed in these film adaptations are concerned.

For example, many films directed at a predominantly teenage audience make fun of the cross and effectively hold it up as something to be ridiculed. In *Love at First Bite* (1979) virtually everything that is associated with the genre of vampirism is parodied, including the cross. The same holds true for Wes Craven's *Vampire in Brooklyn* (1995), particularly in the scene where the vampire Maximillian (played by Eddie Murphy) transforms himself into Preacher Pauley and enters an Afro-American church only to find a number of crosses scattered around the sanctuary.

As an example of the outright replacement of the cross, we note Tony Scott's stylish *The Hunger* (1983). Here we have a sensitive tale of a female vampire named Miriam (played by French actress Catherine Deneuve) in search of a new partner with whom she can spend her life (the extreme loneliness of an ageless vampiric existence being the key theme in the film). What is intriguing about this film is the way in which a cross-necklace is replaced by a similar religious icon, namely the Egyptian ankh. This emblem is worn by Miriam and other vampires within the film and conceals a small knife which is used to slash the throat of victims and start the flow of blood necessary for their existence. Thus, the cross necklace which is traditionally worn by the victims of vampires is replaced by an ankh which the vampires themselves wear. This is an intriguing adaptation of a central feature of many vampire films.

One of the biggest-selling cinematic adaptations of the vampire theme in the 1990s is Neil Jordan's *Interview with the Vampire* (1994); here, too, the cross is something of an irrelevancy as far as the vampires in the story are concerned. This film, one of the biggest money-makers of recent years, is based on the best-selling novel from 1977 by Anne Rice and stars Brad Pitt as the vampire Louis, Tom Cruise as Lestat, Kirsten Dunst as Claudia, Antonio Banderas as Armand, and Christian Slater as the Interviewer. Rice herself wrote the screenplay for the film, along with considerable help from director Neil Jordan,[39] although the original short story of the film was first written by Rice as long ago as 1973.[40] What marks this work out from other vampire stories is the degree to which it humanizes the central characters (it is not unlike the presentation of Vlad/Dracula in Coppola's film in this regard). This is a tale of vampires with human souls and human emotions; this remains the emotional centre of the book and is clearly one of the features of Anne Rice's writing which has made her popular and successful the world over. In effect Rice's vampires are tormented beings who, each in his or her own way, agonize over the complexities of vampiric existence. Thus *Interview with the Vampire* is concerned with the eternal struggle of good versus evil and the universal temptation to be wicked despite the best of intentions. The film makes much of the nightmare that is the vampire's life, with an unending cycle of death and killing, year after year, century after century. The publicity poster of the film contains a conscious allusion to the words of Jesus concerning the celebration of the Eucharist, proudly declaring the vampire's claim, 'Drink from me and live forever!' (see Fig. 3). By the end of the film, however, the viewer is left in no doubt as to the hollowness of that eternal life.

We have already had several occasions to note how central crucifixes are to many of the Dracula/vampire films. Yet, there are only two points in *Interview with the Vampire* where crosses and crucifixes are ever mentioned. The first of these

39. The writing of the screenplay, along with the contribution that Neil Jordan made to it, is discussed in Riley 1996: 205-32.

40. Ramsland 1995: 553-72 provides the text of the original short story.

references occurs early on in the film where Louis is being questioned about certain aspects of his life as a vampire:

> *Interviewer*: What about crucifixes?
> *The Vampire*: Crucifixes?
> *Interviewer*: Yeah. Can you look at them?
> *The Vampire*: Actually, I am quite fond of looking at crucifixes.
> *Interviewer*: What about the old 'stake through the heart' thing?
> *The Vampire*: Nonsense!
> *Interviewer*: Coffins! How about coffins?
> *The Vampire*: Coffins? Coffins, unfortunately, are a necessity.

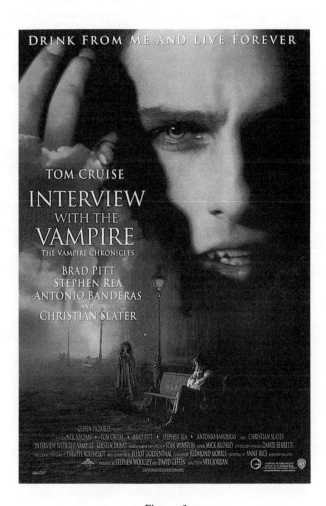

Figure 3

The relative paucity of references to crosses and crucifixes in the film is something of a departure from the novel. Indeed, the book *Interview with the Vampire* has several references to them, most notably the rather extensive section wherein Louis and Claudia go in search of their own identities by travelling through Eastern Europe, including Transylvania. There are several incidents involving crucifixes and peasants crossing themselves in the narrative at this point in the narrative. However, this whole section of the novel is completely downplayed in the film and is condensed into a single exchange between the Vampire and the Interviewer, albeit one which pays due homage to Stoker:

> *The Vampire*: We searched village after village, ruin after ruin, country after country. And always we found nothing. I began to believe we were the only ones. There was a strange comfort in that thought. For what could the damned really have to say to the damned?
> *Interviewer*: You, uh, you say you found nothing?
> *The Vampire*: Peasant rumours. Superstitions about garlic, crosses, the old stake in the heart. But one of our kind? Not a whisper.
> *Interviewer*: So there are no vampires in Transylvania? No…No Count Dracula?
> *The Vampire*: Fictions, my friend. The vulgar fictions of a demented Irishman.

In summary, a growing number of Dracula/vampire films downplay the significance of the cross of Christ within their storylines. This is done either by treating it as an object of contempt and ridicule, or by regarding it as something of no consequence, or by simply removing any reference to it altogether. Indeed in *Interview with the Vampire*, the biggest box-office vampire movie to date, the vampire at the centre of the story declares his affection for the crucifix, something which would have been unthinkable in the Hammer Films of Dracula. In effect this is to evacuate the cross of much of its meaning and to rob it of power, at least as far as the traditional place that it has within the Dracula mythology is concerned.

## Conclusion

I would not want to go so far as to suggest that there is a fixed development with regard to the presentation of crucifixion imagery in *Dracula*-inspired films. It would be misleading to plot a three-stage sequence in which reverence gives way to renunciation, which in turn culminates in ridicule, replacement and rejection. The waters are much more muddied than such a simplistic assessment would allow. One can find examples of reverence, and renunciation, and ridicule and rejection, of the power of the cross at overlapping points over the seven decades that film versions of Stoker's *Dracula* have been produced. A simple glance at the dates of some of the films we have been discussing confirms how difficult it is to trace a straightforward trajectory in this regard. And yet, I cannot think of a major film made in the last ten or fifteen years which unashamedly presents the cross as something from which Dracula or his vampiric followers recoil in fear and terror. Why is this? What does it intimate about the post-Christian societies of the West in which we live? There is certainly a sense in which cinematic releases reflect the values and mores and beliefs of the audience to which they are released. The studios in Hollywood, as well as other film studios around the world, operate within a market-based economy in this regard and must deliver the goods or else risk losing millions on a box-office flop in which no one is interested.

Given this indisputable fact of life, is it too much to suggest that the cross of Christ has lost something of its power for the majority of the contemporary movie-going public? What would happen if the kind of approach adopted by Hammer Films was adopted by a film studio today? Would the same sort of respect and reverence for the cross, which is so integral to the story-line of those films, be accepted in the 1990s? I rather suspect not!—a scene of this kind would probably induce fits of laughter within the cinema audience. In order to be successful today a contemporary filmmaker must either parody the cross, or communicate the substance of its significance by some other means, whether that be love (as in the case of Coppola's *Bram Stoker's*

*Dracula*) or human suffering and anguish (as in the case of Neil Jordan's *Interview with the Vampire*). It may be a sign of the times that respect for the cross has given way to these much more human (some would say marginal) interpretations of its significance. It should come as no surprise that the one place within Anne Rice's novel *Interview with the Vampire* in which reverence for the cross is found and its power discussed (the sequence set in Eastern Europe) is cut completely from the film version. No doubt it was thought insignificant to the story line and it was thus unceremoniously dropped altogether. This in itself is a comment on the power of the cross in the late 1990s. Little wonder then that the story of the sales clerk in the jewelry store (with which I began my study) remains so poignant, and so revealing for those of us who wish to explain the significance of the cross for today's world.

## Works Cited

Arata, S.D.
  1990          'The Occidental Tourist: *Dracula* and the Anxiety of Reverse
                Colonization', *Victorian Studies* 33: 621-45.
Auerbach, N.
  1995          *Our Vampires, Ourselves* (Chicago: The University of Chicago
                Press).
Belford, B.
  1995          *Bram Stoker: A Biography of the Author of Dracula* (London:
                Weidenfeld & Nicolson).
Bentley, C.F.
  1972          'The Monster in the Bedroom: Sexual Symbolism in Bram Stoker's
                *Dracula*', *Literature and Psychology* 22: 27-34.
Bierman, J.S.
  1977          'The Genesis and Dating of "Dracula" from Bram Stoker's Working
                Notes', *Notes and Queries* 24: 39-41.
Case, S.E.
  1991          'Tracking the Vampire', *Differences* 3: 1-20.
Coppola, F. Ford (Dir.)
  1993          *Bram Stoker's Dracula* (Columbia Tristar Home Video).
Cousar, C.B.
  1990          *A Theology of the Cross: The Death of Jesus in the Pauline Letters*
                (Minneapolis: Fortress Press).
Craft, C.
  1984          ' "Kiss Me With Those Red Lips": Gender and Inversion in Bram
                Stoker's *Dracula*', *Representations* 8: 107-33.

Demetrakopoulos, S.
1977        'Feminism, Sex Role Exchanges, and Other Subliminal Fantasies in
            Bram Stoker's *Dracula*', *Frontiers: A Journal of Women's Studies*
            3: 104-13.
Ellis, E.E.
1974        'Christ Crucified', in R. Banks (ed.), *Reconciliation and Hope: New
            Testament Essays on Atonement and Eschatology Presented to
            L.L. Morris on his 60th Birthday* (Exeter: Paternoster Press): 69-
            75.
Eyles, A., R. Adkinson and N. Fry (eds.)
1973        *The House of Horror: The Story of Hammer Films* (London:
            Lorrimer Publishing).
Fitzmyer, J.A.
1978        'Crucifixion in Ancient Palestine, Qumran Literature, and the New
            Testament', *Catholic Biblical Quarterly* 40: 493-513.
Fry, C.L.
1972        'Fictional Conventions and Sexuality in *Dracula*', *The Victorian
            Newsletter* 42: 20-22.
Gelder, K.
1994        *Reading the Vampire* (London: Routledge).
Glover, D.
1996        *Vampires, Mummies and Liberals: Bram Stoker and the Politics
            of Popular Fiction* (Durham, NC: Duke University Press).
Griffin, G.
1980        '"Your Girls That You All Love Are Mine": *Dracula* and the
            Victorian Male Sexual Imagination', *International Journal of
            Women's Studies* 3: 454-65.
Haining, P. (ed.)
1995        *The Vampire Omnibus* (London: Orion Books).
Haining, P., and P. Tremayne
1997        *The Legend of Bram Stoker and Dracula* (London: Constable).
Halberstam, J.
1993        'Technologies of Monstrosity: Bram Stoker's *Dracula*', *Victorian
            Studies* 36: 333-52.
Hatlen, B.
1980        'The Return of the Repressed/Oppressed in Bram Stoker's
            *Dracula*', *Minnesota Review* 15: 80-97.
Hengel, M.
1977        *Crucifixion: In the Ancient World and the Folly of the Message of
            the Cross* (London: SCM Press).
Hennelly, M.M., Jr
1977        '*Dracula*: The Gnostic Quest and Victorian Wasteland', *English
            Literature in Transition* 20: 13-26.
Hogan, D.J.
1988        *Dark Romance: Sex and Death in the Horror Film*
            (Wellingborough: Thorsons Publishing Group).

Howes, M.
1988        'The Mediation of the Feminine: Bisexuality, Homoerotic Desire
            and Self-Expression in Bram Stoker's *Dracula*', *Texas Studies in
            Literature And Language* 30: 104-19.
Hutchings, P.
1993        *Hammer and Beyond: The British Horror Film* (Manchester:
            Manchester Press).
Jancovich, M.
1992        *Horror* (London: Batsford).
Johnson, A.
1984a       'Bent and Broken Necks: Signs of Design in Stoker's *Dracula*', *The
            Victorian Newsletter* 67: 17-24.
1984b       'Dual Life: The Status of Women in *Dracula*', *Tennessee Studies in
            Literature* 27: 20-39.
Jones, S.
1993        *The Illustrated Vampire Movie Guide* (London: Titan Books).
Jordan, N. (Dir.)
1994        *Interview with the Vampire* (Geffen Pictures).
Käsemann, E.
1971        *Perspectives on Paul* (London: SCM Press).
King, S.
1981        *Danse Macabre* (London: Warner Books).
Krumm, P.
1995        'Metamorphosis as Metaphor in Bram Stoker's *Dracula*', *The
            Victorian Newsletter* 88: 5-11.
Leatherdale, C.
1993        *Dracula: The Novel and the Legend* (Brighton: Desert Island
            Books).
Martin, R.P.
1993        'Hymns, Hymn Fragments, Songs, Spiritual Songs', in G.F.
            Hawthorne, R.P. Martin and D.G. Reid (eds.), *Dictionary of Paul
            and His Letters* (Leicester: Intervarsity Press): 419-23.
McDonald, J.
1993        '"The Devil is Beautiful" *Dracula*: Freudian novel and feminist
            drama', in P. Reynolds (ed.), *Novel Images: Literature in
            Performance* (London: Routledge): 80-104.
McGrath, A.E.
1993        'Cross, Theology of the', in G.F. Hawthorne, R.P. Martin and D.G.
            Reid (eds.), *Dictionary of Paul and His Letters* (Leicester:
            Intervarsity Press): 192-97.
McNally, R., and R. Florescu
1975        *In Search of Dracula: A True History of Dracula and the Vampire
            Legends* (London: New English Library).
1995        *In Search of Dracula: The Enthralling History of Dracula and
            Vampires* (London: Robson Books).
Miller, E.
1994        '*Dracula*: The Narrative Patchwork', *Udolpho* 18: 27-30.

Minear, Paul
1979 'The Crucified World: The Enigma of Galatians 6.14', in C. Andresen and G. Klein (eds.), *Theologia Crucis—Signum Crucis: Festschrift für Erich Dinkler* (Tübingen: Mohr): 395-407.

Monette, P.
1979 *Nosferatu: The Vampyre* (London: Pan Books).

Moretti, F.
1983 'The Dialect of Fear', in *Signs Taken for Wonders: Essays in the Sociology of Literary Forms* (London: Verso Press): 83-108.

Nandris, G.
1966 'The Historical Dracula: The Theme of His Legend in the Western and Eastern Literatures of Europe', *Comparative Literature Studies* 3: 367-96.

Porter, R.
1992 'The Historical Dracula', 12-page article posted on the Internet dated 30 April.

Punter, D.
1980 *The Literature of Terror: A History of Gothic Fiction from 1765 to the Present Day* (London: Longman).

Ramsland, K.
1995 *The Vampire Companion* (London: Little Brown).

Riley, M.
1996 *Interview with Anne Rice: An Intimate, Enlightening Portrait of Her Life and Work* (London: Chatto & Windus).

Roth, J.
1977 'Suddenly Sexual Women in Bram Stoker's *Dracula*', *Literature and Psychology* 27: 113-21.

Ryan, A. (ed.)
1987 *The Penguin Book of Vampire Stories* (Harmondsworth: Penguin).

Saberhagen, F.
1992 *Bram Stoker's Dracula* (New York: Signet Books).

Seed, D.
1985 'The Narrative Method of *Dracula*', *Nineteenth-Century Fiction* 40: 61-75.

Senf, C.A.
1979 'The Unseen Face in the Mirror', *Journal of Narrative Technique* 9: 160-70.
1982 '"*Dracula*": Stoker's Response to the New Woman', *Victorian Studies* 26: 33-49.

Silver, A., and J. Ursini
1993 *The Vampire Film: From Nosferatu to Bram Stoker's Dracula* (New York: Limelight Editions, 2nd edn).

Skal, D.J.
1990 *Hollywood Gothic: The Tangled Web of Dracula from Novel to Stage to Screen* (London: Andre Deutsch).

Stevenson, J.A.
   1988          'A Vampire in the Mirror: The Sexuality of *Dracula*', *Proceedings of
                 the Modern Language Association* 103: 139-49.
Stewart, G.
   1995          'Film's Victorian Retrofit', *Victorian Studies* 38: 153-98.
Stoker, B.
   1897          *Dracula* (Westminster: Archibald Constable and Company).
   1983          *Dracula* (Intro. by A.N. Wilson; Oxford: Oxford University Press
                 [1897]).
   1993          *Dracula* (Intro. by M. Kindle; Penguin Classics; London: Penguin
                 Books [1897]).
Stuhlmacher, P.
   1986          *Reconciliation, Law and Righteousness: Essays in Biblical
                 Theology* (Philadelphia: Fortress Press).
Sutherland, J.
   1996          'Why Does the Count come to England?', in *idem*, *Is Heathcliff a
                 Murderer?: Great Puzzles in Nineteenth-Century Literature*
                 (Oxford: Oxford University Press): 233-38.
Thornton, T.C.G.
   1986          'The Crucifixion of Haman and the Scandal of the Cross', *Journal
                 of Theology Studies* 37: 419-26.
Twitchell, J.B.
   1981          *The Living Dead: A Study of the Vampire in Romantic Literature*
                 (Durham: Duke University Press).
   1989          *Preposterous Violence: Fables of Aggression in Modern Culture*
                 (Oxford: Oxford University Press).
Wasson, R.
   1966          'The Politics of *Dracula*', *English Literature in Transition* 9: 24-27.
Weissman, J.
   1977          'Women and Vampires: *Dracula* as Victorian Novel', *Midwest
                 Quarterly* 18: 392-405.
Wicke, J.
   1992          'Vampiric Typewriting: *Dracula* and Its Media', *English Literary
                 History* 59: 467-93.
Wilcox, M.
   1977          ' "Upon the Tree"—Deut. 21.22-23 in the New Testament', *Journal
                 of Biblical Literature* 96: 85-99.
Williams, A.
   1991          '*Dracula*: Si(g)ns of the Fathers', *Texas Studies in Literature and
                 Language* 33: 445-63.
Wolf, L.
   1993          *The Essential Dracula: The Definitive Annotated Edition of Bram
                 Stoker's Classic Novel* (London: Plume Books).

Wood, R.
1979        'The Dark Mirror: Murnau's *Nosferatu*, in R. Lippe and R. Wood
            (eds.), *The American Nightmare* (Ottowa: University of Ottawa
            Press): 43-49.
1983        'Burying the Undead: The Use and Obsolescence of Count Dracula',
            *Mosaic* 16: 175-87.

JUDITH LEE

## Sacred Horror:
## Faith and Fantasy in the Revelation to John

> Which of us is without fear? Who would not fear / when even
> God's eyes shut / and all the angels fall flat / and every creature
> darkens?
>
> (Pilinszky 1976: 41)
>
> To have pain is to have *certainty*; to hear about pain is to have
> *doubt*.
>
> (Scarry 1985: 13)

'My God, my God! Why has thou forsaken me?' This is the cry
to which apocalyptic responds. In the cosmic silence that surrounds this cry, apocalyptic exhorts and consoles a group who
is in danger of losing sight of its divinely ordained identity and
purpose. In rhetoric that is highly conventional and in language
that is shockingly original, the apocalyptic prophet opposes
both anguish and indifference in claiming a two-fold authority:
on the one hand, he is authorized through divine revelation, but
on the other hand he affirms solidarity with the powerless community he addresses. Thus, apocalyptic has contradictory tasks:
to counter complacency by reminding listeners that the God in
whom they believe is mysterious and strange, beyond knowing,
and at the same time to console suffering believers that God is
familiar and faithful to them.

Nevertheless, in reading the Revelation to John we are
prompted to protest, 'What kind of God is this?' How alien is
this God of wrath from the loving and immanent God of much
contemporary Christian theology, how different the fear evoked
by John of Patmos from the engagement and empowerment
called for by many modern Christian prophets. Even liberation
interpretations do not adequately address the ethical ambiguity
of the vengeance that is expressed and promised so insistently

in this text.[1] The strangeness of Revelation reveals a problem
that is at once theological and literary: in combining different
theological traditions, John of Patmos modifies both the Lord of
the Jews and the Father of the Christians; in his attempt to
make the divine presence real without compromising God's
transcendent holiness, he attempts to represent what cannot be
represented.[2] From a theological perspective, the strangeness of
this God expresses the mystery of divinity itself and calls attention to the limits of human language and imagination. From a
literary-critical perspective, however, the monstrous manifestations of this God affirm the power of language to articulate
mystery. The two perspectives converge on the question of representation, and they confront us with the tension between fantasy and faith: between secularizing the text and simplifying its
theology.

Julia Kristeva's theory of abjection provides a framework that
is useful for understanding the tension between reading critically

---

1.   Boesak (1987), writing from a South African perspective, Richard
(1995) from a Latin American perspective, and Schüssler Fiorenza (1991)
argue eloquently that Revelation is a work of protest literature calling for
solidarity with the suffering and oppressed. Pippin (1992, 1994) problema-
tizes the liberation interpretations of Revelation by showing its gender
codes to be so deeply embedded that the reader (specifically the woman
reader) must vigilantly resist its politics. Among the non-liberation theologians who do not see any tension between the theology and ethics of
Revelation, Moltmann (1967) finds here a 'theology of hope', while McGinn
(1979) argues persuasively that 'apocalyptic spirituality' involves an atten-
tiveness and engagement in the present that warrants more exploration. In
a very different approach Bauckham (1993: 51) argues that modern theological resistance to the God of Revelation compromises a belief in God's
transcendence that would allow for the genuinely new, and that the theology of Revelation offers a basis for disinterested political engagement.

2.   By referring to the authorship of John of Patmos and to the coherence of the text of Revelation, I do not ignore the historical, textual and
christological debates that surround Revelation. For the purposes of my discussion, however, it is not necessary to engage directly in these debates. For
a review of them, I am especially indebted to Collins (1992) Harrington
(1993), and Court (1979). Schüssler Fiorenza (1991) and McGinn (1987)
also offer useful historical and critical overviews of pertinent theological
and textual questions.

and reading faithfully that which we confront in Revelation.[3] Kristeva argues that since both literature and theology are cultural constructs, they draw upon communal fears, longings, and language, and encode psychological and social struggles. She defines abjection as a state of consciousness in which one is unsure about the boundaries of one's identity and therefore of one's relationships. In psychoanalytic terms, she identifies it as that stage of development between narcissism (when 'I' am the center within absolute and knowable boundaries, when there is no Other) and the differentiated ego that lives in separation and relationship with an Other. Abjection is a state of grieving and uncertainty: 'The abject is the violence of mourning for an 'object' that has always already been lost' (1982: 15). Abjection is thus in essence a liminal condition, a stage of being 'in between' union and relatedness, the known and the unknowable, the 'I' and the 'not-I'. Because it brings the realization that boundaries are neither absolute nor predetermined, and the awareness that desire is both inescapable and insatiable, Kristeva proposes that the uncertainty and instability one experiences in abjection is the basis for both horror and ecstasy.

Pointing out that it offers a vision, not a philosophical argument, Kristeva (1982: 154) argues that apocalyptic is both a defense against the ambiguity of abjection and an affirmation of its revelatory power. Based on a reading of the novels of Celine, her analysis integrates literary and ontological questions in a way that allows us to mediate among other theories of the fantastic that emphasize either its literary forms (as does Todorov 1973, for example) or its cultural purpose (as does Jackson 1981, for example).[4] Her assumption that the reader of

3.   Keller (1996: 23-24) also finds in Kristeva's theory of abjection a useful framework for reading Revelation, not only for understanding the content of the narrative itself but also for recognizing the reader's liminal position between points of certainty. My own reading of Revelation enters into dialogue with Keller's book, which came to my attention while I was completing my essay.

4.   While the theoretical conversation about the literary fantastic continues to expand, the other theorists whose work has been particularly influential for my own have been Rabkin (1976) and Hume (1984). I am also indebted to the groundbreaking essays in Aichele and Pippin (1992).

apocalyptic is placed in the position of the abject is, as Keller points out (1996: 23-24), especially important for recognizing and negotiating the dialectic between fear and desire that evokes opposing readings of Revelation. For the literary fantastic is a mode that defamiliarizes the world of the reader, and even if we recognize fantasy as the fulfillment of desire that subverts prevailing authority by restoring, albeit momentarily, a sense of freedom and wholeness, Kristeva reminds us that the reader's point of entry is a profound sense of uncertainty and estrangement, a liminal condition that the literary fantastic, and apocalyptic in particular, validates and counters. Her argument that apocalyptic originates in an experience of psychocultural pain is aligned with Elaine Scarry's theory that by eliminating one's power to imagine, bodily pain generates language that encodes the very structures in which pain originates.[5]

At the same time, the dissonance between Kristeva's psycho-analytic and materialist assumptions and Revelation's theology is itself illuminating. For example, her discussion calls attention to the liminality of the early Christians, who proclaimed a salvation accomplished 'already, but not yet' and who struggled to form faith communities without the visible signs of cultural membership shared by non-Christian Jews (who continued to follow the traditional rituals) and Gentiles (who participated in public worship).[6] This liminal condition is reflected in the letters to the seven churches with which Revelation begins (2-3), where Christ's exhortations reinforce unambiguous boundaries between believers and unbelievers, between true and false teachers, and between earthly and divine power. However, we need to remember that John's rhetorical purpose in depicting the horrors of the end time is to jolt the early Christians out of

---

5. Although we do not have space to explore it here, Scarry's brilliant analysis of the relation between pain, imagination, and belief, particularly in her discussion of the significance of biblical scenes of wounding (1985: 181-243), provides a valuable gloss to Revelation, even though she does not address that specific text.

6. More particularly, Kristeva proposes that the essential trait of Christianity is 'the interiorization of abjection' (1982: 113), and that Judeo-Christian monotheism is a 'fulfillment of religion as sacred horror' (1982: 210).

apathy, self-serving compromise, and internal division. Consequently, although we may read the plague sequences as expressions of the extreme ontological uncertainty that Kristeva identifies as abjection, we must also remember that John uses the grotesque as a rhetorical strategy in a theological argument and in a narrative that, as Dewey (1992: 88) reminds us, was to be read aloud and shared communally.[7] Similarly, the modern struggle for God-language, which in Kristeva's terms indicates 'a hollowing out of abjection through the Crisis of the Word' (1982: 208), is radically different from John's recurrent allusions to a wide range of Hebrew and intertestamental texts. Indeed, the dense intertextuality that may make this text so strange for modern readers would have reminded John's audience of how longstanding was their convenantal relationship with God, replacing the unreadable text of contemporary public life with the familiar sacred text of their own history.

In short, the ontological experience of God that is foundational in a theological reading of Revelation would be construed by Kristeva to be a cultural psycho-linguistic construct, a projection of shared fear that is more ambiguous than either self-loathing or awe. In other words, John deconstructs social and political behavior to evoke the awe that must be at the center of a life centered on the God worshiped by the Christians, whereas Kristeva deconstructs apocalyptic language to expose the anguish it expresses. For John, faith is the alternative to abjection; for Kristeva, faith is an expression of and defense against abjection.

Recognizing the narrative mode of the fantastic in Revelation gives us some insight into a fundamental difference between the Christian (Johannine) theology of Revelation and Jewish apocalyptic. The Incarnation of the Word not only made creation sacred, it also made it strange. Human attempts to usurp divine generative power by in effect re-creating the world have both desecrated the world and made it unreadable. As a result, the revelatory power of the world as Word cannot be restored.

---

7.   The combination of argument and narrative in Revelation, indeed in much apocalyptic, raises separate critical questions. Brummett (1991) and O'Leary (1994) offer the best discussions of the non-narrative structures and strategies of apocalyptic rhetoric.

Thus, in contrast to the Jewish intertestamental apocalypses, Revelation represents the end, not the renewal of creation.[8] More significantly, whereas in Jewish apocalyptic God *promises* destruction and renewal of the earth, in Revelation John bears witness directly to the power of the Divine Word to *uncreate* the world. Metaphors of the body in Revelation represent the world as a body deprived of its generative power, and metaphors of textuality represent the world as a text in which God's Word is distorted. God's presence is revealed in two ways: in the destruction of the body/text of the earth, and in the grotesque forms of human usurpation of a generative power that belongs only to the creator.

Throughout Revelation, the grotesque is revelatory. There can be no godless space in the incarnate world; God cannot be represented, but neither can God's absence be imagined. These grotesques thus confront us with the paradox that God is present in what God is *not*.[9] Read with the double vision of literary criticism and theology, the plague sequences thus reveal *both* the monstrous perversion of creation by human oppression *and* the horrors of a God imagined from the midst of pain and fear. A similar 'sacred horror' is expressed in the complementary figures of the woman clothed with the sun in ch. 12 and the whore of Babylon in ch. 17, who reveal God's presence in the midst of desolation and horror. The final vision of the New Jerusalem and the presentation of the new text constitute a fantasy of the abject, a fantasy in which boundaries are paradoxically clear and unconstraining. The New Jerusalem is a new kind of body, and John's writing is a new kind of text; both are fantastically, absolutely, immutable and inviolate, albeit

8.    Despite the similarities between the theologies of Jewish intertestamental apocalypses and Revelation, John of Patmos does not convey the visionary's sense of dialogue with the *person* of God that is conveyed in the other texts, even in 2 Baruch, which is closest to Revelation both historically and theologically. For texts and discussion see Charlesworth (1983). For discussions of the history and genre of Jewish apocalyptic see also J. Collins (1979, 1989), Hanson (1973), and Russell (1978).

9.    Harpham (1982) offers an insightful analysis of the ways that the grotesque operates in a process of 'forming through deformation'. Flannery O'Connor's reflections on the grotesque and the sacred (1969) are usefully compatible with Revelation.

perhaps monstrous to those who are still able to read the (veiled) sacred signs of the incarnate world.

The different beginnings of the three plague sequences outline a ritual progression. The first (6.1-17, 8.1) begins when the four horsemen, called forth by one of the 'four living creatures' who stand around the throne of God, initiate a divine intervention in time and space. The second sequence, the plagues revealed by the seven trumpets (8.2-9, 21; 11.15-19), are sacrificial offerings to God: An angel fills with fire the censer that is used to offer prayers at the altar and throws it to the earth, where it causes storms and an earthquake (8.5). The third sequence (16.1-21) is introduced as a ritual of purification that will allow all who are worthy to enter the heavenly temple: seven angels carry seven golden bowls 'full of the wrath of God...and no one could enter the temple until the seven plagues of the seven angels were ended' (15.7, 8). Thus, the plagues paradoxically delineate an unmistakable boundary between self and Other (believer and unbeliever) while at the same time expressing the horror of living without discernable boundaries—without the power to exclude.

Although each sequence also culminates differently, the final woe in each sequence serves as a narrative pause that both suspends movement (and thereby defers closure) and provides a visionary opening in the narrative. The seventh seal reveals divine substance and presence, in contrast to nothingness: 'When the Lamb opened the seventh seal, there was silence in heaven for about half an hour' (8.1). This silence counterpoints the cries of the martyrs for vengeance (6.9-11), the cries of fear from the inhabitants of the earth (6.15-17), and the hymns of praise sung by the multitudes (7.7-17). In contrast to this blank space—or, more accurately, filling it—the seventh trumpet reveals the opening of God's temple in heaven and the ark of the covenant within the temple (11.15-19) to counterpoint the opening of Sheol and of the Euphrates (9.1-21). What we could not see after the first revelation of woes is now revealed. Finally, the seventh bowl reveals the judgment on Babylon (16.18-21) in a passage that very differently represents a blank space and incomplete closure:

And there came flashes of lightning, rumblings, peals of thunder, and a violent earthquake, such as had not occurred since people were upon the earth, so violent was that earthquake. The great city was split into three parts, and the cities of the nations fell. God remembered great Babylon and gave her the wine-cup of the fury of his wrath. And every island fled away, and no mountains were to be found; and huge hailstones, each weighing about a hundred pounds, dropped from heaven on people, until they cursed God for the plague of the hail, so fearful was that plague (16.18-21).

We shall return below to the devastation described in this passage, but here let us note that its structural parallel to the prior 'last woes' calls attention to the correspondence between the opening of heaven and the destruction of the earth. Like the seventh seal and the seventh trumpet, the seventh bowl celebrates a divine power that cannot be contained within earthly boundaries or within human consciousness—a divine power that knows no bounds.

Metaphors of the body and of textuality in the three sequences of woes further suggest that the God of Revelation is formed from the kind of uncertainty that Kristeva identifies with abjection. The natural disasters, in particular, are very much 'views from the body' (McFague 1993: 198) that reiterate the foundational confusion that a fantasy of absolute power expresses. For example, in the fifth seal (the cry of the martyrs, 6.9-11) and the sixth seal (the earthquake, 6.12-17), the counterpointing voices of the martyrs and the inhabitants of the earth fill the space created by the breaking of earthly forms initiated by the four horsemen. The martyrs' call for vengeance is a call for revelation: '[T]hey cried out with a loud voice, "Sovereign Lord, holy and true, how long will it be before you judge and avenge our blood on the inhabitants of the earth?"' (6.10). The white robes they are given become unmistakable signs of the boundary between them and their 'brothers and sisters' who will suffer before the judgment; they also give their souls a bodily, material reality.

The earthquake revealed by the sixth seal (and again by the seventh bowl in 16.18-21) erases the world-as-text: '[T]he sun became black as sackcloth, the full moon became like blood, and the stars of the sky fell to the earth as the fig tree drops its winter fruit when shaken by a gale. The sky vanished like a scroll rolling itself up, and every mountain and island was removed from its place' (6.12-14). As we saw above, similar language in the description of the seventh bowl suggests that the decreation of the world involves dismembering a body and erasing a text: 'The great city was split into three parts...God remembered great Babylon and gave her the wine-cup of the fury of his wrath. And every island fled away, and no mountains were to be found' (16.19, 20). The wordless breath of God decreates all forms, and the earth becomes blank.

The horror of 'the inhabitants of the earth' shows that the earthquake is an implosion of the earth/body itself that eliminates any boundary between inside and outside. Hiding in caves, they call out to the mountains: ' "Fall on us and hide us from the face of the one seated on the throne and from the wrath of the Lamb; for the great day of their wrath has come, and who is able to stand?" ' (6.15-17). The cry of the inhabitants of the earth is the witness sought by the martyrs, even while it shows the futility of human speech that is opposed to the silent and manifest Word of God.

In the second sequence of woes, what was previously described as natural devastation affecting one fourth of the earth, is revealed to be both more extensive (destroying one third of the earth) and more intense (hail and fire mixed with blood, a fallen star that pollutes the water, the darkening of a third of the sun, moon, and stars for a third of a day and a third of a night). The first four plagues deprive the earth of its power to sustain and regenerate: the burning of vegetation (8.7), the poisoning of waters (8.8-10), the darkening of light (8.12). The blood mixed with the hail (8.7) and the blood of the sea (8.8) point toward the transformation that began in the first sequence when 'the moon became like blood' (6.12), and it reminds us that this devastation fulfills a promise to avenge the blood shed by the martyrs. The blood that pours from the sky and that poisons the sea is the blood of martyrs, now visible. It also evokes the image of a body torn open. The earth, like the bodies of the martyrs, has become a sacrificial offering.

In these two sequences, human abuses of power are depicted in the attacks of grotesque figures who eradicate all human

productivity. The four horsemen bring forth divine power to
override human abuses of power that have de-formed creation
through tyranny, war, economic exploitation, and human claims
to immortality (6.1-8). The personification of Death and Hades
as the fourth horseman and his companion suggests that the
boundary between life and the afterlife no longer holds: '[T]hey
were given authority over a fourth of the earth, to kill with the
sword, famine, and pestilence, and by the wild animals of the
earth' (6.8). The earth has become the territory of death.

The demonic locusts and horses that are announced by the
fifth and sixth trumpets (9.1-4) also represent an opening of the
earth that re-views and extends the commission of the fourth
horseman:

> I saw a star that had fallen from heaven to earth, and he was given
> the key to the shaft of the bottomless pit; he opened the shaft of
> the bottomless pit, and from the shaft rose smoke like the smoke
> of a great furnace, and the sun and the air were darkened with
> the smoke from the shaft. Then from the smoke came locusts on
> the earth, and they were given authority like the authority of
> scorpions of the earth. They were told not to damage the grass of
> the earth or any green growth or any tree, but only those people
> who do not have the seal of God on their foreheads...
> And in those days people will seek death but will not find it;
> they will long to die, but death will flee from them (9.1-4, 6).

The extension of death's provenance, along with its elusiveness
and the intensification of the desire for death, all point toward a
new ambiguity in the body's boundaries. Similarly, when the
angels are commanded to release demonic horses that have
been constrained in the Euphrates (9.13-15), we are reminded
that the form of the earth originates in the creator. In the darkness of these woes, amid the smoke and sulfur, we—with those
who are suffering—can see only the perversion of divine creation. Formed out of distorted images of gods and demons that
would have been familiar in contemporary culture and in Scripture, the locusts and horses are horrifying embodiments of
power that is both gendered and mechanistic:

> On their [the locusts'] heads were what looked like crowns of
> gold; their faces were like human faces, their hair like women's
> hair, and their teeth like lions' teeth; they had scales like iron
> breastplates, and the noise of their wings was like the noise of

> many chariots with horses rushing into battle. They have tails like scorpions, with stingers, and in their tails is their power to harm people for five months...
>
> And this was how I saw the horses in my vision: the riders wore breastplates the color of fire and of sapphire and of sulfur; the heads of the horses were like lions' heads, and fire and smoke and sulfur came out of their mouths...their tails are like serpents, having heads, and with them they inflict harm (9.7-10, 17, 19).

Female and reified, these monsters are paradoxically both what God is *not* and signs of God's presence. In these images, John of Patmos shows what the world looks like from the perspective of those who have unrepentantly appropriated divine generative power, worshiping 'the work of their own hands', be it a kingdom they rule or idols that—in contrast to the one, living God—'cannot see or hear or walk' (9.20).

This sequence depicts the disgorgement of the body of the world in a demonic birth that foreshadows the grotesque maternity of the Whore of Babylon in ch. 17 and the fall of Babylon in ch. 19. Not only is there no refuge within the earth, as was revealed in 6.16, but only God can mark the boundary against the horrifying forces contained inside the earth. It is thus fitting that this part of the plague sequence culminate with the angelic proclamation that the mystery of God the creator will be revealed imminently (10.5-6). When John eats the scroll from which the angel has read, obeying a command reminiscent of the Eucharistic invocation ('Take it, and eat' [10.9]), he thus becomes the embodiment of the new creation that will be fully revealed in ch. 21. He *is* a sacralized body/text, containing and expressing the Word that will bring forth a new heaven and earth, which itself will be a bride/city with unmistakable and impermeable boundaries and a text that will not require (or allow) interpretation.

In the third sequence of plagues (16.1-21), the woes come more rapidly and result from the direct command of God (16.1). There is little distinction between human abuses and natural disasters, and every bowl brings wounds to the body of the earth and to human bodies. When the first bowl is poured, 'a foul and painful sore came upon those who had the mark of the beast and who worshiped its image' (16.2); with the second, the sea 'became like the blood of a corpse' (16.3); and with the third, all the waters of the earth 'became blood' (16.4); the fourth bowl is poured upon the sun, which then scorches the followers of the beast (16.8), who '[c]ursed the name of God' (16.9); the fifth bowl is poured upon the throne of the beast, plunging its kingdom into darkness (16.10); the sixth is poured on the Euphrates and dries its waters, from which three spirits come forth to assemble the armies of the kings of the earth for a final battle (16.12-16); and the seventh bowl is poured into the air and brings about the destruction of Babylon. The refrain throughout this sequence is the defiant blasphemy of the unrepentant followers of the beast even as they 'gnawed their tongues in agony' (16.11). In the tension between these two absolutes—God's judgment and the unbelievers' blasphemy—Revelation marks out divine anger and demonic anguish as the two boundaries of human consciousness.

Chapter 17 functions literally as an opening in the narrative that re-views the judgment on Babylon proclaimed in 16.19. It is worth pausing to look at the familiar and grotesque vision of the body/city of Babylon because it confronts us with the critical and theological questions that are central to reading Revelation. Even if we keep in mind that the scene incorporates mythological and political imagery that would have been less strange to early Christians than it is to us, this episode nevertheless shows how deeply embedded in our mythology and theology is a repulsion for the female body and female power. From a literary critical perspective, the whore of Babylon expresses abject desire and horror in response to the female body—physical and political—and its generative power; as the personification of the city, the whore of Babylon is a miniature of the earth/body that has been reviewed in the plague sequences. However, as we have seen, from a theological perspective, the distortions of the grotesque throughout Revelation are revelatory. In this desecrated world where the Word is no longer manifest, God's presence can be discerned only in the act of uncreation (expressing a power belonging only to the creator) that reveals a space whereby clear boundaries are restored. Thus, theologically, the judgment on Babylon dramatizes not only the triumph of the one living God over the goddess, but also the exorcism of the body/text desecrated by those who have claimed a generative power that belongs only to God and thereby distorted the boundary between creator and creature. The judgment on Babylon erases that false boundary to make possible the transfiguration of the relation between creator and creation in the divine marriage between the Lamb and the Bride.

Chapter 17 is a miniature narrative that condenses the uncreation of the world narrated in the plague sequences. The whore of Babylon herself is a grotesque body/text that blurs the boundaries between animate and inanimate, beast and human, clean and unclean:

> The woman was clothed in purple and scarlet, and adorned with gold and jewels and pearls, holding in her hand a golden cup full of abominations and the impurities of her fornication; and on her forehead was written a name, a mystery: 'Babylon the great, mother of whores and of earth's abominations'. And I saw that the woman was drunk with the blood of the saints and the blood of the witnesses to Jesus (17.4-6).

Covered with layers of cloth and jewelry, 'drunk with blood', the whore's body seems to 'spill over'. The great mother and the great devourer, a parody of the prophet who has eaten the divine scroll, she is the antithesis of the spiritualized bodies that will exist in the new creation and will be erased as the earth has been: '[T]hey will make her desolate and naked; they will devour her flesh and burn her up with fire' (17.17). As Tina Pippin has pointed out, the angel promises a divinely sanctioned sexual murder (1992: 57) that the beast and his followers will commit as a revelatory act of self-hatred and self-destruction. At the same time, the sequence of actions by which the whore's body will disappear—disrobing ('unveiling'), eating, burning—parallels the sequences of woes that afflict the earth and parodies the ritual of sacrifice.

The proclamation of the fall of Babylon (18.2-8) is an exorcism that attributes to the whore an interiority belonging neither to the woman in the wilderness nor to the Bride:

> 'Fallen, fallen is Babylon the great! It has become a dwelling place of demons, a haunt of every foul spirit, a haunt of every foul bird, a haunt of every foul and hateful beast'... 'Come out of her, my people, so that you do not take part in her sins, so that you do not share in her plagues' (18.2, 4).

Echoing Moses' plea to the Pharoah ('Let my people go!' [Exod. 5.1]), God calls his people out of the demonic and polluted body/city/earth in a kind of birthing, thereby reclaiming the generative power that had been usurped by the female. This call, and the comfort God offers to the saved in the new creation (7.16-17; 21.4), which are reminders of God's covenantal relationship with believers, contrasts to the whore's arrogant and narcissistic announcement, '"I will never see grief"' (18.7). The whore absorbs all persons into herself in a grotesque parody of the creator's transcendence.

Thus, one of the central tensions between literary critical and theological interpretations of Revelation is unavoidable in chs 17–19: The narrative mode (the grotesque) calls our attention to the opaque language, while the whore makes visible our own fears and desires (our abjection). In addition, because its narrative purpose is to refer back to and amplify the judgment named in 16.19, it constitutes a pause that opens the narrative and highlights its reiterative structure. A theological interpretation, in contrast, recognizes the whore as the unambiguous embodiment of the mystery of human evil (Boesak 1987: 117) and the density of the language as a sign that this is an unchangeable text (with no openings in which to insert human speculation); in addition, when seen with the eyes of faith, the text is translucent and revelatory, allowing us to discern through it the forms of a divine plan. A secular reading evokes horror, while a theological reading evokes awe. Neither, I would argue, is adequate by itself.

This same tension operates in ch. 12, which also provides a pause in the unfolding narrative and offers a miniature version of the entire story of Revelation and the core of its theological argument (Boring 1989: 150). The mirroring of ch. 17 is apparent from the very beginning, with the vision of the woman clothed in the sun portrayed as the very antithesis to the whore of Babylon: 'A great portent appeared in heaven: a woman clothed with the sun, with the moon under her feet, and on her head a crown of twelve stars. She was pregnant and was crying out in birth pangs, in the agony of giving birth' (12.1-2). The beauty of this heavenly virgin-queen-mother mirrors the garish materialism of the whore-queen-mother, and her agony mirrors the whore's drunken pleasure. The dissonance of a 'queen of heaven' crying out in pain erases the boundary between goddess and woman, just as the whore's gluttony confuses the boundary between human and beast. The woman's bodily reality is underscored like the whore's is, moreover: she is pregnant, gives birth, is nourished, is pursued by the dragon and flies on eagle's wings. Nevertheless, signifying a fusion of Hebrew and pagan iconography (Garrett 1992: 172), this female figure represents both power and pain; although she embodies God's promise of offspring (Boesak 1987: 80) and sustenance in the wilderness, she also embodies a relationship with God experienced only in bodily pain and need. In contrast to the whore's disavowal of grief—and therefore of relationship—this woman exists only in relationship, first in giving birth and then in being nourished by God, remaining within her designated place in the wilderness, 'a place prepared by God' (12.6; 12.14). The clarification of boundaries between heaven and earth signified by this woman and narrated in this story expresses a fantasy of mutuality through the containment of maternal power. Theologically, this story reminds us of the sovereignty of God, who sustains the subordinate goddess-woman and whose judgment contains the power of the dragon, who 'knows that his time is short!' (12.12). Again, however, God's presence is revealed through grotesque images of pain and deprivation.

In the new creation and the new text, represented in chs 19 and 21, the world is at last the Word. The dialectic between horror and desire in the plague sequences and in chs 12 and 17 is suspended. Although the new creation is heaven/earth because space and time as we know them no longer exist, its form is nevertheless familiar. As Pablo Richard has pointed out (1995: 160), 'What is transcended here is not matter or bodiliness, but death, chaos, darkness, suffering, the curse'. The new creation is a fantasy of bodily existence without contingency. Reiterating the promise of 7.16-17 and the story of God's faithfulness to the woman in the wilderness described in 12.6 and 12.14, the healing of bodies (21.4) and of nations (22.2) eliminates all bodily manifestations of pain or separation: no wounds, no hunger, no thirst, no tears.

Moreover, the wall around the City, so large that it fills all imaginable space, is a text so dense that there is no space on it for new inscriptions (21.12-21); in its intricate design and construction with jewels it represents a sacralized and immutable human creation. Even with gates ever open, the wall of the New Jerusalem constitutes an impermeable boundary: 'Its gates will never be shut by day—and there will be no night there. People will bring into it the glory and the honor of the nations. But nothing unclean will enter it, nor anyone who practices abomination or falsehood, but only those who are written in the Lamb's book of life… Nothing accursed will be found there any more' (21.27; 22.3). Neither chaos ('the sea was no more' [21.1]) nor nothingness surrounds the City, but 'the lake that burns with fire and sulfur, which is the second death' (21.8), wherein exist those who have usurped the divine power to create: 'Outside are the dogs and sorcerers and fornicators and murderers and idolaters, and everyone who loves and practices falsehood' (22.15; cf. also 21.8). The specific naming of these outsiders indicates that in this new creation there will be a space in which God's presence will continue to be visible, but its painful and grotesque manifestations will not impinge on the redeemed, who turn always toward God within the city, wherein the last boundary between human and divine—the Temple—is no longer necessary. These redeemed bodies are formed in their mutuality with God, texts inscribed with the divine name and referring only to God: '[H]is servants will worship him; they will see his face, and his name will be on their foreheads' (22.4). Reader and text, vision and visionary, are one; all liminal space has been erased.

The Bride embodies this fantastical condition of existing with boundaries that do not constrain. We never *see* her, but only hear of her in the marriage hymn sung by the multitude after the fall of Babylon and before the final battle: 'Let us rejoice and exult and give him the glory, for the marriage of the Lamb has come, and his bride has made herself ready; to her it has been granted to be clothed with fine linen, bright and pure'—(19.7-8). In this ancient and sacred marriage, an act of completion and reconciliation, the Bride's body is invisible and metaphorical: 'And I saw the holy city, the new Jerusalem, coming down out of heaven from God, prepared as a bride adorned for her husband' (21.2). Like the redeemed, this body/text is apparent only in its mutual relation with God, a readable, unmistakable, sign of God's presence. Inaccessible and inviolable, safe and in safekeeping, absolutely 'I' and absolutely 'Other', the Bride is the fantasy of the abject.

In the end, the text of Revelation itself is presented as a sacred space that contains within it no room for human inscription. It marks out, once and for all, the absolute and unmistakable boundary between divine speech and human writing. Framing John's testimony are the words of God: '"I am the Alpha and the Omega", says the Lord God, who is and who was and who is to come, the Almighty' (1.8); 'I am the Alpha and the Omega, the first and the last, the beginning and the end' (22.13). Spoken by Christ, this last self-naming marks out the boundaries of this new (sacred) text while at the same time proclaiming that (in contrast to the Book of Daniel and like the wall of the City) this is an open book: 'And he said to me, "Do not seal up the words of the prophecy of this book, for the time is near"' (22.10).

We learn that this text itself is part of the new creation when God exhorts John to write in the second of three pronouncements after the old world has passed away: 'And the one who was seated on the throne said, "See, I am making all things new". Also he said, "Write this, for these words are trustworthy and true". Then he said to me, "It is done! I am the Alpha and the Omega, the beginning and the end. To the thirsty I will give water as a gift from the spring of the water of life"' (21.5-6). I make all things new; write this; it is done: With these three statements John's text is literally enclosed in the new creation, a sign and expression of its material reality. In this sacred new world/text, where the World is Word, to insert human words or images is sacrilege. Hence John's famous warning, expressing, as Keller has also noted (1996: 83), the fantasy of every writer: 'I warn everyone who hears the words of the prophecy of this book. if anyone adds to them, God will add to that person the plagues described in this book; if anyone takes away from the words of the book of this prophecy, God will take away that person's share in the tree of life and in the holy city, which are described in this book' (22.18-19). With this exhortation, John of Patmos steps out of the liminal position of the visionary who participates in the suffering of his 'brothers and sisters'. Like so many prophets and theologians responding to these visions after him, he forsakes half of his authority—his solidarity with his fellow believers—and demarcates an absolute boundary between his own immunity and their vulnerability, claiming a divinely ordained authorial power and disempowering them.

Who, then, is the God revealed in the Revelation to John? Whatever the historical circumstances in which it was written, the God of Revelation was formed out of a certitude born of unbearable pain. The presence of this God is revealed in human bodies that are either contorted in agony or without autonomy. Thus it is precisely in their revelatory function that these bodies—both earthly and redeemed—are grotesque. If Kristeva guides us toward seeing the theology of Revelation as a theology of abjection, she also reminds us that 'the speech of faith is pain' (1982: 129). Whether or not we share John's faith, and precisely because both the narrative mode and the theology of Revelation make possible our empathy with the anguish he expresses, we can resist his *form* of God. For in the end, insofar as it describes a new creation that is a reversal, not a transformation, of the world that we know, Revelation offers a theology of exclusion that sacralizes the relationships and structures that perpetuate suffering.

It is in acknowledging and exploring the desire to be free of pain, a desire drawing us to both fantasy and faith, that literary-critical and theological readings of Revelation converge. For while the fantastic narrative mode of Revelation expresses the power of the human imagination to construct a world free of pain and to exorcise the demons we abhor, its theology reveals our complicity in both causing and repressing suffering. McFague (1993) and Keller (1996) have responded with different eschatologies that point toward a new relational theology that bears witness both to the world's suffering and to the transforming activity of a God beyond imagining. Nevertheless, as both theology and fantasy Revelation reminds us that in the liminal time between 'now and then' none of us is immune from the allure of power or from the horror of suffering. Reading with the double vision that the literary fantastic and

Christian theology call for, we must resist making the move that John of Patmos makes in the final lines of his narrative—to the place of God.

## Works Consulted

Aichele, G., and T. Pippin (eds.)
    1992        *Fantasy and the Bible* (Semeia, 60; Atlanta, GA: Scholar's Press).
Bauckham, R.
    1993        *The Theology of the Book of Revelation* (New York: Cambridge University Press).
Boesak, A.A.
    1987        *Comfort and Protest* (Philadelphia: Westminster Press).
Boring, M.E.
    1989        *Revelation* (Louisville: Westminster/John Knox Press).
Brummett, B.
    1991        *Contemporary Apocalyptic Rhetoric* (New York: Praeger).
Charlesworth, J.H. (ed.)
    1983        *The Old Testament Pseudepigrapha*. I. *Apocalyptic Literature and Testaments* (New York: Doubleday).
Collins, A.Y.
    1984        *Crisis and Catharsis: The Power of the Apocalypse* (Philadelphia: Westminster Press).
    1992        'Revelation', in D.N. Freedman (ed.), *The Anchor Bible Dictionary* (5 vols.; New York: Doubleday): V, 694-708.
Collins, J.J. (ed.)
    1979        'Apocalypse: The Morphology of a Genre', *Semeia* 14.
    1989        'The Genre Apocalypse in Hellenistic Judaism', in D. Hellholm (ed.), *Apocalypticism in the Mediterranean World and the Middle East* (Proceedings of the International Colloquium on Apocalypticism in Uppsal, 1979; Tübingen: JCB Mohr, 2nd edn): 531-44.
Court, J.M.
    1979        *Myth and History in the Book of Revelation* (Atlanta: John Knox Press).
Dewey, J.
    1992        'Response: Fantasy and the New Testament', in Aichele and Pippin (eds.): 83-89.
Garrett, S.R.
    1992        'Revelation', in C.A. Newsom and S.H. Ringe (eds.), *The Women's Bible Commentary* (Louisville: Westminster/John Knox Press): 377-82.
Hanson, P.D.
    1973        *The Dawn of Apocalyptic* (Philadelphia: Fortress Press).
Harpham, G.G.
    1982        *On the Grotesque* (Princeton: Princeton University Press).
Harrington, W.J., OP
    1993        *Revelation* (Sacra Pagina, 16; Collegeville, MN: Liturgical Press).

Hume, C.
1984        *Fantasy and Mimesis* (New York: Methuen).
Jackson, R.
1981        *Fantasy: The Literature of Subversion* (New York: Methuen).
Keller, C.
1996        *Apocalypse Now and Then* (Boston: Beacon Press).
Kristeva, J.
1982        *Powers of Horror* (trans. L.S. Roudiez; New York: Columbia University Press).
McFague, S.
1993        *The Body of God* (Minneapolis: Fortress Press).
McGinn, B.
1979        'Introduction', in *Apocalyptic Spirituality* (New York: Paulist Press): 1-16.
1987        'Revelation', in R. Alter and F. Kermode (eds.), *The Literary Guide to the Bible* (Cambridge, MA: Harvard University Press): 523-41.
Moltmann, J.
1967        *Theology of Hope* (New York: Harper & Row).
O'Connor, F.
1969        'Some Aspects of the Grotesque in Southern Fiction', in S. Fitzgerald and R. Fitzgerald (eds.), *Mystery and Manners* (New York: Farrar, Straus & Giroux): 36-50.
O'Leary, S.D.
1994        *Arguing the Apocalypse* (New York: Oxford University Press).
Pilinszky, J.
1976        'Introitus', in *Selected Poems* (trans. T. Hughes and J. Czokits; Manchester: Carcanet New Press).
Pippin, T.
1992        *Death and Desire: The Rhetoric of Gender in the Apocalypse of John* (Louisville: Westminster/John Knox Press).
1994        'The Revelation to John', in E. Schüssler Fiorenza (ed.), *Searching the Scriptures: A Feminist Commentary* (New York: Crossroad): 109-30.
Rabkin, E.S.
1976        *The Fantastic in Literature* (Princeton: Princeton University Press).
Richard, P.
1995        *Apocalypse: A People's Commentary on Revelation* (Maryknoll, NY: Orbis Books).
Russell, D.S.
1978        *Apocalyptic: Ancient and Modern* (Philadelphia: Fortress Press).
Scarry, E.
1985        *The Body in Pain* (New York: Oxford University Press).
Schüssler Fiorenza, E.
1991        *Revelation: Vision of a Just World* (Proclamation Commentaries; Minneapolis: Fortress Press).
Todorov, T.
1973        *The Fantastic: A Structural Approach to a Literary Genre* (trans. R. Howard; Cleveland: Case Western Reserve University Press).

# INDEXES

## *Index of References*

OLD TESTAMENT

| Genesis | | 10.1 | 140 | Job | |
|---|---|---|---|---|---|
| 1.1–2.3 | 109 | 10.20 | 140 | 38.4 | 70 |
| 2–3 | 15, 28, 43, | 10.27 | 140 | | |
| | 50, 55, 56 | 11.10 | 140 | Psalms | |
| 2.9 | 45 | 14.4 | 140 | 22.1 | 208 |
| 3.1-5 | 26 | 14.9 | 140 | 69.22 | 191 |
| 3.3 | 45 | 33.11 | 13 | | |
| 3.5 | 50 | 33.23 | 13 | Isaiah | |
| 3.6 | 27 | 40.34-38 | 191 | 45.7 | 66, 139 |
| 3.8 | 13, 52 | | | 62.5 | 191 |
| 3.16 | 27, 32 | Deuteronomy | | | |
| 3.17 | 27, 31 | 12.23 | 192 | Jeremiah | |
| 3.22-23 | 140 | 21.22-23 | 169-72 | 36 | 152 |
| 3.22 | 51, 53 | 21.23 | 184 | | |
| 3.23 | 52 | 28.66 | 170 | Ezekiel | |
| 5.24 | 191 | | | 21.10 | 171 |
| 5.27 | 191 | Joshua | | | |
| 8.8-12 | 191 | 8.29 | 171 | Daniel | |
| 11.6-8 | 140 | 10 | 143 | 7 | 137 |
| 11.6 | 52 | 10.9-11 | 143 | | |
| 15.45 | 28 | 10.12-13 | 143 | Hosea | |
| 18.25 | 70 | 10.15-43 | 143 | 1.2 | 70 |
| 22 | 45, 46 | 10.26 | 171 | | |
| 32.30 | 13 | | | Amos | |
| 40.19 | 170, 172 | 1 Samuel | | 3.6 | 139 |
| | | 2.4 | 138 | | |
| Exodus | | 2.6-7 | 138 | Malachi | |
| 1–15 | 137 | 15.7-9 | 65 | 1.2-3 | 139 |
| 2.22 | 192 | | | | |
| 4.21 | 140 | 2 Kings | | 2 Esdras | |
| 4.24-26 | 13 | 19.10 | 49 | 7.118 | 28 |
| 5.1 | 233 | | | | |
| 6–15 | 139 | Esther | | | |
| 7.3 | 140 | 2.23 | 171 | | |
| 9.12 | 140 | 8.17 | 64 | | |

NEW TESTAMENT

| Matthew | | 8.38 | 94, 95 | 24.47 | 165 |
|---|---|---|---|---|---|
| 4.9 | 191 | 9.2-8 | 97 | | |
| 10.29-31 | 190 | 9.7 | 96 | John | |
| 13.1-9 | 190 | 9.9 | 95 | 3.29 | 190 |
| 13.33 | 142 | 9.12 | 95 | 6.1-15 | 191 |
| 14.13-21 | 191 | 9.31 | 95 | 7.37-39 | 178 |
| 14.26-27 | 14 | 10.33 | 95 | 7.53–8.11 | 155 |
| 25.1-10 | 190 | 10.42-44 | 138 | 19.30 | 208 |
| 26.39 | 193 | 10.45 | 95 | 19.33-37 | 178 |
| 27.46 | 208 | 11.25 | 94 | | |
| | | 13.6 | 95 | Acts | |
| Mark | | 13.14 | 99 | 5.30 | 172 |
| 1.1 RSV | 93 | 13.21-22 | 95 | 10.39 | 172 |
| 1.9 | 96 | 13.26 | 95 | 13.29 | 172 |
| 1.11 | 96 | 13.32 | 94 | 14 | 148, 163, |
| 1.13 | 98 | 14 | 98 | | 165 |
| 1.15 | 99 | 14.21 | 95 | 14.3 | 163 |
| 1.24 | 93 | 14.36 | 94, 193 | 14.27 | 163, 165 |
| 2.10 | 95 | 14.41 | 95 | 28.27 | 165 |
| 2.28 | 95 | 14.61-62 | 93, 95 | | |
| 3.12 | 93 | 14.62 | 95 | Romans | |
| 3.21 | 97 | 14.66-72 | 98 | 6.6 | 183 |
| 3.22-27 | 98 | 15.29-32 | 98 | | |
| 3.28 | 95 | 15.34 | 208 | 1 Corinthians | |
| 3.31-32 | 97 | 15.39 | 93 | 1.13 | 183 |
| 3.33-34 | 97 | 16.8 | 93 | 1.17 | 183 |
| 4.1-9 | 190 | 16.16-20 | 94 | 1.18 | 183 |
| 4.22 | 92 | | | 1.23 | 183 |
| 5.7 | 93 | Luke | | 2.2 | 183 |
| 5.25-30 | 97 | 4.7 | 191 | 2.8 | 183 |
| 5.39-43 | 97 | 8.4-8 | 190 | | |
| 6.3 | 94, 96 | 9.10-17 | 191 | 2 Corinthians | |
| 6.32-33 | 191 | 9.20-21 | 94 | 13.4 | 183 |
| 6.56 | 97 | 12.6-7 | 190 | | |
| 7.24-30 | 97 | 22.42 | 193 | Galatians | |
| 8 | 98 | 23.46 | 193 | 2.19 | 183 |
| 8.22-26 | 97 | 24 | 163 | 3.1 | 183 |
| 8.24 | 190 | 24.12 | 164 | 3.13 | 171, 184 |
| 8.29-33 | 98 | 24.14 | 164 | 3.15 | 116 |
| 8.29-31 | 93 | 24.27 | 159, 164 | 5.11 | 183 |
| 8.30 | 94 | 24.31 | 164 | 5.24 | 183 |
| 8.31-33 | 94 | 24.32 | 148, 164 | 6.4 | 183 |
| 8.31 | 95 | 24.37 | 164 | 6.12 | 183 |
| 8.33 | 98 | 24.41 | 164 | 6.14 | 183 |
| 8.34-35 | 138 | 24.45 | 165 | | |

| | | | | | |
|---|---|---|---|---|---|
| *Ephesians* | | 8.1 | 226 | 16.12-16 | 231 |
| 2.16 | 183 | 8.2-9 | 226 | 16.18-21 | 226, 227 |
| | | 8.7 | 228 | 16.19 | 228, 231, |
| *Philippians* | | 8.8-10 | 228 | | 233 |
| 2.6-11 | 182 | 8.8 | 228 | 16.20 | 228 |
| 2.8 | 183 | 8.12 | 228 | 17–19 | 233 |
| 3.18 | 183 | 8.21 | 226 | 17 | 225, 230- |
| | | 9.1-21 | 226 | | 33 |
| *Colossians* | | 9.1-4 | 229 | 17.4-6 | 232 |
| 1.15-20 | 182 | 9.6 | 229 | 17.17 | 232 |
| 1.20 | 182, 183 | 9.7-10 | 230 | 18–20 | 137 |
| 2.14 | 183 | 9.13-15 | 229 | 18.2-8 | 232 |
| | | 9.19 | 230 | 18.2 | 232 |
| *Hebrews* | | 9.20 | 230 | 18.4 | 232 |
| 12.2 | 184 | 10.5-6 | 230 | 18.7 | 233 |
| | | 10.9 | 230 | 19 | 230 |
| *1 Peter* | | 11.15-19 | 226 | 19.7-8 | 235 |
| 2.24 | 172 | 12 | 225, 233 | 19.21 | 234 |
| | | 12.1-2 | 233 | 21 | 146, 230 |
| *Revelation* | | 12.6 | 234 | 21.1 | 235 |
| 1.8 | 236 | 12.12 | 234 | 21.2 | 236 |
| 1.16-18 | 13 | 12.14 | 234 | 21.4 | 233, 234 |
| 4–5 | 137 | 12.17 | 234 | 21.5-6 | 236 |
| 6.1-17 | 226 | 14.1-21 | 230 | 21.8 | 235 |
| 6.1-8 | 229 | 15.7 | 226 | 21.12-21 | 235 |
| 6.8 | 229 | 15.8 | 226 | 21.27 | 235 |
| 6.9-11 | 226, 227 | 16.1-21 | 226 | 22.2 | 234 |
| 6.10 | 227 | 16.1 | 230 | 22.3 | 235 |
| 6.12-17 | 227 | 16.2 | 230 | 22.4 | 235 |
| 6.12-14 | 228 | 16.3 | 230 | 22.10 | 236 |
| 6.12 | 228 | 16.4 | 231 | 22.13 | 236 |
| 6.15-17 | 226, 228 | 16.8 | 231 | 22.15 | 235 |
| 6.16 | 230 | 16.9 | 231 | 22.18-19 | 236 |
| 7.7-17 | 226 | 16.10 | 231 | | |
| 7.16-17 | 233, 234 | 16.11 | 231 | | |

OTHER ANCIENT SOURCES

| | | | |
|---|---|---|---|
| Talmuds | | Christian Authors | |
| *b. Šab.* | | Augustine | |
| 127 | 68 | *City of God* | |
| | | 14.13 | 29 |

# Index of Authors

Abrahams, I. 65
Adkinson, R. 196
Aichele, G. 12, 15, 25, 86, 222
Alder, D. 65
Aldiss, B.W. 175
Alter, R. 148
Apte, M.L. 62, 63
Arata, S.D. 189
Auerbach, N. 176, 188, 203

Balzac, H. de 86
Barber, P. 175-78
Barr, J. 44, 45, 53, 55
Barthes, R. 86, 87, 94, 135
Bartusiak, M. 110
Bauckham, R. 221
Bechtel, L.M. 58
Belford, B. 175, 186, 188
Benjamin, W. 90
Bentley, C.F. 189
Berger, P.L. 140, 146
Bierman, J.S. 186
Blackmore, T. 97
Blanchot, M. 149, 152, 157
Blatty, W.P. 201
Boer, R. 55, 82
Boesak, A.A. 221, 233, 234
Bonhoeffer, D. 29, 30
Boozer, J. 22
Boring, M.E. 233
Bouissac, P. 71
Boyer, J. 71
Braudy, L. 23
Bray, H. 22
Bronowski, J. 106, 130
Brooke-Rose, C. 12
Brown, N.O. 148-50, 161, 162

Brueggeman, W. 44, 48, 135
Brummett, B. 224
Burke, D.G. 150

Card, O.S. 52, 53
Carroll, C. 16
Case, S.E. 188
Cassuto, U. 48, 50, 53, 54
Charlesworth, J.H. 225
Clapham, C. 125, 129
Clarke, J. 150
Collins, A.Y. 221
Collins, G. 22
Collins, J.J. 225
Connelly, J.T. 178
Cornwell, N. 11, 12
Coulthard, E. 124
Courant, R. 110, 123
Court, J.M. 221
Cousar, C.B. 182
Craft, C. 188
Crossan, J.D. 44, 136

Davies, P. 120
Deleuze, G. 92
Demetrakopoulos, S. 189
Desser, D. 21
Dewey, J. 224
Dick, P.K. 21
Dickey, J. 19, 38
Dickinson, E. 70
Dirac, P. 110
Donaldson, M. 15
Donaldson, M.E. 33
Doty, W.G. 148, 156-58, 160, 161,
    165
Dowell, P. 22

Downing, C. 162
Dresser, N. 177
Dummelow, J.R. 169, 170

Eco, U. 78, 79, 82, 85, 87, 88, 90, 91, 99
Efrid, J.M. 28
Einstein, A. 63, 102, 107, 118, 120
Eliade, M. 136, 143
Ellis, E.E. 183
Emerson, R.W. 67
Eyles, A. 196

Fanu, S. Le 187
Farnell, R.L. 148, 149, 160
Farson, D. 186
Faulkner, W. 140
Feiffer, J. 80, 81, 83, 84, 90
Fitzmyer, J.A. 184
Florescu, R.R. 168, 173-75, 186
Frei, H.W. 138
Freud, S. 89
Fry, C.L. 188
Fry, N. 196
Frye, N. 108, 112

Gabel, J.B. 108, 113, 115, 116
Garrett, S.R. 234
Gates, H.L. Jr 88
Gauss, C.F. 106, 110, 122
Gelder, K. 195
Glover, D. 189
Golubitsky, M. 109
Gonzales, P. 114
Gottlieb, F. 70
Graves, R. 152, 156
Gray, W.R. 20
Greene, G. 58
Gribbin, J. 115, 121
Griffin, G. 188
Grundmann, R. 20
Guattari, F. 92
Guiley, R.E. 176

Hahn, L.-s. 122
Haining, P. 186, 187
Halberstam, J. 189
Hanson, P.D. 225

Harpham, G.G. 225
Harrington, W.J. 221
Harris, K. 36
Hatlen, B. 189
Hawking, S.W. 15, 102-105, 107, 110, 111, 113-24, 126-28
Heldreth, L.G. 21
Hengel, M. 184
Hennelly, M.M. Jr 189
Hillman, J. 151-53, 161
Hogan, D.J. 188
Horgan, J. 108
Howe, I. 71
Howes, M. 188
Hume, C. 222
Hutchings, P. 196
Hyers, M.C. 62

Inge, M.T. 76, 77, 80, 90

Jabes, E. 151, 152
Jackson, R. 12, 14, 31
Jacoby, S. 114
Jakobson, R. 86
Jameson, F. 81
Jancovich, M. 189
Janes, R. 143
Jewett, R. 77-81, 84, 90
Jobling, D. 52
Johnson, A. 187, 189
Johnson, G. 106, 110
Jones, S. 195
Joyce, J. 140
Jung, C.G. 150

Kafka, F. 12, 90, 140
Kaplan, R.A. 116
Käsemann, E. 182
Kazantzakis, N. 99
Keller, C. 222, 223, 237
Kerenyi, C. 150
Kerenyi, K. 148, 150, 153, 156, 157, 159, 160
Kerman, J. 15, 21
Klein, R. 157, 158, 161
Kolb, W.M. 20, 21, 35
Kramer, J. 15, 130
Kreitzer, L. 16

Krenz, E.J. 136
Kristeva, J. 16, 222-24, 227
Krumm, P. 188

Langer, S. 72
Lanser, S.S. 32
Lawrence, J.S. 77-81, 84, 90
Leary, T. 71
Leatherdale, C. 186, 188
Lee, J. 16
Lewis, C.S. 14
Lindley, D. 110
Lotman, J. 113
Ludlam, H. 186
Luthi, M. 108, 118, 121
Lyotard, J.-F. 104

Manlove, C. 14, 33, 176
Márquez, G.G. 16, 137, 140-46
Martin, R.P. 182
McDonald, J. 189
McFague, S. 227, 237
McGinn, B. 221
McGrath, A.E. 182
McMurray, G.R. 145
McNally, R. 168, 173-75
McNerney, K. 144, 186
Melville, H. 43
Merleau-Ponty, M. 150, 151
Metz, C. 122
Metz, J. 25
Miles, M. 23
Miller, E. 187
Miller, S.H. 63
Milne, P.J. 51
Milton, J. 33
Minear, P. 183
Moltmann, J. 221
Monette, P. 197
Moore, S. 99
Moretti, F. 189
Morris, E. 15
Mostern, K. 90
Mueller, J.R. 116
Mueller-Vollmer, K. 158

Nandris, G. 186
Nietzsche, F. 77, 90, 91, 158

O'Connor, F. 225
O'Leary, S.D. 224
Ochs, E. 114
Oring, E. 70, 71
Ostriker, A. 66
Otten, T. 19, 26, 33
Otto, W.F. 135, 152, 154, 155, 157,
    158, 160, 161, 165
Overbye, D. 112, 118, 121

Page, D. 120, 121
Palumbo, D. 11
Paris, G. 152, 157, 162
Penchansky, D. 15
Phillips, G.A. 86
Pilinszky, J. 220
Pippin, T. 12, 25, 221, 222, 232
Plaskow, J. 30
Poe, E.A. 12
Porter, R. 186
Propp, V. 113
Punter, D. 187

Rabkin, E.S. 222
Rad, G. von 28
Ramsland, K. 210
Rice, A. 210
Richard, P. 221, 234
Richardson, A. 28
Richardson, M. 177
Ricoeur, P. 29, 31
Riley, M. 210
Robbins, H. 110, 123
Roth, J. 189
Russell, B. 120
Russell, D.S. 225
Ryan, A. 187

Saberhagen, F. 202
Saiving, V. 30
Sakenfeld, K.D. 116
Sartre, J.-P. 67
Scarry, E. 220, 223
Schenda, R. 111, 113
Schickel, R. 20, 22
Schlobin, R. 43
Schüssler Fiorenza, E. 221
Schwartzman, S. 110, 123

Schweitzer, A. 139
Scott, B. 21, 22
Seed, D. 187
Senf, C.A. 187, 189
Shakespeare, W. 159
Silver, A. 195
Simpson, J.C. 23
Skal, D.J. 195
Stegemann, H. 168, 169
Stevens, W. 59
Stevenson, J.A. 188
Stewart, I. 109
Stoker, B. 175, 181, 184, 185, 187, 189, 203, 213
Strassfeld, M. 65, 66
Stratton, B. 27, 32
Strong, J. 170
Stuhlmacher, P. 182
Suchocki, M.H. 19, 30
Suggs, M.J. 116
Summers, M. 175, 176
Sutherland, J. 189

Tavis, A. 109, 110, 113
Thiselton, A.C. 153
Thompson, L. 138
Thornton, T.C.G. 184
Tillich, P. 27, 33
Todorov, T. 12, 13, 15, 19, 24-26, 135
Torgovnick, M. 136
Torrance, T.F. 153, 158
Tremayne, P. 186
Trible, P. 31
Turner, V. 62
Twichell, J.B. 187, 198
Ursini, J. 195

Varma, D.P. 176

Walsh, R. 15
Waskow, A. 65-67
Wasson, R. 189
Weeden, T.J. Sr 94
Weinberg, S. 120
Weissman, J. 188
Wenham, G.J. 55
Wertheim, M. 127
Westermann, C. 28
Wex, M. 67, 69
Wheeler, C.B. 108, 113, 115, 116
White, H.C. 58, 121
White, M. 115
Wicke, J. 189
Wilcox, M. 184
Willeford, W. 62, 63
Williams, A. 189
Williams, J.G. 51
Williams, R.L. 143, 144
Wilson, A.N. 187
Winquist, C.E. 158, 162
Wisse, R. 66
Wolf, L. 189
Wood, R. 188
Worley, L. 16
Wylie, P. 77

Yadin, Y. 169
York, A.D. 108, 113, 115, 116
Young, R.M. 106, 109

Zipes, J. 14, 112
Žižek, S. 14
Zucker, W.M. 63